I0123904

Cultural practices and transitions in education

the Tufnell Press,

London,
United Kingdom

www.tufnellpress.co.uk

email contact@tufnellpress.co.uk

British Library Cataloguing-in-Publication Data
A catalogue record for this book is
available from the British Library

paperback	*ISBN*	*1872767486*
	ISBN-13	*978-1-872767-48-2*
hardcover	*ISBN*	*1872767532*
	ISBN-13	*978-1-872767-53-6*

Copyright © 2012 Tarja Tolonen, Tarja Palmu, Sirpa Lappalainen and Tuuli Kurki
The moral rights of the authors have been asserted.
Database right the Tufnell Press (maker).

All rights reserved. No part of this publication may be reproduced, stored in a retrieval
system, or transmitted in any form or by any means, electronic, mechanical, photocopying,
recording or otherwise, without the prior permission of the publisher, or expressly by law, or under
terms agreed with the appropriate reprographic rights organisation.

Printed in England and U.S.A. by Lightning Source

Cultural practices and transitions in education

editors
Tarja Tolonen, Tarja Palmu, Sirpa Lappalainen and Tuuli Kurki

UNIVERSITY OF HELSINKI
FACULTY OF BEHAVIOURAL SCIENCES

FINNISH YOUTH RESEARCH SOCIETY
FINNISH YOUTH RESEARCH NETWORK

Contents

Cultural practices and transitions in education

Authors

Sanna Aaltonen is Senior Researcher at the Finnish Youth Research Network, Finland. She received her Ph.D. in Social Sciences from the University of Helsinki under the supervision of Tuula Gordon and Elina Lahelma.

Sinikka Aapola-Kari is Adjunct Professor of Social Sciences, University of Helsinki, Finland. She currently works as executive director at the Finnish Association for Child and Family Guidance. She has worked and studied together with Tuula Gordon and Elina Lahelma since the late 1980s.

Anne-Lise Arnesen is Professor of Education at Østfold University College. She has collaborated with Elina Lahelma since the mid-1980s, and in later years as a co-convener of the Nordic Research Network NordCrit. She also collaborated with Tuula Gordon and Elina Lahelma and their research group on ethnographic work on difference and marginalisation.

Dennis Beach is Professor of Education at the University of Gothenburg, Sweden. He collaborated with Tuula Gordon and Elina Lahelma in establishing the Nordic Research Network Ethnoped and in the establishment of the international journal Education and Ethnography.

Kristiina Brunila works as a post doctoral researcher at the Institute of Behavioural Sciences, University of Helsinki, Finland.

Janet Holland is Professor of Social Research in the Weeks Centre for Social and Policy Research, London South Bank University, UK, and Co-Director of the Timescapes study. She carried out ethnography in London secondary schools parallel to that of Tuula Gordon and Elina Lahelma in Helsinki schools and comparative qualitative longitudinal studies of Youth Transitions.

Päivi Honkatukia is Senior Researcher at the National Research Institute of Legal Policy, Finland. She received her Ph.D. in Sociology at the University of Helsinki under the supervision of Tuula Gordon.

Kati Kasanen, Ph.D., is University Lecturer at the Educational Sciences and Psychology Department, University of Eastern Finland.

Mary Jane Kehily is Professor of Gender and Education at the Open University, UK.

Seija Keskitalo-Foley is University Lecturer in the Sociology of Education and Docent in the Feminist Sociology of Education, University of Lapland, Finland.

Katri Komulainen, Ph.D., is Professor of Psychology at the Educational Sciences and Psychology Department, University of Eastern Finland.

Maija Korhonen works as a researcher at the Educational Sciences and Psychology Department, University of Eastern Finland.

Tuuli Kurki is a doctoral student at the Institute of Behavioural Sciences, University of Helsinki, Finland, supervised by Elina Lahelma.

Riitta Kärkkäinen, Ph.D., works as a researcher at the Educational Sciences and Psychology Department, University of Eastern Finland.

Sirpa Lappalainen is Adjunct Professor, University of Helsinki. She works as a post doctoral researcher at the Research Unit of Cultural and Feminist Studies in Education founded and directed by Elina Lahelma.

Jukka Lehtonen is Adjunct Professor, University of Helsinki. He works as University Lecturer and is a member of the research project directed by Elina Lahelma.

Kirsti Lempiäinen is University Lecturer in Gender Studies at the University of Lapland, Finland.

Lisbeth Lundahl is Professor of Educational Work at Umeå University, Sweden. She has collaborated with Elina Lahelma for many years and is a co-convener with Lahelma, Öhrn, Arnesen and others of the Nordic Research Network NordCrit.

Elina Paju is a doctoral student at the Department of Social Research, University of Helsinki, Finland. Tuula Gordon is her Ph.D. thesis supervisor.

Tarja Palmu works as a post doctoral researcher. She received her Ph.D. in Education at the University of Helsinki, Finland under the supervision of Tuula Gordon and Elina Lahelma.

Thomas S. Popkewitz is Professor at the University of Wisconsin-Madison, USA. He was awarded a Ph.D. (h.c.) of the University of Helsinki, Finland in 2007.

Hannu Räty, Ph.D., is Professor of Psychology at the Educational Sciences and Psychology Department, University of Eastern Finland.

Päivi Siivonen, Ph.D., works as a post doctoral researcher at the Teacher Education Department, University of Helsinki, Finland.

Beverley Skeggs worked at the Universities of Keele, York, Lancaster and Manchester before joining the Department of Sociology at Goldsmiths, London, UK.

Liisa Tainio is Professor of Finnish Language and Literature Education at the Department of Teacher Education, University of Helsinki, Finland. She has worked on the project Gender Awareness in Teacher Education (Tasuko) directed by Elina Lahelma.

Rachel Thomson is Professor of Childhood and Youth Studies in the Faculty of Health and Social Care at the University of Sussex, UK. She collaborated with Tuula Gordon and Elina Lahelma on comparative qualitative longitudinal studies of Youth Transitions.

Tarja Tolonen is Adjunct Professor, University of Helsinki, Finland. She currently works as Senior Inspector at the Finnish Ministry of Education and Culture. She has worked as a researcher in many research projects with Tuula Gordon and Elina Lahelma.

Elisabet Öhrn is Professor of Education at the University of Gothenburg, Sweden. She has collaborated with Elina Lahelma for many years, lately especially in the Nordic Research Network NordCrit.

Preface

This book is a *festschrift* to the respected academics, professors and docents Elina Lahelma and Tuula Gordon whose research, teaching and supervising have fascinated and inspired people in the fields of sociology, education, youth research and women studies. Elina and Tuula introduced feminist thinking into the sociology of education in Finland, which was a new and radical opening in the 1980s. After that they have built up imaginative research methods, and collective ways of working. They have analysed educational policies and practices by using feminist methodologies.

Internationally, they have collaborated especially with colleagues in the Nordic countries, United Kingdom and the United States. This book has been written as a tribute to the inspiring work they have done.

The book is divided into five parts, each reflecting themes central to Elina and Tuula's work. In *Part 1: Methodology*, the authors concentrate on methodological questions. In the 1990s, Elina and Tuula carried out a cross-cultural research project with Janet Holland. Together they conducted collective ethnographical research in Helsinki and in London, moving towards a new way of thinking about methodology in educational research (see Gordon et al., 2000). In the first chapter of the book, Tarja Palmu and Sirpa Lappalainen reflect on the strengths and challenges of collective ethnography. Tuula and Elina have always paid special attention to ethical sensitivity in all the stages of the research process. Ethical issues are discussed in two chapters of the book. Anne-Lise Arnesen problematises the ethnographic gaze in classroom contexts in relation to tensions between reciprocity and objectification. In their chapter, Sanna Aaltonen and Päivi Honkatukia highlight how the relationship between the researcher and young people is regulated and promoted in institutional contexts, such as in youth work, child protection and prison.

Citizenship is a highly theorised concept in social sciences. In their work, Elina and Tuula have brought theoretical sophistication to the empirical research of citizenship in the everyday life of schools. In their ethnographic project *Citizenship, difference and marginality at school—with special reference to gender* (funded by Academy of Finland), they analysed how citizenship is constructed in school. By focusing on differences and hidden inequalities behind the abstract concepts of the pupil and that of citizenship, they challenged the New Right politics as a sufficient framework for democratic education (Gordon,

2006; Gordon, Lahelma and Beach, 2003). This discussion continues in *Part 2*: Dennis Beach, Lisbeth Lundahl and Elisabet Öhrn examine how democracy is lived out in Swedish upper secondary education practices, whereas Thomas S. Popkewitz's interest is in education in the United States. He focuses on the systems of reason which produce the future citizen. Features of the future citizen are also discussed in the chapter written by Hannu Räty and Katri Komulainen with their colleagues, who focus on the discourse of educability in the era of neoliberalism.

Part 3: Transitions explores transitions in education and in life more broadly. Tuula and Elina have pursued an interest in transitions from school to the labour market; however their interest in the thematic of transitions has also extended beyond this. They have focused, for example, on young people's friendships, gendered identities and growing adults, moving from home and going to the army (Gordon and Lahelma, 2002; Lahelma and Gordon 2003). They see transitions not as a developmental or naturalised and self-evident process, but as intertwined with gender, social class, locality, and ethnicity. In this part, Janet Holland and Rachel Thomson, Sinikka Aapola-Kari, Tarja Tolonen and Beverley Skeggs analyse their empirical data through these traditions. These authors interpret their material from the perspectives of class, locality, age and gender, stressing cultural and social processes.

Gender and embodiment are discussed in the *Part 4: Girlhood*. Tuula Gordon's and Elina Lahelma's research interest in gender and embodiment has interweaved with a wide range of issues related to schooling, but also with hierarchical gender relations and sexuality (Lahelma et al., 2000; Lahelma and Lehtonen, 2002); and with the analysis of different life situations including girlhood (Gordon et al., 2000), adulthood (Gordon and Lahelma, 2002, 2004, Gordon et al., 2005, 2008; Lahelma and Gordon, 2003) and motherhood (Gordon and Lahelma, 2004). In their work—as in recent social and feminist research in general—they approach agency as a critical analytical concept to make sense of the intersectional relations between gender and other cultural and social differences. In this part of the book, Mary Jane Kehily, Elina Paju and Seija Keskisalo-Foley focus on research on girlhood from the perspectives of embodiment and agency, which continue to be highly important themes in feminist research.

Elina and Tuula are both committed and persistent promoters of equality and social justice. In the concluding *Part 5: Equality*, the authors discuss questions of equality in education and interpret/analyse how these intersect with concepts introduced in previous chapters, such as agency and differences connected to class, gender and ethnicities. Kirsti Lempiäinen explores how agency is negotiated in the context of higher education and how these negotiations can be explained along the axes of class, gender and other intersecting differences. Although like other Nordic countries Finland is often considered a model country in terms of gender equality, both Liisa Tainio's and Jukka Lehtonen's chapters make visible gender biases in the context of education in Finland. In the last concluding chapter, Kristiina Brunila focuses on the very core of the work of Tuula and Elina: she examines equality work from different positions and practises, and thus ends up analysing the meaning of equality itself.

When editing this book, we have had the pleasure to be in touch with many wonderful colleagues of Tuula and Elina; we want to thank all of you. We are grateful to Silja Rajander, Ph. D. for revising the language, and to trainee Kristiina Vainio for editorial assistance. This book has been peer reviewed; therefore, we want to thank our anonymous referees for their important work. The support of the Institute of Behavioural Sciences, University of Helsinki and the Finnish Youth Research Society has made this book possible.

Most importantly, Elina and Tuula, we want to thank you for being academic mothers, inspirers, friends and leaders of several research projects.

Tarja, Tarja, Sirpa and Tuuli
Helsinki, 29 August, 2012

References

Gordon, T., (2006) Girls in education: Citizenship, agency and emotions, *Gender and Education*, 18(1): 1-15.

Gordon T., Holland J. and Lahelma L., (2000) *Making spaces. Citizenship and difference at school*, London: Macmillan Press Ltd.

Gordon, T., Lahelma, E. and Holland, J., (2000) Friends or foes? Interpreting relations between girls in schools, in Walford, G. and Hudson, C., (eds.) *Genders and sexualities in educational ethnography, Studies in Educational Ethnography*, vol. 3., Amsterdam: JAI, 7-25.

Gordon, T., Holland, J., Lahelma, E. and Thomson, R., (2005) Imagining gendered adulthood: Anxiety, ambivalence, avoidance and anticipation, *European Journal of Women's Studies*, 12(1): 83-103.

Gordon, T., Holland, J., Lahelma, E. and Thomson, R., (2008) Young female citizens in education: Emotions, resources and agency, *Pedagogy, Culture and Society*, 16(2): 177-191.

Gordon, T. and Lahelma, E., (2002) Becoming an adult: Possibilities and limitations—dreams and fears, *Young*, 10(2): 2-18.

Gordon, T. and Lahelma, E., (2003a) From ethnography to life history: Tracing transitions of school students, *International Journal of Social Research Methodology,* 6(3): 245-254.

Gordon, T. and Lahelma, E., (2004) Who wants to be a woman? Young women's reflections on transition to adulthood, *Feminist Review,* 78, 80- 97.

Gordon, T., Lahelma, E. and Beach, D., (2003) Marketisation of democratic education, in D. Beach, T. Gordon and E. Lahelma (eds.) *Democratic Education. Etnographic challenges,* London: Tufnell Press.

Lahelma, E. and Gordon, T., (2003) Home as a physical, social and mental space: Young people's reflections on leaving home, *Journal of youth studies,* 6(4): 377-390.

Lahelma, E. and Lehtonen, J., (2002) Learning the power of sexuality, *Pedagogy, Culture and Society,* 10(1): 141-148.

Lahelma, E., Palmu, T. and Gordon, T. (2000) Intersecting power relations in teachers' experiences of being sexualized or harassed by students, *Sexualities: Studies in Culture and Society,* 3(4): 463-481.

Part 1: Methodology

Chapter 1

Collaborative reflections on collective ethnography

Tarja Palmu and Sirpa Lappalainen

In this chapter, we explore the contribution of Elina Lahelma and Tuula Gordon's work to educational ethnography. Moreover, we discuss the strengths and challenges of a collective research frame through reflecting on our research projects. We have conducted ethnographic research in different educational contexts ranging from preschool to post-compulsory education (Lappalainen in preschool and vocational education, Palmu in secondary school). Common features of our projects include the contextualisation of our analyses in current educational policy; the generation and collection of many kinds of data (fieldnotes, interviews, policy documents, text books etc.); and the utilisation of similar analytical strategies. Moreover, we share the view that writing occupies a central position throughout the research process: from the generation of data to its analysis (Coffey, 1999). The fundamental difference between our works is that the framework for Tarja's work was a collective ethnography. She had the opportunity to share her experiences with five researchers with whom she spent her time in the field, while Sirpa worked alone as a researcher in the field. In this chapter, we discuss the special features of collective ethnography compared to the 'individual' ethnographic approach, and reflect on ethnographic writing in the current academic culture.

Starting the ethnography

In the mid-nineties, six researchers Tuula Gordon, Elina Lahelma, Pirkko Hynninen, Tuija Metso, Tarja Palmu and Tarja Tolonen started to plan a joint research project. Each of them had their own research interests, but having worked together in a gender studies network, they decided to conduct collective ethnographic research in secondary schools in Finland. Tuula and Elina carried out a cross-cultural project jointly with Janet Holland, who conducted a similar research in London (e.g. Gordon et al., 2000a/b/c). For all the others, in addition to a concrete research group, the project provided a social, mental and physical space (see Lefebvre, 1991; Rajander, 2010) for writing their doctoral theses. Due to the project's strong influence on Finnish and Nordic traditions of school ethnography (see Beach, 2010; Lahelma and Gordon, 2007), we refer to it as a 'mother project'.

The ethnographic project (funded by the Academy of Finland) was named *Citizenship, Difference and Marginality at School—with Special Reference to Gender* to encompass the central concepts that guided the planning of the research. The group started their ethnographic fieldwork during the first school day in August 1994 (see Lahelma and Gordon, 1997) and followed more than 900 lessons during one school year in two different secondary schools in Helsinki. At the time, educational ethnography in Finland was in a state of becoming. A few ethnographies conducted in educational institutions had been published (e.g. Laine, 1997; Pösö, 1993; Strandell, 1994; Syrjäläinen, 1990), and methodological influences were sought from elsewhere. The group chose to utilise methodological approaches offered by British sociology of education in particular (Lahelma and Gordon, 2007). However, they developed their own collective way of working. They observed and wrote notes during lessons, breaks and different school events and ceremonies. The group interviewed one hundred and sixty students, forty-four teachers, other school staff and forty-one parents, and collected curriculum texts, teaching materials and other texts during the lessons and essays written by students. Each researcher wrote her own fieldnotes and diary that framed the collective data. The collective discussions about activities in the field helped develop reflexive interpretations. Through analytical discussions in project meetings, the multi-layered everyday life of the schools started to unveil as a rich chain of both predictable and unexpected events. (Gordon et al., 2006.)

Six years later, Sirpa began her ethnographic PhD project under the supervision of Elina and Tuula. Her work was part of the project *Inclusion/ exclusion in educational processes*, directed by Elina and funded by the Academy of Finland. She decided to study intertwined constructions of nationality, ethnicity and gender in the preschool context. She conducted one-year ethnographic fieldwork in two kindergartens in the Helsinki Metropolitan Area. Ethnography was still a relatively marginal approach among educational researchers at the time, although some work had just been finalised (e.g. Salo, 1999) and quite a few works were in process (e.g. Hakala, 2007; Kankkunen, 2004; Kasanen, 2003; Käyhkö, 2006). Sirpa constructed her methodological approach in close interaction with the collective research group. Her research proposals, first pieces of analysis and preliminary interpretations were commented on in PhD seminars attended by members of the mother project who were in the process of finalising their work. Her insights about what it means to do research were pretty much based on the practices of the collective research group. In other words, her way of knowing was partly framed by the collective ethnography. However, her work was an individual project in the sense that she was the only researcher with embodied experience of her particular field (see Atkinson et al., 2001).

Drawing on the idea of collaborative reflexivity (Cherry et al., 2011), we analyse how the framework of collective ethnography gains significance in individual projects such as academic dissertations. We share our experiences of fieldwork and writing in order to analyse how the joint ethnography, joint fieldwork and joint analyses have shaped ethnographic knowing in our research projects. In the following section, we discuss collective and individual ways of working and knowing during fieldwork.

In the field

One of the challenges in ethnography is gaining access to the field. When studying educational institutions, formal permission is required. However, this does not guarantee the willingness of all the actors in the field to participate to the research. Tarja Tolonen (2001, p. 51) describes fieldwork as 'knocking the doors', referring to the continuous negotiations about entry. For the researchers involved in the mother project, access to the schools was no easy matter, and they went through several negotiations before they had permission to enter the schools, City Park and Green Park. As it was a research project, some negotiations were made jointly. In addition, everyone had to negotiate their own entry into different classes, to different occasions, celebrations or meetings and ask permission for interviews.

When Sirpa started her ethnography, her access to the field went relatively smoothly. Both Sirpa and Tarja had a research project behind them. However, the way in which these projects were present in the field was different. When Tarja conducted her fieldwork, the project was present in the field in a concrete embodied way. Teachers and students met the people with whom Tarja collaborated. Tarja was part of the project; she was one of them. Although Sirpa expressed that her research was part of a larger project, the project behind her research was more or less as an abstraction to research participants; Sirpa was considered more as an individual student 'collecting' data for her PhD. The following example from fieldnotes illustrates her position in the field:

I was on my way to the preschool when I met Meri [the teacher] in the street. She sang out to me: 'Just like a preschool kid with a heavy backpack, you're so small and invisible'. I answered: 'This is probably the only place I can make use of it' [of being small]. She continued: 'They [the staff of the preschool] wondered whether it's annoying when someone is there, but somehow you aren't even noticed, maybe it's because you don't evaluate ...   (Fieldnotes, translated by SL)

Sirpa had worked to avoid causing any extra work to the staff, and the staff saw Sirpa as a relatively harmless outsider. As an individual researcher, she was less visible than six women in the everyday life of the educational institution she observed, and her position as a critical educational researcher was easily forgotten (see Lappalainen, 2007a). During the fieldwork of the mother project, the situation was quite different. The schools were reminded of the researchers' presence in a concrete way when the main newspaper in Finland referred to an article written by members of the group (Gordon et al., 1995). The way the results were reviewed in the newspaper was not very complimentary towards schools, which led to serious discussions in the field. Although the results reviewed in the newspaper were not based on the ethnographic data generated during this fieldwork and these schools, the researchers' critical stance towards institutionalised school practices[1] became visible due to this incidence. The confidence between the researchers and teachers was shaken, and the researchers needed to negotiate to re-establish their position as observers. This was an important reminder of the delicate nature of the relationship between the researcher and the field. In addition, the incident demonstrated that researchers have relatively limited possibilities to control the ways in which their research is interpreted. A more or less established practice in fieldwork is to avoid disturbing the 'normal order of things' as much as possible. When reflecting afterwards on her own work, Sirpa is inclined to think that maybe it would have been more fair to be more visible; to ask more critical questions; to maybe even actively disturb the everyday life of the institution sometimes to make the critical gaze of the researcher visible (Lappalainen, 2007a, p. 74). Katariina Hakala (2007), who was also one of the Elina and Tuula's students, has developed the idea of dialogical ethnography, in which the goal is to base the analysis and interpretations on

---

1   Individual teachers or the individual schools were never as subjects of evaluation or criticism.

dialogue between the researcher and informants, and in which the possibility for controversial interpretations is kept in mind during the research process.

The mother project researchers decided to conduct intensive collective ethnography for the first two months, observing the same seventh grade classes. In addition to writing fieldnotes, they filled in an observation form they had developed together. The observation form was filled in every lesson, and it included information on the school, lesson, teacher, date, time, school subject, and what was most important: some quickly made reflections on significant, interesting or extraordinary events and questions that came to their mind during the lessons observed. This can also be interpreted as a very early preliminary analysis while in the field. This was also the way Tarja wrote her fieldnotes and filled in observation forms during the mother tongue lessons she observed. After the two months period, each researcher started to focus more on her own topics. However, the mother project still offered emotional and intellectual support. The six researchers could share and discuss their experiences of the field. This was something Sirpa yearned for during her fieldwork. Through following the practices established by the mother project, she learned to write her fieldnotes in a disciplined way. However, when writing her fieldnotes she was painfully aware that these represented her way of seeing (e.g. Emerson et al., 2001, p. 353; Arnesen, this book). For example, she saw some common disciplinary practices as being quite startling. In these situations, she struggled between her empathy for the children and her loyalty to staff, which permitted her to be there. She would have hoped for another 'pair of eyes'—someone who knows the context—to be present. She yearned for someone who she could discuss her interpretations with, and who could challenge her gaze (see Gordon et al., 2005). We do not argue that six pairs of eyes increased the objectivity of the research, but we do argue that the mother project supported its members in different ways. Collective work helped to situate their individual experiences within a wider context and see the habits, practices, power relations and different kinds of positions teachers, students and researchers had in the school structure, which, we argue, was one of the main strengths of the collective ethnography.

Reflections on the positioning of the researcher self, being an outsider or insider and the questions of who is the knower, are crucial to ethnographic research. These discussions are often undertaken assuming a singular researcher or ethnographer (e.g. Coffey, 1999, pp. 17-37). The strength of collective ethnography and collective working lies with the opportunity to reflect together, and besides asking, 'what do I know' and 'how do I know it' (Hertz, 1997, p. viii;

Cherry et al., 2011, p. 235) there are also questions of 'what we know' and 'how we know it'. During the fieldwork, the ethnographic project had weekly meetings. The meetings had different functions during different periods; from preparing for fieldwork, to sharing experiences and engaging in analytical discussion (see more Gordon et al., 2006). Analysis through discussion (ibid., pp. 9-10) comes close to the 'collaborative reflexivity' that Cherry, Ellis and DeSoucey (2011) describe in their analysis. They claim 'reflexivity benefits from collaborative analysis because it provides variations in perspective and experience' (ibid., p. 235). In the collective ethnography, the 'collectiveness' reflected a collective way of working, but also a commitment to feminist methodologies (Lahelma et al., 2011).

The mother project shared methodological commitments to feminist ethnography's ideas of reflexivity, gender awareness and fragmentariness (Skeggs, 2001, p. 429). Also social justice, equality, agency and power relations are crucial to critical studies of ethnography (Gordon, Lahelma and Beach, 2003). In order to focus their collective gaze in the field, the group discussed the practices and processes they were especially interested in and adopted a layered response to the school: the official, informal and physical school (see more Gordon et al., 1999, 2006; Gordon, Holland and Lahelma, 2000a). The official school is defined in curricula, other formal school documents and everyday life in school as teaching methods and materials, contents of teaching pedagogical interaction and formal hierarchies in school. The informal school refers to unofficial interaction during lessons and breaks. It also refers to unofficial hierarchies in students' cultures and classroom interactions. The physical school refers to space, movement, voice, time and regulation of embodiment at school. (Gordon et al., 2006, p. 5.) These layers helped to focus the gaze in the field, but also helped to formulate the research and interview questions in certain frames and further the analysis and discussions. This way to approach observation and analysis developed by the mother project has made a significant contribution to Finnish school ethnography (e.g. Berg, 2010; Rajander, 2010; Souto, 2011). Sirpa applied these layers, originally developed in a school context, to her study conducted in kindergarten. The context of early childhood education differs from school in the sense that the pedagogical orientation is extended from teaching situations like lessons to reproductions of everyday activities like meals, dressing and freshening up, which makes the borders between the layers more vague (Lappalainen, 2006, p. 24). However, they helped her to discern things she saw and heard in the flow of everyday life. Moreover, when writing her PhD she could focus her analysis on particular layers of the kindergarten (e.g. Lappalainen, 2009). These layers helped her to deal with the 'messiness' of the ethnographic research process.

Collective knowing and analysing—individual writing and academic demands

In this chapter, one starting point is to reflect how the joint ethnography, joint fieldwork, joint analyses and joint knowing are reflected in our own studies. Tuula and Elina with Janet Holland carried out a cross-cultural research project with their research teams.[2] The practice of 'analysis through discussion' was generated both within and between the research teams in Helsinki and London. (Gordon et al., 2000a, pp. 204-5.) The idea was that particular pieces of data were chosen for joint focus in order to grasp general and particular links between them (Gordon et al., 2000c, p. 11). The 'analysis through discussion' turned out to be an inspiring way of working among the 'children' of the mother project. For example, when sharing an office, Sirpa and Reetta Mietola, who conducted her ethnography in the context of special education (Mietola, forthcoming) jointly discussed and analysed discourses of worry in their data generated in different educational contexts (Mietola and Lappalainen, 2006).

In addition to, or rather as a part of the mother project, everyone had their own research questions and data. In the university, academic studying, researching, career and merits are usually individualised. Knowledge and intelligence are seen to reflect an individual's personal capacity and extensive reading. The dissertation is one demonstration of individual learning. When a thesis is the product of collective work, there can be some ambivalence in estimating 'whose knowledge is this?'

In the mother project, the researchers shared their methodological commitments and data. After one year of fieldwork, sharing the data turned out not to be only easy, unambiguous and rich, but also problematic. In several meetings, the group discussed the use of the two months' joint ethnographic data and the data that was based on everyone's own research questions and

2   Tarja, as a one researcher in the ethnographic project reflects her own dissertations that were made as part of this mother project in Helsinki. Also Tuija Metso (2004) who studied relationships between schools and parents and Tarja Tolonen (2001) who studied youth and student cultures at school wrote their dissertations within this project. Pirkko Hynninen studied careers guidance (Hynninen 1998; Hakala and Hynninen 2007). Tuula and Elina with Janet Holland carried out a research project and wrote together book (Gordon et al., 2004), several articles and joint seminar presentations. Janet conducted similar ethnographic research in London with her group.

observations of different grades, specific subjects and leisure time. Tarja, as well as all the other researchers, had access to all the ethnographic data. She utilised the data by reading and comparing it with her own findings, but for more detailed analysis she used only the data collected by herself. Regardless of the collective nature of the mother project, fieldwork is subjective, personal and experienced through and by our body. The thought of the 'researcher as a tool' with her own history, knowledge, emotions and body were fundamental to Tarja's decision to concentrate on her own observations (Coffey, 1999). The collective project and the joint data was described as the context, the 'table of interpretation' (Tolonen, 2001, p. 44) or the mirror for each researcher's own experiences, data and analysis. The knowledge, data and methods were shared, but how each researcher reflected on and portrayed them in their own analysis and writing acquired different emphases. The use of 'own' data was a significant methodological choice emphasising embodiment, gaze, experience and presence. With hindsight it can also be interpreted to having demonstrated academic and individual competency.

The dialogue between the collective and the individual, 'us' and 'me', is one thread or discussion in every dissertation made in the mother project. As Tarja has written in her thesis:

> This dialogue between the project and individual researcher is present in my work in how I write. Depending on the situation, I use 'us' or 'I'. 'Us' refers to shared knowledge and experiences, analysis and interpretations; the border is not clear or static, but the joint experiences, knowledge and discussion are inevitably present also in the analysis and interpretations made in 'I' form.   (Palmu, 2003, p. 2.)

The above citation reflects how difficult it was to make a division between the individual and the collective. It also shows how vital it was not only to reflect on personal knowing, but also to recognise and acknowledge the importance of collective work. Tuija and the other Tarja have also engaged in similar discussion of knowing in their theses (Metso, 2004, p. 59, 65; Tolonen, 2001, pp. 44-45). All researchers involved in the mother project discussed the joint ethnography widely in their thesis, as well as the uniqueness and importance of collective working. The collective work was the starting point and basis for their dissertations, but each researcher moved more towards her own thinking and writing after the tough and intensive fieldwork. However, their findings, results or research products would not have acquired their present form without the collective production of knowledge and analytical discussions.

The changing conditions of conducting research

In the field of social sciences, the culture of academic writing has fundamentally changed during the last two decades. The mother project actually was ahead of its time in many ways. In the 1990s, generating and analysing data, and writing PhD dissertations were supposed to be conducted more or less individually, and the final report was usually a monograph written in the author's own language. This had its impact on how the four PhD researchers of the mother project framed their work. They had a huge data set available to them, but they all decided to focus on the data they had generated themselves, partly due to the pressure of the academic conventions of the time. Today, the pressure has shifted towards using data as effectively as possible, which has entailed new discussions about the ownership of data, for example. This presents particular challenges to ethnographers. Ethnographic fieldnotes are usually text written by an ethnographer for her/himself. The mother project developed a disciplined fieldwork practice in order to make sense their observation for each other. Today, funding, for example, encourages/pressures[3] researchers to recycle and archive their data (Kuula, 2006; Lappalainen, 2007b), which brings fieldwork practices into consideration in new ways.

When writing this chapter in 2011, the culture of writing PhDs is different. There is more and more pressure to publish in international journals and to write PhD reports as a compilation of articles. Monographs written in the author's own language have lost their value in the academic world. The members of the mother project had the opportunity to write a book of their own. Besides their own books, all the students of the group published internationally with their supervisors. (Gordon et al., 1999, 2005, 2006; Lahelma et al., 2000.) However, these monographs have had a lot of relevance in the professional field of education. Sirpa's work took place in a transition moment. She had the privilege to choose between a monograph and a compilation of articles. She chose the latter because she felt more comfortable with the compactness of the article format. Due to this decision, she probably missed a wide audience of students and educational professionals.

---

3   Whether it is encouraged or pressured depends on researcher's stance towards archiving and recycling data. Many of our colleagues share extremely critical view on that. However Sirpa's current project collaborates with Finnish National Data Archive.

Today, neo-liberalism and new public management policy in universities appear as demands and competition for results, effectiveness and funding, and this creates considerable pressure on individuals to 'perform' (Acker and Armanti, 2004, p. 12). In spite of tightening funding and demands for rapid outcomes, ethnographic research is regarded as inviting and relevant. During the past years, some ethnographic dissertations (Honkasalo 2011; Souto, 2011) and small ethnographic projects (Hoikkala et al., 2009) have been conducted successfully. Both Tarja and Sirpa supervise PhD students who conduct ethnographic research and go against the grain. From the mother project they have all acquired as their heritage a sense of ethnographic thinking, trust towards collaborative working and sharing ideas, as well as feminist political thought. Feminist research and its questions of hierarchies, equality, power and knowledge have been and still are part of the university, but at the same time feminist research also challenges new managerial policy and struggles for social justice, multiple ways of knowing and collectiveness (Mohanty, 2003; Skeggs, 2001). As Virginia Woolf's (1929) metaphoric call for 'a room of one's own', we also presume that furthermore fruitful, inspirational, reflexive collective working and collaboration we need to have, not only metaphoric but also very concrete, 'room and book of our own' in the academy. During the process of brainstorming, thinking, looking, finding, reading, analysing, discussing and writing that is involved in writing the 'book of our own', we need each other so that through collective reflection and analysis we can seek answers to the questions 'What do we know?' and 'How do we know it?'

References

Acker, S. and Armanti, C., (2004) Sleepless in academia, *Gender and Education*, 16(1): 3-24.

Atkinson, P., Coffey, A., Delamont, S., Lofland, J. and Lofland, L., (2001) Editorial introduction, in Atkinson, P., Coffey, A., Delamont, S., Lofland, J. and Lofland, L., (eds.) *Handbook of ethnography*, London: Sage, 1-8.

Beach, D., (2010) Identifying and comparing Scandinavian ethnography, Comparisons and influences. *Ethnography and Education*, 5(1): 49-63.

Berg, P., (2010) Shifting positions in physical education—notes on otherness, sameness, absence and presence, *Ethnography and Education*, 5(1): 65-79.

Cherry, E., Colter, E. and DeSoucey, M., (2011) Food for thought, thought for food: Consumption, identity, and ethnography, *Journal of Contemporary Ethnography*, 40(2): 231-258.

Coffey, A., (1999) *The ethnographic self. Fieldwork and the representation of identity*, London: Sage Publications.

Emerson, R. M., Fretz, R. I. and Shaw, L. L., (2001) Participant observation and fieldnotes, in Atkinson, P., Coffey, A., Delamont, S., Lofland, J. and Lofland, L., (eds.) *Handbook of ethnography*, London: Sage, 352-368.

Gordon, T., Holland, J. and Lahelma, E., (2000a) *Making spaces. Citizenship and difference at school*. London: Macmillan Press Ltd.

Gordon, T., Holland, J. and Lahelma, E., (2000b) Moving bodies/still bodies. Embodiment and agency in schools, in McKie, L. and Watson, N., (eds.) *Organizing bodies*. London: Macmillan, 81-101.

Gordon, T., Holland, J. and Lahelma, E., (2000c) Friends or foes? Interpreting relations between girls in schools, in Walford, G. and Hudson, C., (eds.) *Genders and sexualities in educational ethnography, Studies in Educational Ethnography*, vol. 3., Amsterdam: JAI, 7-25.

Gordon, T., Holland, J., Lahelma, E. and Tolonen, T., (2005) Gazing with intent. Ethnographic practice in classrooms, *Qualitative Research,* 5(1): 113-131.

Gordon, T., Lahelma, E. and Beach, D., (2003) Marketisation of democratic education: Etnographic insights, in Beach, D., Gordon, T. and Lahelma, E., (eds.) *Democratic education: Ethnographic challenges*, London: Tufnell Press, 1-9.

Gordon, T., Lahelma, E., Hynninen, P., Metso, T., Palmu, T. and Tolonen, T., (1999) Learning the routines. "Professionalisation" of newcomers to secondary school, *International Journal of Qualitative Studies in Education*, 12(6): 689-705.

Gordon, T., Lahelma, E. and Tolonen, T., (1995) "Koulu on kuin..." Metaforat fyysisen koulun analysoinnin välineinä, [School is like ... Metaphors as tools to analyse physical school], *Nuorisotutkimus (Finnish Journal of Youth Research),* 13(3): 3-12.

Gordon, T., Hynninen, P., Lahelma, E., Metso, T., Palmu, T. and Tolonen, T., (2006) Collective ethnography, joint experiences and individual pathways, *Nordisk Pedagogik (Nordic Studies in Education),* 26(1): 3-15.

Hakala, K., (2007) *Paremmin tietäjän paikka ja toisin tietämisen tila. Opettajuus ja tutkijuus pedagogisena suhteena. [The position of knowing better and the space for knowing otherwise. Pedagogical mode of address in teaching (and in research)].* Helsinki: University of Helsinki.

Hakala, K. and Hynninen, P., (2007) Etnografisesta tietämisestä [About ethnographic knowing], in Lappalainen, S., Hynninen, P., Kankkunen, T., Lahelma, E. and Tolonen, T., (eds.) *Etnografia metodologiana: lähtökohtana koulutuksen tutkimus. [Ethnography as a methodology: The study of education as a starting point]*, Tampere: Vastapaino, 209-225.

Hertz, R., (1997) Introduction: Reflexivity and voice, in Hertz. R., (ed.) *Reflexivity and voice*. Thousand Oaks: Sage Publications, vii–xviii.

Hoikkala, T., Salosuo, M. and Ojajärvi, A., (2009) *Tunnetut sotilaat. Varusmiehen kokemus ja terveystaju [Well-known soldiers. Draftee's experience and sense of his own health]*, Helsinki: Finnish Youth Research Society.

Honkasalo, V., (2011) *Tyttöjen kesken: monikulttuurisuus ja sukupuolten tasa-arvo nuorisotyössä. [Among girls: Youth work, multiculturalism and gender equality]*, Helsinki: Finnish Youth Research Society.

Hynninen, P., (1998) 'Juicy Henna' and a boy in a 'dress'. Sexuality lurking in school counseling. *JFPF Congress in Lahti, 12-15 March 1998.*

Kankkunen, T., (2004) *Tytöt, pojat ja 'erojen leikki'. Sukupuolen rakentuminen koulun kuvataideopetuksen arjessa [Girls, boys and 'gender play'. Gender construction in the everyday context of school art education]*, Helsinki: Taideteollisen korkeakoulun julkaisusarja A 52.

Kasanen, K., (2003) *Lasten kykykäsitykset koulussa [Children's perceptions of ability in school]*, Joensuu: Joensuu University Press, publications 58.

Kuula, A., (2006) *Tutkimus etiikka. Aineistojen hankinta, käyttö ja säilytys. [The ethic of research. Data generation, use and archiving]*, Tampere: Vastapaino.

Käyhkö, M., (2006) *Siivoojaksi oppimassa. Etnografinen tutkimus työläistytöistä puhdistuspalvelualan koulutuksessa [Learning to become a cleaner. Ethnographic study of working- class girls in cleaning services education]*, Joensuu: Joensuu University Press.

Lahelma, E. and Gordon, T., (1997) First day in secondary school: Learning to be a "professional pupil", *Educational Research and Evaluation*, 3(2): 119-139.

Lahelma, E. and Gordon, T., (2007) Taustoja, lähtökohtia ja avauksia kouluetnografiaan [Backgrounds, staring points and openings into school ethnography], in Lappalainen, S., Hynninen, P., Kankkunen, T., Lahelma, E. and Tolonen, T., (eds.) *Etnografia metodologiana: lähtökohtana koulutuksen tutkimus [Ethnography as a methodology: The study of education as a starting point]*, Tampere: Vastapaino, 17-38.

Lahelma, E., Palmu, T. and Gordon, T., (2000) Intersecting power relations in teachers' experiences of being sexualized harassed by students, *Sexualities*, 3(4): 463-481.

Lahelma, E., Lappalainen, S., Mietola, R. and Palmu, T., (2011) Discussions that 'tickle our brains': Constructing interpretations through multiple ethnographic data sets, *Ethnography and Education Conference, 19-20 September 2011 Oxford*.

Laine, K., (1997) *Ameba pulpetissa: Koulun arkikulttuurin jännitteitä.* [The ambivalences of everyday school], SoPhi. Jyväskylän yliopisto: Yhteiskuntatieteiden, valtio-opin ja filosofian julkaisuja 13 (University of Jyväskylä: Research Reports of Political Sciences, publications 13.).

Lappalainen, S., (2009) Making differences and reflecting on diversities: Embodied nationality among preschool children, *International Journal of Inclusive Education*, 13(1): 63-78.

Lappalainen, S., (2007a) Rajamaalla. Etnografinen tarina kenttätyöstä lasten parissa [On the border line: ethnographic story about fielfd work among children], in Lappalainen, S., Hynninen, P., Kankkunen, T., Lahelma, E. and Tolonen, T., (eds.) *Etnografia metodologiana: lähtökohtana koulutuksen tutkimus. [Ethnography as a methodology: The study of education as a starting point]*, Tampere: Vastapaino, 65-88.

Lappalainen, S., (2007b) Havainnoinnista kirjoitukseksi, [From observation towards ethnographic writing], in Lappalainen, S., Hynninen, P., Kankkunen, T., Lahelma, E. and Tolonen, T., (eds.) *Etnografia metodologiana: lähtökohtana koulutuksen tutkimus. [Ethnography as a methodology: The study of education as a starting point]*, Tampere: Vastapaino, 113-133.

Lappalainen, S., (2006) *Kansallisuus, etnisyys ja sukupuoli lasten välisissä suhteissa ja esiopetuksen käytännöissä. [Nationality, ethnicity and gender in children's peer relations and preschool practices]*, University of Helsinki: Department of Education, publications 205.

Lefebvre, H., (1991) *The production of space*, 3rd ed., Translated by Nicholson-Smith, D. Oxford: Blackwell Publishing.

Metso, T., (2004) *Koti, koulu ja kasvatus. Kohtaamisia ja rajankäyntejä. [Home, school and education—encounters and detting boundaries]*, Research in Educational Sciences 19, Helsinki: Finnish Educational Research Association.

Mietola, R., (forthcoming) *Hankala erityisyys. Etnografinen tutkimus erityisopetuksesta ja erityisopetuksen oppilaista. [Troubling special. Ethnography of special education and students in special education].*

Mietola, R. and Lappalainen, S., (2006) Storylines of worry in educational arenas, *Nordisk Pedagogik (Nordic Studies in Education)*, 3: 229-242.

Mohanty, C. T., (2003) *Feminism without borders. Decolonizing theory, practicing solidarity*, Durham: Duke University Press.

Palmu, T., (2003) *Sukupuolen rakentuminen koulun kulttuurisissa teksteissä. Etnografia yläasteen äidinkielen oppitunneilla. [Construction of gender in cultural texts in school: An ethnographic study on mother tongue lessons in secondary school]*, Research studies 189, University of Helsinki: Department of Education.

Pösö, T., (1993) *Kolme koulukotia. Tutkimus tyttöjen ja poikien poikkeavuuden määrittelykäytännöistä koulukotihoidossa. [Three approved schools. Ethnographic study of defining abnormality]*, Acta Universitatis Tamperensis ser A vol 388: University of Tampere.

Rajander, S., (2010) *School and choice: An ethnography of a primary school with bilingual classes*, Helsinki: Finnish Educational Research Association.

Salo, U-M., (1999) *Ylös tiedon ja taidon mäkeä. Tutkielma koulun maailmoista ja järjestyksistä. [Up the hill of knowledge and skill. The worlds and orders of the school.]*, Acta Universitatis Lapponiensis 24. Rovaniemi: Lapin yliopistopaino.

Skeggs, B., (2001) Feminist ethnography, in Atkinson, P., Coffey, A., Delamont, S., Lofland, J. and Lofland, L., (eds.) *Handbook of ethnography*, London: Sage, 426-442.

Souto, A-M., (2011) *Arkipäivän rasismi koulussa. Etnografinen tutkimus suomalais- ja Maahanmuuttajanuorten ryhmäsuhteista. [Everyday racism at school. Ethnographic study of group relations between Finnish and immigrant youth]*, Helsinki: Finnish Youth Studies Society.

Strandell, H., (1994) *Sociala mötesplatser för barn: aktivitetsprofiler och förhandlingskulturer på daghem. [Social meeting places for children: Activity propfhiles and negotiation culture in kindergarten]*, Helsinki: Gaudeamus.

Syrjäläinen, E., (1990) *Oppilaiden ja opettajan roolikäyttäytyminen luokkahuoneyhteisössä. Etnografinen tapaustutkimus peruskoulun ja steinerkoulun ala-asteen 4. vuosiluokalta. [The role behaviour of pupils and teachers in classroom, ethnographic case study among 4 graders in primary school and Steiner school]*, University of Helsinki: Department of Teacher Education, publications 78.

Tolonen, T., (2001) *Nuorten kulttuurit koulussa. Ääni, tila ja sukupuolten arkiset järjestykset. [Voice, space and gender in youth cultures at school]*, Helsinki: Gaudeamus and Finnish Youth Research Society, publications 10.

Woolf, V., (1929) *Room of one's own*, London: Hogart Press.

Chapter 2

The gaze in the classroom: Marginalisation with a focus on objectification and reciprocity

Anne-Lise Arnesen

My studies on marginalisation, starting in the early 1990s, were initially inspired and informed by the work of Elina Lahelma and Tuula Gordon. Their thinking was an important catalyst that inspired new ways of investigating marginalisation and challenging hegemonic perspectives in understanding and explaining social phenomena in educational research in this area. Gordon and Lahelma (1995) connected marginality to the production of othering and the positioning of gendered subjects in that production. Their ethnographic works were also dedicated to exploring the part played by the school in the production of difference within a wider scope; in terms of economic, social and cultural background, as well as gender, ethnicity and locality. They argued that marginalities could be seen as multiple social axes intertwined in relations of structural and cultural power (Gordon and Lahelma, 1994). In the book *Making spaces: Citizenship and difference in schools* (Gordon et al., 2000) everyday life at schools is analysed using the metaphor of dance, paying particular attention to the official and informal processes of the school and the way in which the physical space affected pedagogy and practice (p. 2). They wanted to trace a 'curriculum of the body', referring to Lesko (1988), and their analyses focus primarily on the physical school and embodiment. The gaze is central in ethnographic research, and in their research it is connected to reflections on the ethnographer's positions and practices in the classroom and aimed to sensitise the gaze of the researchers (Gordon et al., 2005). In this chapter, I examine and reflect on the gaze as embedded in and played out as part of the complex social relations of the classroom, with a particular interest in its power to include and exclude. I will explore the gaze using the terms objectification and reciprocity, which involve complex processes of defining and locating students as insiders/outsiders, normal/deviant, as 'the other', or of different/equal value. This chapter[4]

---

4   The chapter is an elaboration of the article 'Forskerblikk på blikket i klasserommet' (The research gaze on the gaze in the classroom), published in *Norsk Pedagogisk Tidsskrift*, nr. 6/2002: 460-472.

is a tribute to Elina Lahelma and Tuula Gordon whose amazing scholarship has been a rich source from which I have drawn in my own academic research.

The gaze in the classroom

The gaze has fascinated people for thousands of years. Each and every one of us has rich experiences of what the gaze means, and we understand its importance in human interaction. It is therefore surprising that education researchers, particularly those doing ethnography, have shown so little interest in the gaze in the classroom. In this chapter, I attempt to illustrate[5] how the gaze contributes to relations of intimacy and distance, to reciprocity and objectification.

One spring day I was observing an eighth grade class during their annual mathematics examination. Examinations are considered to be critical incidents of 'anxiety-making situations' which produce 'fears, nervousness and disappointment—as well as pleasure and a sense of accomplishment for students who have good results' (Gordon et al., 2000, p. 124). I noted the following observations:

> Ronny looks up briefly, wearing a look of bottomless despair. I notice that he has not managed to get much down on paper yet. I feel as if I can see his anxiety, just beneath the surface, desperation waiting to erupt. His look seems to say: Am I the only one who can't do math? He carefully steals a look at a classmate's paper, but the classmate responds with a demonstrative movement and a self-righteous stare, covering his answer sheet with his arms to block Ronny's view. Ronny looks like he has given up. He sits for a moment, seemingly lost in his own thoughts. He rearranges a few items on his desk and takes a slurp of the coke he has brought along. He makes another desperate attempt to tackle the questions. He looks down at his paper, then up in the air, chewing on his pencil, before leaning over his paper, writing furiously. He'll show them—he knows what he's doing. But it seems to me to be only an act, and his sad face reveals that nothing came out of it. He loses his pencil on the floor. As he stands up to retrieve it, he catches the eye of one of his fellow students, a student who responds by giving him a sympathetic look. Some support, a friend. Some consolation, encouragement? He

5 I draw on material from the projects *Difference and marginalization in school* (1996-2001) and *Inclusion and exclusion in professional work: Institutional relations and dilemmas in school*, funded by the Norwegian Research Council (2002-2006).

quickly eats his packed lunch. Time is running out. The bell rings, ending the lesson. I take a look at Ronny's paper, left on his desk after he has gone; it is sweaty, slightly crumpled and almost devoid of any substantial writing.

In analysing this text, I was intrigued by the gazes involved in the observation, my own as well as Ronny's and his classmates. I started to inquire into this particular aspect of ethnographic work by reading John Berger's book *Ways of seeing* (1982). He discusses the complex network surrounding the gaze; how fundamental the ability to see is, how it determines our place in the world, how verbal explanations fall short compared to spontaneous experience. We are embedded in the world. The concrete way we see things is, according to Berger, affected by where we are, when, what we know, and what we believe.

The researcher's gaze is directed toward certain objects and excludes others, focuses on some things and dismisses others (Gordon et al., 2005). Berger (1982) argues that we see only what we choose to see. This means the act of seeing is determined by our choices; we focus on what we find valuable. Another important aspect that Berger mentions is that we never simply see an object. What we see is always the relationship between the thing and ourselves. As soon as we open our eyes and see, we discover that we can also be seen. Our first contact with the eyes of others makes it clear to us that we are a part of the visible world.

The many dimensions of the gaze

The gaze is connected to the body and to sensual perception. Merleau-Ponty (1962/2000) links existence and experience to the body whereby the individual is both a subject and object. He is critical of both the speculative gaze that reduces the gaze to mental processes and scientific knowledge (theory), and the empirical gaze that alleges that sensual impressions are 'pure' reflections of an external world produced by stimuli outside a passive, receptive sensual apparatus (Crary, 1990). Merleau-Ponty claims that the world we see, via our bodies, is tied to the simultaneous experiences of seeing and being seen. It is through the body, for example through the gaze, that we gain experience, insight, and understanding of the world and become part of that world.

The gaze is dependent on emotions. There are many expressions that allude to the gaze; something catches our attention, we perceive with our senses, we see, or we are touched by the gaze. Such expressions emphasise the fact that we focus on some things and exclude others. Even as researchers, we are influenced by our emotions; they move us and determine the perspective or point of view from which we view objects (Fausing, 1999).

The experience and insight that we gain through the gaze, the pictures that we create and use when we see and interpret the world, are both subjective and objective, or perhaps rather beyond experience and 'reality'. Experience, which is always founded on a particular culture, is projected from qualities of the experience onto the objects. Our emotions are projected onto the object, although they may belong to the subject (Løvlie, 2002).

The gaze comprises a language of relationships that relates and expresses feelings and intentions. It is a language that is learned and gains meaning within a particular culture through the everyday practice of seeing. Based on these ideas, I look at the gaze as a special point of view, always situated and anchored in social, professional and cultural processes and positions.

The classroom is the location or stage for the special dramaturgy that I want to explore in this chapter. I see the classroom both as a room for face-to-face interaction where the gaze has direct pedagogic and ethical implications and as a symbolic room where the layout and organisation of the room itself reflects the way the gaze or gazes are positioned, the relations between actors and between knowledge and power. A change in the positions of students and teachers in the room simultaneously changes the relations of the gaze. The teacher standing at the front of the class is perhaps a relic of the past, but rows of desks, with students sitting behind each other so that their gazes are synchronically directed toward a common point, the teacher or the blackboard, still exist in many classrooms. New cooperative teaching methods have dissolved the central, omniscient and scrutinising gaze of the teacher. The centralised perspective of Modernism has been replaced by a decentralised perspective, based on the increasing degree of face-to-face interaction between students. This gives students greater control over the gaze, and teachers more possibilities for reciprocal gaze relationships with individual students. At the same time, it is possible to see the contours of a stronger, although less conspicuous role as observer for the teacher. This actualises issues of the positions of the gaze; on the one hand as technology for surveillance, control, and objectification, and on the other as an important mode of relating to others requiring reciprocity. I will in the following look at the gaze in classrooms in relation to the tension between *reciprocity* and *objectification*.

The reciprocal gaze

Eva, one of my young informants, told me she was especially fond of one of her teachers because that teacher 'looked' at her in a way that made her feel liked. Experiencing the approving gaze of another creates a foundation for motivation and participation. This applies to both students and teachers. The teacher who has students who sit with wide open eyes and who look as if they are greedily soaking up information—as one of the teachers in my material describes them—has her need for self-confirmation fulfilled. How fortunate the teacher is who is met with open, interested, and receptive gazes! Eye contact can be spontaneous or calculating and judgmental, but it lays the foundation for reciprocity between the teacher and student, strengthening the contact.

Georg Simmel (1908/1969) has developed what he called 'sociology of the senses'. He underlines that the unification of and interaction between individuals is based on the reciprocal gaze, and looking into each other's eyes is 'perhaps the most direct and purest form of reciprocity in existence' (ibid., 358). He believes that it is important to know how we perceive and understand each other through the senses and the processing of impressions. He differentiates between two forms of understanding of the other, 'apprehension' and 'comprehension'. The first is spontaneous and non-cognitive and catalyses emotions in the meeting with the eyes of the other. The second refers to understanding the other, a gaze that can create a bridge between oneself and the other and enables us to gain access to the other's 'real self'. His sociology is based on the second form, because 'sociation', a term Simmel uses to describe the founding and regulation of social relations, is made possible because individuals have shared forms of interaction and cultural patterns. To Simmel, sociation always involves harmony and conflict, attraction and repulsion, love and hatred. Sociation is always the result of both categories of interaction, and he claims that in order to function together with others it is necessary to know whom you are relating to and, to a certain extent, what you can expect of the other.

The basis of Simmel's 'sociology of the senses' is that the eye has unique sociological functions for constituting society, without the help of the objectified forms primarily exercised through language. According to Simmel, the reciprocal gaze creates a connection between subjects that cannot be reduced to an objective structure. It exists in the moment; it is vulnerable and disappears the very moment that eye contact is broken. The reciprocal, interactive form that Simmel recommends is based on 'give and take'. When one wishes to understand the other, one opens oneself to the gaze of the other. This reciprocity involves both risk and trust. The knowledge gained is based on participation; a knowledge that cannot be reached through observation, but only by offering oneself as a gift to the other. Simmel speaks of the unmediated perception of the other as the intuitive experience of a gestalt, a complete person. It is this first impression that is retained, Simmel claims, and functions as the key to further knowledge of the other.

In *The Power of the eyes* Webbink (1986) argues that the direct gaze signals involvement with the other and reciprocal acceptance of a shared humanity. The eyes are expressive and can project, signal and express intense emotions. Reciprocity is connected to the emotions (Fausing, 1999), and the intensity and focus of a relationship form the basis for identification, learning and development of the self. Emotional ties and dependence make others into significant others (Mead, 1934/1974). Both students and teachers are influenced by this premise; both can be stimulated by and are vulnerable to the gaze of the other. In my own work, I observed situations where the teachers used the gaze to convey recognition and respect to some of their students (Arnesen, 2002, p. 211). For example, one teacher placed herself in a position where her eyes and the eyes of the student were on the same level and sent a look that clearly signalled 'I see you', and 'This is good'.

The gaze is flexible and facilitates contact in ways that are difficult to manage through the other senses, and our sense of sight is also the sense that can be consciously controlled. It allows us to communicate across distances and makes it possible to signal intimacy and attention, and to maintain control even when there are many students in the classroom. Quick glances may stimulate concentration on the subject being taught.

The gaze of recognition gives those who feel recognised the freedom to forget themselves, allowing them to immerse themselves in their work. Sartre (1943/1980) claims that although the gaze of the other on us may inhibit our actions, it may also form the basis of new understanding. He says that our world is reconstructed when we become aware of the gaze of the other directed at our self because it enables us to see situations and possibilities from the outside, through the gaze of the other. The fact that subjects see something in a viewed world means that they change—and the way they see and experience the world also changes. The object they look at changes.

Simmel (1908/1969) is concerned with all the different forms of social interaction between people, and emphasises that they are the glue in social relations, and the gaze is part of this. However, he does not romanticise or build a utopian vision. He studies and describes different conventions regulating the contact between gazes that have been developed and continue to develop in complex situations. According to Simmel, social conventions influence how one may show interest in the other or create a comfortable distance between oneself and the other. Goffman (1963) describes a special way of creating distance, which he calls 'civil inattention'. This happens when one pays the other enough attention through the gaze to signal that one realises and recognises that the other exists, but then breaks eye contact to signal that one is not interested in closer contact. One perhaps does not intend to dismiss the other, but we still see a potential problem with regard to reciprocity.

Many students who perhaps need contact must often make do with this type of (in)attention. The classroom situation itself, which comprises a teacher and many children, is an arena where attention is differentiated; some students experience the reciprocal gaze of recognition and respect, whereas others must manage on more random eye contact. This means that the gaze may facilitate the creation or concretisation of class hierarchies. When a teacher pays attention and demonstrates positive involvement with some students through the gaze, she signals the importance of these students. Those who fall within the teacher's field of vision can easily be perceived as more important than those who land outside or are 'completely in the periphery' (Arnesen, 2002, p. 234), whether this is due to recognition or a reprimand. My observations showed that some students never or very seldom fell within the teacher's field of vision. Being invisible in relation to the gaze of the teacher in a community with other invisible students is different to being invisible among many visible students, especially where visibility is valued. It is difficult being overlooked when being seen gives status. What Goffman (1963) describes as 'civil inattention', can easily be perceived as a simple lack of interest, rejection, and exclusion. 'Inattention' may even be interpreted as animosity, as demonstrated in the case of Tonje, who had individual tutoring and was usually alone every school recess throughout elementary school. She described the teachers as 'grumpy and nasty and ... they were kind of grumpy and they were just grumpy all day, sort of, it seemed like I'd done something to them, sort of, the whole school was sort of against me' (Arnesen, 2002, p. 377, my translation). Busy teachers, who barely cast a glance at students they meet when they hurry past with a pile of papers to be graded, can easily cause an unhappy, lonely child to feel 'invisible', non-existent, like a nobody.

However, being seen or not seen has both positive and negative aspects from the perspective of actors. Reciprocity is accompanied by the risk of being exposed and means to a certain extent that one surrenders oneself to the mercy of the other. In asymmetrical relationships this is a clear danger. There is a very weak boundary between reciprocity and dominance and objectification; this is obvious in the teacher's mandatory double vision. She must develop equal relations with her students and simultaneously evaluate and rank them according to their accomplishments, within a framework that allows little time for the development of reciprocity. Time, of course, is exactly what is needed if a teacher is to be able to find her way into 'the real self of the other' when students have problems. The objectification of students is not simply due to lack of time and attention; it is also caused by the perspective the teacher chooses to view her students from. Professional behaviour is, for example, connected to the ability to 'see' and judge which students to report as entitled to special educational resources.

Objectification: The professional gaze

It has been claimed that the accuracy of the teacher's gaze is an important premise of a teacher's work. The Norwegian framework curriculum (1999) claims that 'teachers must have a *knowledgeable gaze* that enables them to identify and encourage positive social behaviour and to intervene in negative student behaviour and bullying' (my emphasis and translation, p. 17). It is considered an ideal that teachers develop a competent gaze that enables them to see what is hidden and problematic long before an untrained person could manage to discover anything deviant. The teacher observes students in a relatively inconspicuous manner to capture a plausible representation of 'reality', based on a general trust in the 'objective' gaze. The professional gaze is developed in order to 'read the students', for example to 'see' which students need help, and they are expected to maintain order and control, demands that tend to exacerbate the development of the 'suspicious' gaze. The act of seeing is influenced by the professional literature, the media and the experiences of the teacher. These influences help form the expectations and interpretations of student behaviour, which become the basis on which troublemakers or students who have 'special needs' can be identified. A selective process is activated where the teacher focuses only on what appears to be relevant—other signs are ignored. This focus determines what is included or excluded, and it creates a constellation between teachers and students of 'powerful invisibility' (the teachers) and 'powerless visibility' (the students) because the teacher, as the one who sees, is considered to be irrelevant in terms of what must be documented.

Foucault (1977) talks about surveillance and how it is manifested in disciplinary institutions through techniques on a continuum, from the most penitentiary-like, to self-disciplining. This variety presents a continuum of normality that develops scales for types of deviance. Subtle forms of exclusion and rejection have replaced more repressive technologies. The gaze in this connection functions as a medium for detailed observation of 'inmates' (prisons), 'patients' (health clinics), or 'students' (schools). The determination of deviance requires that it is detected by a trained eye. Teachers are expected to have the ability to 'see' when students fail to meet the norms or requirements set by the institutions. The protocols for discovering problems can in this sense be perceived as technologies for intrusive surveillance. Foucault points out that the 'objectified gaze' may be internalised by the individuals under surveillance, who come to see themselves in view of the criteria of normality and subordinate to them, bringing about the production of 'docile and useful bodies' (Foucault, 1977).

This description of the gaze contrasts sharply with the reciprocal perspective that Simmel and Merleau-Ponty argue for. The actors' experiences and self-consciousness of their positions in the world are absent in Foucault's perspective. Sartre shares his scepticism with regard to the gaze, or perhaps it is more appropriate to say he shares Foucault's belief in the animosity of the gaze. At the same time, Sartre focuses first and foremost on the bodily and existential qualities of the gaze. We are all objects of the gaze of others, and our self-understanding hinges on the way we are perceived by others. In our interaction with others we expose sides of ourselves that are available for others to 'read' and interpret. This makes us vulnerable (Gordon et al., 2005). Many of the students I interviewed told me about their own or others' anxiety when exposed to the gaze of others, and the risk they ran of making fools of themselves or being laughed at. The classroom is a place where students are occasionally expected to expose themselves in the limelight. This turns it into a threatening location for some and a place for positive exposure for others.

Becoming an object in the gaze of the others

Sartre (1943/1980) focuses first and foremost on 'the state of being observed', having the gaze turned towards oneself and the importance this has for human development and alienation. The existential experience of being subjected to the gaze of the other is central. Sartre argues that shame and pride reveal the gaze of the other to the self and establish the position of the self in this gaze. The experience of being seen and judged causes one to become self-conscious and calculating with regard to the impression one makes on others. Under the gaze of the teacher, students can develop different survival strategies, which Simmel (1908/1969) refers to as masking strategies. The experience of being looked upon with a denigrating or revolted gaze can contribute to subterfuge; one desires to please others or protect one's self. For Sartre (1943/1980) this subterfuge has a high cost. It reduces the individual's freedom, his or her possibilities of living authentically.

All social situations involve power in one shape or another (e.g. Giddens, 1993). When relationships are asymmetrical, as in the relationships between adults and children, the likelihood of objectification is clearly present. This involves specifying who has the right to see and define reality. Objectification is manifested in all relations between groups where there is a relationship of dominance and subordination. A lot has been written about how seeing and being seen is manifested as dimensions of gender. In *La domination masculine* from 1998 Bourdieu claims that dominance keeps women in a constant state of bodily insecurity through the gaze of the other, and hence as objects which are congenial, attractive and at men's disposal (Bourdieu, 1998/2001). The division between the symbolic categories of feminine and masculine creates stereotypes that operate even when they are in conflict with forms of reality that contradict these stereotypical images. In most places in the world, men, because they are men, still have greater power than women with regard to seeing, and their gazes exercise more control; we see this fact manifested in its most extreme form in the dictates of the Taliban regime requiring women to be covered from head to toe, including their eyes. Men's privileged gaze, especially with regard to the ways men and women, boys and girls are perceived, is obvious in the way they are presented in films, on TV, on gallery walls and in the coloured press, where they are still to a great extent framed in and chosen by and for the male gaze. This tendency is perhaps expressed most strongly in pornography (Berger, 1982; Bonner et al., 1992; Mulvey, 1975).

The power of the gaze, objectification, is a central point in literature about different kinds of discrimination and suppression. In addition to gender, the gaze has been studied in relation to majorities/minorities, 'black' and 'white', 'master' and 'slave'. Power relations are not static, however. Relations can be changed and

can be reversed, turning the gaze in the opposite direction. In the introduction
to an anthology of African texts Sartre wrote:

> I want you to feel, as I, the sensation of being seen. For the white man
> has enjoyed for three thousand years the privilege of seeing without
> being seen. It was a seeing pure and uncomplicated; the light of his eyes
> drew all things from their primeval darkness. The whiteness of his skin
> was a further aspect of vision, a light condensed. The white man, white
> because he was a man, white like the day, lighted like a torch all creation;
> he unfolded the essence, secret and white, of existence. Today, these black
> men have fixed their gaze upon us and our gaze is thrown back into our
> eyes. … By this steady and corrosive gaze, we are picked to the bone.
>
> (Qtd. in Jay, 1993, p. 294).

Changes in power relations change gaze relations. The ideals of reciprocity
and equality face severe challenges when for example students no longer assume
the same 'natural' attitude of subordination as they did in the past when faced
with the gaze of the teacher. In a society based on equality, the teacher's gaze
no longer has indisputable authority. However, social relations in school still
operate by the 'rules' of the teachers' privileged gaze, which have their roots in
another time, but are taken for granted until they are broken. When students
demonstratively meet the gaze of the teacher, this can be perceived as a strong
provocation, because the student transgresses unspoken rules regarding who
has the right to see and control the gaze.

The gaze of the researcher

I have witnessed episodes like the one I described in my introduction many times
in the course of many years as a teacher and researcher, although with certain
variations. It was exactly such a situation, an examination requiring silence and
no verbal contact, which made the gaze 'speak' and express meaning in very
obvious ways. I was surprised at how strongly this aspect of communication
was portrayed in this little introductory ethnographic note. Haraway (1996)
describes the researcher as a witness. Scientific practice, the role of the researcher
and the production of knowledge she claims, are all related to different aspects
of 'witnessing'. The roles of observer and researcher, which were created during
the scientific revolution during the 1600s, aimed 'in all modesty, to mirror reality
in a systematic and accurate manner and the researcher was not supposed to

disturb this reflection of reality with his subjectivity' (Asdal et al., 1998, p. 76, my translation). As a witness, the producer of knowledge, paradoxically, in spite of his presence and attentive gaze, was supposed to be invisible. This is an ideal still argued for in our modern-day understanding of scientific objectivity; i.e. sight is a sense that allows us to grip the world, sight offers a direct connection between science and reality; one can test whether knowledge is true simply by seeing for oneself. Even though the ideal of the objective, distanced observer has been examined critically since then, Haraway argues that researchers continue to carry this ideal with them in their practice (Asdal et al., 1998, p. 78), and, I would like to add, it has a strong influence on their view of the professional gaze, including that of teachers. Seeing is all about power: about the power to see and have control over the way in which things are seen. The gaze of the researcher resembles all the gazes that operate from a position of power. Haraway prescribes a measure of modesty for the researcher; this involves describing one's own point of view and a responsible attempt to discover what is or could be perceived and interpreted differently. I see this simultaneously as a call for critical awareness and as a basis for agency and action. Being critically aware implies demonstrating how power and opportunity are produced, distributed, designated and unfairly allocated. Haraway launches the terms 'diffraction' and 'interference' as metaphors for critical consciousness. Diffraction means breaking something up into several components. Interference refers to the interaction between wave movements; waves with the same or different frequencies either increase or decrease each other (Lille Fokus, 1973). These metaphors seem suitable for disturbing, making waves and getting involved in the exploration of the complexity of power and the ways in which the gaze is part of processes of inclusion and marginalisation. The school is characterised by control and surveillance—and of reciprocity and mutual exchanges. Teachers and researchers gaze with some power, but as Gordon et al. (2000) suggest, the situation is complex, and both teachers and pupils may experience objectification and reciprocity, and thus seem to balance between power and vulnerability.

References

Arnesen, A.L., (2002) *Ulikhet og marginalisering—med referanse til kjønn og sosial bakgrunn: En etnografisk studie av sosial og diskursiv praksis i skolen. [Difference and marginalisation—with reference to gender and social background: An ethnographic study of social and discursive practice in school]*, HiO-rapport 2002: 13, Oslo: Høgskolen i Oslo.

Asdal, K., Berg, A.J., Brenna, B., Moser, I. and Rustad, L.M., (1998) *Betatt av viten. Bruksanvisninger til Donna Haraway. [Infatuated with knowledge. Instructions for using the work of Donna Haraway.]*, Oslo: Spartacus Forlag A/S.

Berger, J., (1982) *Ways of seeing*, British Broadcasting Corporation and Penguin Books.

Bonner, F., Goodman, L., Allen, R., Janes, L. and King, C. (1992) (eds.) *Imagining women. Cultural representations and gender.* Issues in Womens' Studies. Cambridge, UK: Polity Press in association with The Open University.

Bourdieu, P., (1998/2001) *Masculine domination,* Stanford, CA: Stanford University Press.

Crary, J., (1990) *Techniques of the observer. On vision and modernity in the nineteenth century.* London: October Books, MIT Press.

Fausing, B., (1999) *Bevægende billeder. Om affekt og billeder. [Moving images. On affect and images]*, København: Tiderne Skrifter.

Foucault, M., (1977) *Discipline and punish: The birth of the prison*, translated by Sheridan, A., London: Penguin Books.

Giddens, A., (1993) *New rules of sociological method. A positive critique of interpretative sociologies*, 2nd edition, Cambridge, UK: Polity Press.

Goffman, E., (1963) *Behavior in public places. Notes on the social organisation of gatherings*, London: The Free Press, Macmillan.

Gordon, T. and Lahelma, E., (1994) Citizenship, difference and marginality in schools with special reference to gender: From restructuring of education to the physical school, *European Conference on Ethnocentrism and Education,* May 1994 Delphi.

Gordon, T., and Lahelma, E., (1995) Citizenship, difference and marginality in schools — with special reference to gender. Presentation of a Finnish Project. Being, having and doing gender in schools, in *Gender, modernity, postmodernity — New perspectives on development/construction of gender*, Arbeidsnotat 2/95, Oslo: Centre of Womens' Research, University of Oslo.

Gordon, T., Holland, J. and Lahelma, E., (2000) *Making spaces: Citizenship and difference in schools*, London: Macmillan Press.

Gordon, T., Holland, J., Lahelma, E. and Tolonen, T., (2005) Gazing with intent: Ethnographic practice in classrooms, *Qualitative Research,* 5(1): 113-131.

Haraway, D., (1996) Modest witness: Feminist diffractions in science studies, in Galison, P. and Stump, D. J., (eds.) *The disunity of science. Boundaries, contexts, and power*, Stanford, CA: Stanford University Press.

Jay, M., (1993) *Downcast eyes. The denigration of vision in the twentieth-century French thought,* Berkeley, CA: University of California Press.

Lille Fokus leksikon (1973) *[Focus encyclopedia]*, Oslo: Aschehoug A/S (Nygaard).

Løvlie, L., (2002) The promise of Bildung, *Journal of Philosophy of Education,* 36(3): 467-486.

Mead, G.H., (1934/1974) *Mind, self and society from the standpoint of a social behaviorist.* Vol. 1, Edited and with an Introduction by Morris, Charles W., Chicago: The University of Chicago Press.

Merleau-Ponty, M., (1962/2000) *The phenomenology of perception*, translated by Colin, S., New York: Humanities Press.

Mulvey, L. (1975) Visual pleasure and narrative cinema, *Screen,* 16(3): 6-18.

Norwegian Ministry of Education and Research (1999) *Rammeplan og forskrift for 4-årig allmennlærerutdanning. [Framework curriculum for 4-year teacher education]*, Oslo: Norwegian Ministry of Education and Research.

Sartre, J. P. (1943/1980) *Erfaringer med de Andre. Kapitler om sosiale relasjoner [Experiences with the Others. Chapters on social relations]*, selection from L'étre et le Néant. Introduction and translation (from French to Norwegian) by Østerberg, D., Oslo: Gyldendal Norsk Forlag.

Simmel, G., (1908/1969) Sociology of the senses: Visual interaction, in Park, R.E. and Burgess, W.W., (eds.) *Introduction to the science of sociology*, Chicago: Chicago University Press, 356-361.

Webbinck, P., (1986) *The power of the eyes,* New York: Springer Publishing Company.

Weinstein, D. and Weinstein, M., (1984) On the visual constitution of society: The contributions of Georg Simmel and Jean-Paul Sartre to a sociology of the senses, *History of European Ideas,* 5(4): 349-362.

Chapter 3

Interviewing young people in institutional contexts—methodological reflections

Sanna Aaltonen and Päivi Honkatukia

The ethical and reflexive turns in the social sciences have contributed towards consolidating new principles of research practices. This means that researchers informed by a commitment to using reflexive and ethical approaches aim to make explicit the power relationships between researcher(s) and research participants as well as the context and the process that has led to particular interpretations of the data. While these principles are widely agreed upon, among the feminist researchers in particular, there is still confusion on how to achieve and practice reflexivity (e.g. Guillemim and Gillam, 2004; Mauthner and Doucet, 2003; Pillow, 2003; Ramazanoglu and Holland, 2002).

This chapter deals with challenges concerning reflexivity in studies on young people in institutional settings.[6] It contemplates how institutions, as administrative contexts, shape research practices (cf. Gordon et al., 2000, p. 53) and the ways in which institutional contexts influence the interaction between different actors when producing the data on young people in marginal positions in society. Thus, the aim is to highlight the complicated relationship between researchers and young research participants in institutional contexts, particularly to discuss how issues such as the researcher's access to the field and the research participants' informed consent are regulated and promoted in institutional settings.

Based on our individual research experiences this chapter is intended to contribute to developing critical and collective reflection on the ethics and practicalities of empirical fieldwork, specifically, of interview based research on young people who can be considered to be in vulnerable life situations. Thus this chapter aims to practice reflexivity both backwards and forwards: documenting and investigating reflexivity in-practice during fieldwork as well as considering how this reflexivity has the potential to inform the analysis of data and the representations produced (cf. Gillies and Alldred, 2002; Riach, 2009).

6   With this article Tuula Gordon and Elina Lahelma are credited with the methodological reflexivity that the authors have learned from them and aim for in their current research projects.

The chapter draws on two research projects that are both based on young people's interviews in institutional settings and that share similar ethical and methodological starting points. Both research projects aim to produce knowledge on the lived experiences of marginalised young people to which qualitative methods are particularly well suited. There is no single label that would do justice to the informants, but referring to our informants as being in the margins is an attempt to acknowledge their position in relation to the socially constructed ideal of a life career. We believe that it is important to study how these particular young people make sense of their life situations, choices, past and future. This, in turn, requires particular theoretical and methodological sensitivity.

Within the context of this anthology, our chapter focuses on cultural practices in doing research on struggles that young people go through in making transitions in education and in other areas of their lives. Aaltonen's study[7] explores what the imaginable prospects and actual choices are of ninth graders who are considered at risk of becoming marginalised from education or from their peer groups. The data was produced in metropolitan areas of Finland and consists of thirty-two thematic biographical interviews with fifteen to seventeen year old young women and men who participated in multi-professional services offering young people support to complete comprehensive school and to prevent their marginalisation. The research participants were recruited from two multi-professional programs or services, Pilot and My Own Career (MOC), that both implemented activities either in or outside schools with the aim of supporting young people, eighth and ninth graders in particular, with such methods as activity based learning, small group teaching and offering positive experiences within leisure time activities.

Honkatukia's study[8] focuses on the criminality of young men categorised as belonging to ethnic minorities in Finland. Her data consist of twenty biographical interviews with sixteen to twenty-five year old young men whose criminal acts had been dealt with in the criminal justice system. The aim of the study was to analyse their personal accounts of their criminality as part of their life course and in relation to central transitions, such as moving from one country to another, changing schools and starting working life. Twelve informants were

7   The research project was funded by the Academy of Finland 2008-2010, and the Youth Research Society 2011-2013.
8   This study was conducted together with Dr Leena Suurpää (Honkatukia and Suurpää, 2007). While the study has been a joint project in this text the study is referred as Honkatukia's study.

interviewed in prison, and the remaining eight were recruited via child protection, probation services and mediation offices.

Why to choose a beaten path?
Conducting interviews within institutions

While having separate research problems, we shared an interest towards capturing empirical knowledge on phenomena and processes such as disadvantage, criminality and marginality. Our aim was to produce in-depth information on how issues seen as youth problems by adult society are experienced and made meaningful by young people themselves. In the process of considering who would be apt, accessible and willing to share their experiences and viewpoints on such topics, and how these topics could be studied, we chose first, to interview individuals and second, to recruit them through institutions. Both of these decisions can be considered common solutions. Interviewing is one of the most used qualitative research methods in social as well as youth studies, but at the same time, it is sometimes considered an outworn and tame way to produce knowledge. Particularly within child and youth studies, traditional one-to-one question-answer type interviews have been disparaged for being neither productive for researchers nor especially enjoyable for participants. As Karen Nairn and her colleagues (2005, p. 228) state, despite our good intentions, it is difficult to break the formal structure of an interview and thus avoid reproducing relations of authority.

In order to improve interviews as sources of varied information on meanings and experiences, and to address the unequal power relationship between the researcher and the researched, a range of participatory and often long running or sequential research techniques have been developed by youth researchers (e.g. Conolly, 2008; Renold et al., 2008, pp. 431-32; Sanders and Munford, 2007). Although we appreciate the development of these stimulating research techniques and alternative routes of access that have enabled researchers to listen to young people in new ways and in new contexts, we propose that both interviewing and gaining access to young people through institutional settings still have value in producing knowledge of their lives. Our claim is not based on practical reasons only; we believe that these solutions embody particular advantages in some research contexts.

While a participatory approach is valuable, keeping the research and the researcher marginal in the lives of young people, at least time-wise, may be well suited for many of the potential informants. Volunteering to a one-off interview may be more inviting to some young people than the option of committing to a long-term research relationship. Moreover, a simple interview setting functions to remind informants of the context and power relations of data production, and of the fact that discussion is initiated by the researcher for a particular purpose. In more long-lasting fieldwork, the role and function of the research may become unclear and blurred. In reporting on their longitudinal, ethnographic research on young people in care, Emma Renold and her research team (2008) pointed out that empowering young people as active research participants over a longer period of time made some of the informants regard research more as a social event or a club than as the purposeful production of data.

Some forms of interaction are of course missed in a short-term research encounter. Tuula Gordon, Janet Holland and Elina Lahelma (2000, p. 62) state that since they as ethnographers spent a lengthy time in their research schools, they hopefully 'had some impact to the lives of students and teachers we met and came to know'. A researcher doing one-off interviews can hardly dream of making a significant impact, or coming to know the informants anything but superficially; and during a single interview it may be challenging to establish rapport between a research participant and an interviewer, who remains an abstract researcher rather than becoming a personalised adult (cf. Gordon and Lahelma, 2003, pp. 248-49).

Institutions are the main access routes for the recruitment of young people for all kinds of studies (see Heath et al., 2007). In our research projects, accessing young people via institutions meant acknowledging that while institutionally produced categories of normalities and pathologies should be critically examined, the institutional groupings still reveal something about the material and social differences among young people. Consequently, approaching specific institutions meant choosing targeted samples that were strategically located and apt to illuminate experiences of being underprivileged or marginalised (cf. Gerson and Horowitz, 2002). Honkatukia wanted to interview young men who had committed crimes and whose offences had been dealt with in the criminal justice system. An obvious context for the research was prison (in addition to child protection and probation services). Aaltonen's decision to recruit informants in specific educational and youth outreach programs was an attempt to operationalise concepts she identified in the early phases of her research that grasp the nature of unfavourable positions in society.[9]

---

9   During her field study Aaltonen ended up, however, abandoning the very same concepts, such as disadvantaged, as inadequate, too limiting and stigmatising.

We will now turn to discuss in more detail the institutional contexts of data production sites and the role of gatekeepers in the course of gaining access and informed consent. These processes have been acknowledged as being problematic and as demanding ethical consciousness from the researcher not only in the beginning of, but throughout the research process (see Guillemin and Gillam, 2004; Miller and Bell, 2002; Renold et al., 2008). In the following, we focus on the multiple roles of the staff who acted not only as focal gatekeepers, but also as informants, mediators and motivators.

Multiple roles of gatekeepers in institutions

During our fieldwork, we both negotiated practical agreements with the staff members of each institutional setting where contact persons had helped to organise the interviews. The staff worked as mediators between us and the young people, which meant that we as researchers were throughout dependent on their motivation to assist us. Aaltonen's study provides an example of a multi-phased procedure of gaining access. First, there were the institutional gatekeepers that consisted of the staff working in Pilot and MOC units and the departments[10] that co-operated in administering the multi-professional programs. Second, there were familial gatekeepers. Both the programs and the administrating departments insisted that parents had to be well informed of the research and their consent had to be obtained in writing. Even at the cost of alienating some of the young people or parents with this formal procedure (cf. Miller and Bell, 2002, p. 65), the justification for it was the programs' aim to prevent the research interviews from producing any distrust or confrontations that could, in turn, aggravate the already delicate co-operation between them and the families. Therefore, the gatekeepers can be seen as protecting not only the young people, but also the institutions from any possible harm caused by the research. Young people were given forms with information on the aims of the study; the source of research funding and the confidentiality of the interviews and these were to be brought to Aaltonen with both their and their guardian's signature.

According to our experiences and the remarks made by several of our colleagues, many of the institutions in Finland appear to be amenable to youth researchers' requests to recruit informants in their premises, and this applied also to our research settings. This may be due to the fact that background organisations, such as universities and research institutes administered by

10   Youth Department, the Social Services Department, the Education Department and the Health Centre of the City of Helsinki.

government departments, are considered reliable. Further, we suggest that having interviews as our principal method facilitated access to the field at least compared to time-consuming methods requiring ongoing presence of the researcher. In the opening interviews with the staff conducted by Aaltonen, some of the units described the process of building trust with the young people as being too delicate to be interfered by the extended presence of a researcher.

Another possible rationale for the amenability of institutions is that institutional gatekeepers look to possible benefits of the research to the institutions in general and to the young people in particular. In the youth services, staff members considered young people's participation to the research to support the program's aims of rehabilitation and extracurricular learning. Therefore, in Aaltonen's study the paper traffic involved in collecting formal permission from guardians, as well as ensuring the young people arrived on time for the interviews, was monitored and supported by staff. Their aim was to foster a sense of responsibility among the young people and to urge them to take made promises seriously. From the program's viewpoint, the data production provided a real-life opportunity to practice these skills. Thus Aaltonen was positioned not only as a researcher, but also as a responsible adult who was implicitly expected to comply with the aims of the program. One could ask whether this pedagogical aim to promote participation compromised young people's fully informed consent (see also Curtis et al., 2004, p. 169; Heath et al., 2007, pp. 412-13).

Although staff can be seen as posing a barrier that has to be crossed to gain access to young people (e.g. Honkatukia et al., 2003, p. 327), the gatekeepers referred to in this chapter appeared to make the fieldwork smoother and to work hard to motivate the young people to take part in the research. This is not to say that the gatekeepers did not shut the gate when they deemed it necessary. For example, according to a youth worker in Aaltonen's study, a girl who was suffering from depression and who had first agreed to be interviewed, later reversed her decision, which the youth worker accepted without further persuasion. Revealing this to the researcher can be understood to demonstrate that the staff members were sincere in their efforts to recruit participants, but that they were also able to estimate who were in danger of becoming upset because of an interview.

We regard the observations above as also relevant to the analysis, for when the participation of young people in a study is sought through institutions; there is a particular need to reflect on whose voices are included in the study and whose voices are left out. Besides the decisions made by contact persons in the field (gatekeepers), this is related to actions of both researchers and young people themselves as research participants. Researchers are claimed to be inclined to listen to voices that are most easily reached (e.g. Honkasalo and Suurpää, 2009), which in turn can be seen as narrowing down the voices that get represented. Also, in institutional settings such as schools, there are always those who have been excluded from school, who do not participate in organised activities and to whom it is problematic to gain access for different reasons (see also Conolly, 2008, p. 206).

Establishing rapport with gatekeepers is one of the preconditions for conducting fieldwork, but at the same time the researcher is expected to maintain a degree of social distance to them for ethical reasons. It is not uncommon for gatekeepers to expect researchers to co-operate with them and to share their impressions and information on the informants. After all, they may offer general and particular information on the informants and expect this exchange to be reciprocal. For example, one youth worker interviewed by Aaltonen mentioned a particular girl who she anticipated would be thrilled to participate in the research. The girl the youth worker referred to indeed participated in the interview and was very talkative. However, she appeared to be selective in what she revealed for she chose not to disclose some difficult circumstances in her life that the youth worker shared with Aaltonen. Thus institutions and institutional connections may provide unrequested information on informants that alters the image they would like to create of themselves.

In the prison context, Honkatukia's research team sometimes found themselves in ambiguous positions in terms of loyalty to the gatekeepers on one hand, and to informants on the other. These feelings might relate to the nature of prison as a so-called total institution where relations between staff and the inmates have a tendency to become tense and oppositional. Even if anonymously done, revealing some aspects of the interviews felt like a betrayal of the confidentiality promised to the interviewees; whereas refraining from answering appeared impolite (see also Gordon et al., 2007). Besides uneasiness, typical for these encounters between researchers and gatekeepers were the difficulty to determine, even afterwards, what would have been the most ethically sound way to act in each situation.

From potential to actual informants—informed consent and the meaning of trust

Obviously, passing by the gatekeepers and gaining access to the informants do not automatically mean gaining young people's consent to participate in research (cf. Miller and Bell, 2002). In the youth services, two-thirds of the potential informants participated in the interviews. In comparison, in the prison only a few of those asked to be interviewed refused. This may tell something about the prison as an institution: for some, meeting outsiders for an interview may have meant a refreshing break from the greyness of prison life. The same can be said to apply to school environments, where the opportunity to skip a class because of an interview was an additional incentive for many of the students. An additional and more material incentive to participate in the interviews was provided in the form of two movie tickets offered to the informants.[11] These tickets were also meant to be a gesture of reciprocity.

Considering that we claim to live in an interview society, it was not surprising that most young people we interviewed had some idea of what was expected of them right from the beginning when their initial informed consent was sought. At this stage, they were asked to present their opinions and experiences orally, and most appeared to be aware that they had the opportunity to regulate the scope and depth of their responses. However, we encountered some young people with, for example, a refugee background who were unfamiliar with the discursive nature of conventional one-to-one interviews (cf. Curtis et al., 2004, p. 168). This emphasises the point that all young research participants cannot be expected to be fully aware of what participating in a research means and how their comments will be used and framed in future reports. Since the research process is somewhat unpredictable and is dependent on the data produced, this is rarely clear to the researcher, either, when conducting interviews. In this sense, the notion of informed consent remains fundamentally problematic (see also Heath et al., 2007; Miller and Boulton, 2007).

The key difference between research and 'curing' encounters is that researchers are able to listen without having to act (Sanders and Munford, 2007, p. 196). However, young people may be uncertain of how to interpret the position of a researcher; for example, we encountered expectations that the researchers would help the informants with their acute problems. While we aimed to establish rapport with the young people and create a safe atmosphere where they could

11 Unfortunately this could not be done in a closed institution such as prison.

speak out, through seeking the informed consent of the young people at the beginning of the interviews—Honkatukia describing her research project to the informants and Aaltonen introducing two copies of a research contract for the young people to sign—the attitude of the informants towards the research was interlinked with their general feelings towards the institution in which they were involved. Conducting interviews in premises where young people are subjects of education, guidance or control by adults occupying positions of authority, calls for negotiating and alleviating the relations of authority between the young participants and researchers, although this may be challenging. For example, a young man interviewed in prison stated in his interview that he did not trust the researchers because he had previously had bad experiences with authorities. Some informants expressed they did not want to disclose the offences they had committed or their former home country. Such comments can be met with both disappointment and delight: disappointment because of missing information but delight because it means that young people feel able to regulate the information they are prepared to provide of themselves (cf. Heath et al., 2007, p. 413).

Institutional contexts of interaction

Many features of interaction are intertwined with the particular institutional settings in which they occur. An example of this is the timing of an interview in terms of the informants' 'institutional career'. The lives of some young people who had just entered the youth services appeared to be so chaotic and unplanned that at the time of the interviews, they were unable to disclose information because they had not had time to process it themselves yet (Curtis et al., 2004). Some of the young people could be argued as belonging to an 'over-surveilled' social group that had already had their share of being counselled and monitored by different institutions and services in the criminal justice, health, youth and social sectors (cf. Honkatukia et al., 2003; Renold et al., 2008). Informants' present and past institutional encounters may provoke either well 'rehearsed' and abundant narratives of oneself, or a refusal to 'confess' once more and produce a forced telling about oneself (cf. Aaltonen forthcoming; Skeggs, 2004). Some of our informants were silent even though they had volunteered to be interviewed. This may be linked to the fact that young people have different resources and capabilities to reflect on their lives, but also to their possible interpretation of the research interviews as voyeuristic, as yet another means of surveillance or as a simulation of social intervention (see also Conolly 2008, p. 206; Honkatukia et al., 2003, p. 320).

By contrast, the interviews with the young men who had just entered prison in Honkatukia's study were productive in their content. At the same time, the interviews raised some ethical concerns. The newcomers had to spend some days in a cell by themselves and without many activities. They therefore had time to think about their past, present and future. In this situation, the research interview offered the young men the possibility to reflect on issues that occupied their mind together with someone who was willing to listen. Some talked about very intimate and psychologically complicated feelings, and expressed strong emotions, for instance, crying. The possibility to speak to researchers at this particular moment, together with the knowledge that the interview would be a one-time occasion, made some informants very open.

In methodological literature, the concept of 'emotion work' has been used to describe the work with other people's emotions (Dickson-Swift et al., 2007, pp. 335-36). In conducting interviews, one has to be ready to encounter the interviewee in a humane way and at an emotional level. The boundary between the researcher and the researched is sometimes broken, and some interviewees may also experience interviews as therapeutic (ibid., p. 336; Maynard, 1994, p. 6). This can mean feeling being heard; but talking to an empathetic listener can also lead to such unplanned openness that is even regretted later on (Corbin and Morse, 2003, p. 338; Dickson-Swift et al., 2007, p. 331).

In these situations, researchers need to reflect on their responsibility in raising difficult emotions. Some interviewees in the prison revealed such serious problems and expressed them in a manner that the researchers considered breaking the promise of confidentiality and sharing their worries with the prison staff. They talked about their worries at a more abstract and general level, to ensure that the staff were informed and prepared to encounter the possibly complex consequences of the interviews. However, in the end, the researchers were not sure whether any measures were taken since access to and knowledge about possible aftercare was institutionally regulated most strictly in the prison context.

Aaltonen conducted interviews with young people in programs offering support. This institutional context meant that a more efficient emotional 'safety net' was in place (Reiter, 2003, p. 275) compared to the prison context. In other words, the young people had the possibility to reflect on the interview afterwards with an adult, if they wanted to. To the best of Aaltonen's knowledge, only one interviewee used this opportunity. The youth worker involved in the program mentioned how an interview conducted the previous day appeared to have been 'tough' because the interviewee had phoned her and told her that the researcher had started crying during the discussion. Indeed, tears had filled the researcher's eyes when the interviewee had described the sudden death of a close person, and she had mentioned this reaction to the interviewee. Although neither the interviewee nor the youth worker accused the researcher of anything, she felt puzzled and guilty for allowing her feelings to show. Had the interviewee simply been surprised that an adult researcher reacted in such a way, or was she offended because the reaction implied that her life is sorrowful? The course of events was a valuable reminder that while we as researchers should not be impassive or callous either, it may sometimes be better to prevent the display of strong emotions as this deflects attention away from informants to ourselves; at the same time, it was reassuring to notice that the 'safety net' does, indeed, work.

Conclusion

In this chapter, we have unravelled our experiences of conducting interviews in formal institutions with young people in vulnerable positions. We have examined how the institutional context plays a significant part in shaping the research process. According to our experience, structural aspects of the studied institutions and institutional power relations and tensions have an impact on the research process in at least the following ways:

First, they have impact on the composition of informants. This occurs based on the understandings, values and decisions of the researcher, institutional gatekeepers as well as young people themselves. The analysis is heavily influenced by who is selected for the study, and researchers need to critically reflect on the consequences of whose voices and knowledge are represented in the study, and whose experiences are left out. For various reasons, the voices of the most vulnerable young people tend to remain silent in research practice. In youth research, sensitivity to this issue has, however, increased, and innovative methods have been developed to seek out 'hard-to-reach' informants, such as spending a longer time in the field and using a wide range of contact persons (e.g. MacDonald and Marsh, 2005).

Second, institutional settings affect the ways in which young people decide to represent themselves in the interviews: what they talk about, what they leave untold. Young people negotiate their relationship to the questions they are asked from the institutional positions through which researchers approach them, even if not in any straightforward way. A researcher should be sensitive towards the ways in which institutional discourses and definitions become part of the self-understandings of young people when they make sense of their lives.

Third, institutional settings include interactional and emotional processes, which influence both the interviews with young people and the regulation of researchers' access to the field by adult gatekeepers. These interactional settings often involve ethical dilemmas and contradictory loyalties, which can be hard to foresee but often need an immediate reaction from the researcher in the field. Relatedly, it is also important to acknowledge that the research intervention itself can have an impact on the relations and interactive processes in the field.

We suggest that scrutinising the above-mentioned aspects of data production is important to the analysis of the cultural significance of the interview data. The aspects above deserve a careful analysis not only in their own right, but also because they have an impact on the results of the study and the knowledge that is being produced. In concrete research practice, examining these aspects means discovering numerous ethically challenging and emotionally uncomfortable moments, exploring 'messy' examples of fieldwork and engaging in 'uncomfortable reflexivity' that acknowledges our knowing as tenuous (cf. Pillow, 2003). All this messiness and emotionality can be claimed to be reverberated in the interview. Our responsibility as researchers is not to tidy it away but to highlight it and incorporate it to the analysis of the data to produce reflexive knowledge on the everyday lives of young people in marginal positions.

References

Aaltonen, S., (forthcoming) Subjective orientations to the schooling of young people on the margins of school, *Young*.

Conolly, A., (2008) Challenges of generating qualitative data with socially excluded young people, *International Journal of Social Research Methodology*, 11(3): 201-214.

Corbin, J. and Morse, J.M., (2003) The unstructured interactive interview: Issues of reciprocity and risks when dealing with sensitive topics, *Qualitative Inquiry*, 9(3): 335-354.

Curtis, K., Roberts, H., Copperman, J., Downie, A. and Liabo, K., (2004) How come I don't get asked no questions? Researching 'hard to reach' children and teenagers, *Child and Family Social Work*, 9: 167-175.

Dickson-Swift, V., James, E.L., Kippen, S. and Liamputtong, P., (2007) Doing sensitive research: What challenges do qualitative researchers face, *Qualitative Research*, 7(3): 327-353.

Gerson, K. and Horowitz, R., (2002) Observation and interviewing: Options and choices in qualitative research, in May, T., (ed.) *Qualitative research in action*, London: Sage, 199-224.

46   *Interviewing young people in institutional contexts—methodological reflections*

Gillies, V. and Alldred, P., (2002) The ethics of intention: Research as a political tool, in Mauthner, M., Birch, M., Jessop, J. and Miller, T., (eds.) *Ethics in qualitative research*, London: Sage Publications, 33-49.

Gordon, T., Holland, J. and Lahelma, E., (2000) *Making spaces: Citizenship and difference in schools*. Houndsmill, New York: Macmillan.

Gordon, T., Hynninen, P., Lahelma, E., Metso, T., Palmu, T. and Tolonen, T., (2007) Koulun arkea tutkimassa. [Researching the everyday school], in Lappalainen, S., Hynninen, P., Kankkunen, T., Lahelma, E. and Tolonen, T., (eds.) *Etnografia metodologiana: lähtökohtana koulutuksen tutkimus. [Etnography as methodology from the point of view of education research]*, Tampere: Vastapaino, 41-64.

Gordon, T. and Lahelma, E., (2003) From ethnography to life history: Tracing transitions of school students, *International Journal of Social Research Methodology*, 6(3): 245-254.

Guillemim, M. and Gillam, L. (2004) Ethics, reflexivity, and "ethically important moments" in research, *Qualitative Inquiry*, 10(2): 261-280.

Heath, S., Charles, V., Grow, G. and Wiles, R., (2007) Informed consent, gatekeepers and go-betweens: Negotiating consent in child and youth-oriented institutions, *British Educational Research Journal*, 33(3): 403-417.

Honkatukia, P., Nyqvist, L. and Pösö, T., (2003) Sensitive issues in vulnerable conditions. Studying violence in youth residential care, *Young*, 11(4): 323-339.

Honkatukia, P. and Suurpää L., (2007) *Nuorten miesten monikulttuurinen elämänkulku ja rikollisuus. [Young men's multicultural life course and criminality]*, Helsinki: Oikeuspoliittisen tutkimuslaitoksen julkaisuja 20 and Nuorisotutkimusverkosto/ Nuorisotutkimusseura, julkaisuja 80.

Honkasalo, V. and Suurpää, L., (2009) Tutkijoiden kiistellyt roolit rasismin ja nuorten tutkimuksessa. [Researchers' contested roles in research on racism and young people], in Keskinen, S., Rastas, A. and Tuori, S. (eds.) *En ole rasisti mutta … Maahanmuutosta, monikulttuurisuudesta ja kritiikistä. [I'm not a racist but … on immigration, multiculturalism and critique]*, Tampere: Vastapaino, 145-155.

MacDonald, R. and Marsh, J., (2005) *Disconnected youth? Growing up in Britain's poor neighbourhoods*, Basingstoke: Palgrave.

Mauthner, N. and Doucet, A., (2003) Reflexive accounts and accounts of reflexivity, *Sociology*, 37(3): 413-431.

Maynard, M., (1994) Methods, practice and epistemology: The debate about feminism and resesarch, in Maynard, M. and Purvis, J. (eds.) *Researching women's lives from a feminist perspective*, London: Taylor and Francis, 10-26.

Miller, T. and Bell, L., (2002) Consenting to what? Issues of access, gate-keeping and 'informed' consent, in Mauthner, M., Birch, M., Jessop, J., and Miller, T. (eds.), *Ethics in qualitative research*, London: Sage Publications, 53-69.

Miller, T. and Boulton, M., (2007) Changing constructions of informed consent: Qualitative research and complex social worlds, *Social Science and Medicine*, 65: 2199-2211.

Nairn, K., Munro, J. and Smith, A. B., (2005) A counter-narrative of a 'failed' interview, *Qualitative Research*, 5(2): 221-244.

Pillow, W. S., (2003) Confession, catharsis, or cure? Rethinking the uses of reflexivity as methodological power in qualitative research, *Qualitative Studies in Education*, 16(2): 175-196.

Ramazanoglu, C. with Holland, J., (2002) *Feminist methodology: Challenges and choices*, London: Sage.

Reiter, H., 2003. Past, present, future: Biographical time structuring of disadvantaged young people, *Young*, (11)3: 253-279.

Renold, E., Holland, S., Ross, N. J. and Hillman, A., (2008) 'Becoming participant': Problematizing 'informed consent' in participatory research with young people in care, *Qualitative Social Work*, 7(4): 427-447.

Riach, K., (2009) Exploring participant-centred reflexivity in the research interview, *Sociology*, 43(2): 356-370.

Sanders, J. and Munford, R., (2007) Speaking from the margins — implications for education and practice of young women's experiences of marginalisation, *Social Work Education*, 26(2): 185-199.

Skeggs, B., (2004) *Class, self, culture*, London: Routledge.

Part 2: Citizenship

Chapter 4

Cosmopolitanism, making the nation and the citizen as a salvation theme of turn of the twentieth century pedagogy

Thomas S. Popkewitz

I begin with a simple historical observation about the modern school that crosses Europe and the Americas. That observation is that the pedagogies of the school are ordered through principles of governing that relate to the Enlightenment's notion of cosmopolitanism. Cosmopolitanism embodies a radical historical thesis about the power of human reason and science. The aspiration of cosmopolitanism was a mode of life in which individual liberty and freedom produced universal human progress and individual happiness. Central to the liberty and freedom of the citizen was the secularisation that placed value on human agency guided through reason and rationality (science). The cosmopolitan conceptions of reason and human agency were embedded in the French and American republics, for example. Government was premised and dependent on the citizen who adhered to cosmopolitan principles. The enlightened self-interest of the citizen who enables progressive change was a salvation theme continually accompanied by fears about degeneration and decay (McMahan, 2001). Early American educators spoke about the fears of the barbarians and savages coming in through the gates of the Republic and destroying its future if education did not do its job properly.

Although the actual word *cosmopolitanism* is rarely used in today's reforms, its foundational assumptions are embedded in school pedagogy, curriculum and teacher education. The modern American comprehensive high school in the first decades of the twentieth century was initially called 'the cosmopolitan high school' (Drost, 1967). Cosmopolitan theses travel as foundation assumptions in European reforms about intercultural education and the lifelong learner.

Cosmopolitanism, human agency and the curriculum

The Enlightenment pushed to the side the received order given by the grace of God and replaced it with another eternal human purpose: the reason and science of happiness in life and the possibility of general social good (Becker,

1932). This notion of human intention was instituted into the nineteenth century school curriculum through concepts related to the idea of agency of the citizen. New forms of government and theories of human agency constituted people as autonomous subjects of motives and perceptions that were independent of theology.

The notions of agency have become so much a part of the modern orthodoxy that a theory of childhood, schooling and society that without signifying the autonomous agent who acts to improve the self and world is almost unthinkable, or at least not politically correct. The *doxa* is that without theories of agency we are left with an anti-humanist and deterministic world that dehumanises. Notions of agency bring into focus the qualities that are to enable personal realisation and social betterment, and in these distinctions of hope are possibilities of rescue for those who have fallen from the graces of progress.

Change was directed to the social and individual matters found in 'the city of man' through human agency; a notion of intervention and change no long controlled by the static hierarchies of aristocracies and religious cosmologies. The redemptive projects of the human agency are central from Comte and Marx; and given new life in correcting social wrongs after World War Two. The War on Poverty in the United States during the 1960s was premised on eliminating poverty through psychologies that defined the problem of poverty through the individual agency who lacked self-esteem or motivation.

Notions of agency were shaped and fashioned through multiple historical trajectories that link the secular and the sacred. The American Republic was no exception. The salvation themes of the Reformations and Counter Reformation were transported and translated as redemptive themes in the secularism of Republican (see, Tröhler, 2006; also Lilla, 2007). New England Puritans, a Calvinist group that came to America in the seventeenth century to escape persecution, gave recognition to the site of their colony as the New World. The colony was God's chosen place, with the Puritans serving as God's elect to make possible 'the day of God's judgment and the new reign of Christ on earth' and thus reverse the corruption of Europe (McKnight, 2003, p. 17).

America as the new world in comparison to the Old World of Europe had a double significance as a secular and sacred place. The saga of the nation was told of as an evangelical purity and political goodness of its land and its people. Calvin's edict about each individual entering and participating in the world to fulfil the greater corporate mission of America becoming a 'city upon a hill' was transmogrified into narratives of National Exceptionalism and 'The Chosen

People' (McKnight, 2003, p. 2). The nation was 'errand in the wilderness' that served as the terra profane 'out there' yet to be conquered, step by inevitable step, by the advancing armies of Christ (Bercovitch, 1978, p. 26). The nation and its people embodied a divine plan of constructing community without the old traditions that put the universality of progress in danger. The redemptive stories of the nation's exceptionalism told of 'boundless sources of energy through which individuals discovered who they were: personality flourished only through exploration and growth' (Wiebe, 1995, p. 186).

The assembly of salvation themes embodied a transcendent cosmopolitan ethics of the enlightenments in the new republics' notions of citizenship. Cosmopolitanism was initially to transcend the provincialism and localism associated with the nation state, but in the context of the formation of the new nation, the citizen of the republic told a radical historical thesis about human reason and rationality as progressive human forces.

The redemptive hope of the future of the Republic was told in the story of the school. The school embodied the narratives that joined cosmopolitan reason with the common good as a salvation narrative about a redemptive nation. The U.S. Department of Interior, Bureau of Education report on American education (U.S. Government Printing Office, 1874) spoke of American national destiny in the founding of a civilisation that transformed the wildness. It asserted the history of the United States as 'the founding [of] a civilisation [in the peculiar] "character in the American people"'(US Government Printing Office, 1874, p. 13). The saga of the evolutionary development of the U.S. as the embodiment of enlightenment ideals was reiterated twenty years later in a speech given to the National Education Association meeting of educational leaders (Martin, 1895). The American Republic was told as the culmination of 'five hundred years of passionate struggles for liberty, of breaking chains and abolishing formulas'. Drawing on a notion of civic virtue, education is the march of the Republic,

> to develop common standards and 'a common weld' in which personal interest are set aside for public ends. The civilising of the child is to combine social and personal obligation. The past, present and future are joined as education civilises by bringing back new patriotism ... to penetrate this system and bring back personal responsibility and social harmony that combines social and personal obligations (Martin, 1895, p. 138).

The progressive epic of the people's 'errand in the wilderness' implied fears of an imperilled people and of the hope of the nation continually in 'a state of *un*fulfillment of the future' (Bercovitch, 1978, p. 23, italics in original). The enlightened and civilised of American Exceptionalism were set in relation to darkness and the backwardness of the 'Others'. John Adams, signer of the Declaration of Independence and second U.S. President (1797-1801) and a strong devotee to the republican ideal of civic duty, spoke about the settlement of America as 'the opening of a grand scene and design in Providence for the illumination of the ignorant, and the emancipation of the slavish part of mankind all over the earth' (Wood, 1991, p. 191). That citizen was expressed through a biological metaphor of growth and decay that juxtaposed the hope and fear of the Enlightenment.

The separation of light and darkness fell upon science and technology in the political and social reforms associated with American Progressivism and the development of the modern school. Various U.S. progressive reforms were narrated as a struggle between darkness and light and 'the civilising mission' of the nation. The evangelistic hope of exceptionalism was to bring the Protestant gospel to Christians and non-Protestant Christians alike in order to produce civic virtue as principles of everyday life. Fears were expressed as double gestures—as the need to provide legislation and conditions to enable immigrants and others to embody the sensitivities and dispositions articulated as civic virtue in American Exceptionalism; and as fears of the qualities and characteristics of the life of the immigrant that stood as dangers to the realisation of the hope of the cosmopolitanism of the nation.

Progressive social and educational sciences: From planning for the pursuit of happiness to planning 'the unhappy'

The social science disciplines appeared in the second half of the nineteenth century and were institutionalised in the new scientific universities. The social and related education sciences were practices related to Progressive reform movements. The interventions related to a variety of social changes associated with industrialisation, urbanisation, and immigration. The sciences were projects to change the conditions of society that also changed people.

Two particular qualities of the intervention strategies of the social sciences are addressed here. One quality related to science as a salvation theme. American Exceptionalism tied to the finding of The New World and reclaiming the Puritan inspired evangelical past was (re)visioned. That (re)visioning gave science and technology a sacred place in the problem of change and progress. The historian Nye (1999) calls the new salvation narrative of the nation 'the technological sublime'. Foundation stories of technological changes were told about Americans transforming the wilderness into 'a prosperous and egalitarian' cosmopolitan society whose landscape and people had a transcendent presence (Nye, 2003, p. 5). The marvels of the railroad, electricity, bridges, skyscrapers as well as the natural power of the Niagara Falls and the Grand Canyon were placed in a cultural dialogue about the nation in an inevitable developmental process. The triumphs of science were spoken about as the liberation of the human spirit to be realised by the republic.

The new epic tale of the nation of the Technological Sublime was told by Charles Horton Cooley, an early American sociologist and Progressive reformer interested in education. Cooley (1909) saw the United States as 'nearer, perhaps, to the spirit of the coming order' (p. 167) that is totally different from anything before it. Evoking Exceptionalism, Cooley wrote that 'the new industrial modernity' of America was close to being the first real democracy that is 'totally different from anything before it' because it places a greater emphasis on individuality and innovation in a land that 'does not inherit the class culture of Europe' (in Ross, 1972, p. 245). The narratives placed the nation as 'the apotheosis of reason' in bringing progress that removed corruption and brought democracy and freedom to all of human kind.

The second quality related to the Enlightenment hopes and fears in Progressivism and the social sciences. The epic tale of the nation was being challenged by what was called *The Social Question* posed by the conditions and people of the new urban life—the poor, immigrants, and racial groups (Rodgers, 1998). Cross-Atlantic reform Protestant movements of American Progressivism, the British Fabian Society, the German Evangelical Social Congress, the French *Musée Social*, and the Settlement House movement in many countries had 'an intense preoccupation with the social problems of industrial society, whether in the literacy form of Dickens, the aesthetically and reform-oriented writings of Ruskin and Morris, the romantic historical work of Carlyle, the activities of the emerging labour movement, or in the connections with government activities proper' (Wittrock et al., 1991, p. 33).

In this context of *The Social Question* and the forming of the citizen, the Progressive sciences 'were meant to contribute to the amelioration of social evils and provide a basis for the rational and enlightened ordering of societal affairs' (Wagner et al., 1991, p. 2). For some of the early American social scientists and social reformers, the Old World cultures had to be purified through re-socialising the immigrant family and child. Massachusetts Institute of Technology (MIT) President Francis Amasa Walker, a statistician involved in the censuses in 1870 and 1880, saw the outcome of immigration as the destruction of the American family and nation. Jane Addams, a leader of the Settlement Movement in Chicago's Hull House and close colleague to John Dewey, searched for ways 'to transform social relations and establish patterns of thinking so that increasing numbers of people, from increasing numbers of cultural traditions, could live together in crowded, urban conditions and still maintain a sense of harmony, order, beauty, and progress' (Lagemann, 2000, p. 55). Addams thought that the influx of foreigners brought people who were 'densely ignorant' of American customs and institutions (cited in Lybarger, 1987, p. 181).

The new Progressive school was spoken about through the double gestures of the hope of the republic and fears of dangerous populations whose dispositions challenged the moral ground necessary for the enlightened future. Schools were designed as urban institutions to teach moral behaviour and conduct and aid society by preventing disease, vice, or future crime (Bloch, 1987, pp. 52-55). Thomas Jesse Jones, affiliated with the New York Settlement House and instrumental in the forming of social studies as a curriculum subject, was interested in the transformation (social evolution) of the immigrant to embody 'the Anglo-Saxon ideal' (Lybarger, 1987, p. 185). Jones talked about the educational needs of different immigrant groups in terms of their dispositions and social judgements. The notion of 'need' was 'the social judgment ... about what ideals and traits ought to be inculcated in the weak by the strong through instruction in the social studies' (Lybarger, 1987, p. 187).

The Social Question, schooling and the pedagogical sciences reversed the enlightenment expression about the individual's 'pursuit of happiness' that was written into The United States Declaration of Independence. With the formation of the modern welfare state, Progressive reforms gave focus to the dangers and dangerous populations that were seen as threatening to the hope of freedom.

Whereas the focus of social policy and public discussions from the American Revolution in the late eighteenth century engaged in how people can engage in 'the pursuit of happiness', that focus can be thought as having been reversed by the turn of the twentieth century. One might think of the emergence of the new social science as making its object those populations who could not pursue happiness and what might be called the 'unhappy populations' targeted as in need of rescue and redemption. Education was to change the individual who was poor, 'backward', immigrant so they could pursue 'happiness' in what the educational psychologist Edward L. Thorndike (1909/1962) thought of education would enable these kinds of people to become part of the democratic processes of the Republic, through which the given civic virtues defined as the common good were produced.' The making of the virtuous citizen simultaneously inscribed fears about moral disorder and dangerous populations. The new scientific psychologies were directed to those populations that constituted the dangers to the common good. Thorndike's Connectionism was placed in the dual language of the moral characteristics needed for happiness and what prevents this kind of person: 'to enable men to satisfy their wants more fully, the crude curiosity, manipulation, experimentation and irrational interplay of fear, anger, rivalry, mastery, submission, cruelty and kindliness must be modified into useful, verified thought and equitable acts' (Thorndike, 1912/1962, p. 76).

Thorndike was not alone in the pursuit of the unhappy populations who did not embody civic virtues. The pragmatism of Dewey was to counter the debilitating effects of modern conditions and its modes of living through science as the method of living. 'The existence of scientific method protects us also from a danger that attends the operation of men of unusual power; dangers of slavish imitation partisanship, and such jealous devotion to them and their work as to get in the way of further progress' (Dewey, 1929, p. 11).

But at the same time, there were fears that travelled with that hope. The systematic training in 'thinking' was to prevent 'the evil of the wrong kind of development [that] is even greater ... the power of thought ... [as it] frees us from servile subjection to instinct, appetite, and routines' (Dewey, 1929, p. 23). Lester Frank Ward, one of the founders of American sociology, spoke about moving the immigrant family of the settlement house away from the habits of the savage and the barbarian. Ward argued that education needs an 'absolute universality' that was intended 'to neutralise the *non-civilised* or it will lower all of society.' Educational methods were to take 'the lesser of a civilisation,' 'the savage and used by stagnant people' (Ward, 1883, p. 159-60) in order 'to raise the *uncivilised* classes up toward its level' (Ward, 1883, p. 595, italics in original).

The different historical practices entailed a grid that linked schooling to the making of the citizen and its Others. What became possible to see, think about and act on as the child entailed different and uneven historical processes that come together in pedagogy as political, social, cultural and scientific rationalities intersected in notions of instruction, curriculum and psychologies of the child.

The unfinished cosmopolitanism and the new social question: Cultural theses and the lifelong learner

Contemporary reforms enunciated the capabilities and capacities of the citizen through a (re)visioning of the cosmopolitanism of the citizen and fears that are embodied in the new Social Question. That cosmopolitanism embodies an agency that is *unfinished*, a mode of life signified by the mode of living of the lifelong learner. The mode of life is not directed to an overt notion of the social, but to an individuality of never-ending processes of making choices, innovation and collaboration. Biography is managed through self-monitoring processes that include 'survival learning, adaptive learning, and generative learning, learning that enhance the capacity to create' (Simon and Masschelein, 2006, p. 1). Personal responsibility and self-management of one's risks is tied to continual problem solving that serves as the correct application of reason and rationality. Life is a series of rationally ordered paths for finding solutions that is never complete and always defers the present to the future.

The salvation theme of the lifelong learner is the citizen who lives in both the uncertainty and certainty of time. The lifelong learner is a citizen of the nation, but he or she also communicates through Internet and computer games played simultaneously around the world, and with multiple identities and disjointed narratives, just as in the television comedy of Seinfeld's that had no overarching coherence in the storyline of the mundane daily events of its four main characters.

Paradoxically, this individuality is shaped and fashioned by the social, which is today named as The Knowledge Society or The Innovative Society. Belonging and 'home' are placed within the context of a transnationalism in which Europe as a cultural and social space of its 'social model' and science provides its exceptionalism in the competition its research documents call as becoming world champions (Popkewitz and Martin, forthcoming 2013). The lifelong learner in the US is expressed as its liberalism and entrepreneurial culture.

In research on educational governance and social exclusion, this relation of the social and the individual placed, oddly enough, the certainty of change and the freedom of choice in the fatalism of the processes of globalisation (Lindblad and Popkewitz, 2004). Teachers, school administrators and government officials in a European Union study spoke about the inevitable march of globalism that teachers needed to respond to through curriculum changes. The ubiquitous future of globalism makes it impossible for the individual, to quote a French high school textbook, 'to escape the flux of change' (Soysal et al., 2005, pp. 24-25). The ubiquitous boundaries of globalism are naturalised and go unquestioned to intern and enclose the spaces of freedom and participation.

Connecting the public with the personal: Collaboration in community

Earlier twentieth century classrooms were places of socialisation that presumed the child internalised pre-established universal norms of collective identity; today the child is to live as the future citizen in spaces of responsibility no longer traversed through the range of social practices directed toward a single public sphere—the social. Responsibility is located today in diverse, autonomous and plural communities. These notions of community are seemingly perpetually constituted through one's own practice of learning. The 'learning' and 'discourse' communities, however, do not erase the social but relocate the telling of the collective obligation of the political community.

The assumption of collaboration is linked to the governing practices of communication systems and the procedures of interaction in which the common good and hospitality to others are to be produced. Choice in individual life is sanctioned as double acts of contributing to individual self-realisation and collaboratively to justice and equity. Individuality and sociality are told as foundational stories of participation, collaboration, and reflection that form the hope of the democracy of the nation.

The salvation themes of collaboration and participation in policy and research obscure how negotiations and communication are assembled in the cultural theses of the unfinished cosmopolitanism. Collaboration and participation inscribe a hermeneutic objectivism in the name of the new democracy. The 'barriers' breached across groups in narrations of collaboration join individual agency with the general development of society.

Empowerment is talked about as if there are no enclosures. The redemptive figure is the teacher as the agent of change. Contemporary American teacher education reform talks about the teacher as the new leader in the making of the citizen. The teacher is 'energised' to 'work with others,' 'to ensure that America and its children will have the schools they require and deserve' (American Council on Education, 1999, p. ii) and to provide 'a down payment to renewal and reform' that the 'American public' demands so 'the nation's schools can and must serve better the citizens of our democracy' (p. 1).

Classrooms and instruction become 'participatory structures' organised by constructivist and learning psychologies rather than the early twentieth century Connectionism of Edward L. Thorndike. Contemporary psychologies are related, in part, to changing cultural patterns through the technologies of communication practices. Social and learning psychologies iconically cite the American John Dewey and the Russian Lev Vygotsky in the (re)visioning of the cosmopolitanism of the 'reason' of schooling. (Popkewitz, 1998a). An assumption is that each set of actors has unique experiences and points of views that are negotiated through collaborative practices. It is within these psychologies of communication, interaction, and participation that recognition of diversity and inclusion are enacted. In one sense, this is expressed in the discourses about teachers, parents, and researchers coming to understand and respect different perspectives as a method of arriving at the truth.

Whatever the merits of problem solving and community, they are not merely descriptive of some natural reasoning of the child that research recoups. 'Democratic participation', to borrow from Cruikshank (1999), is 'not clear cut or naturally occurring; it [is] something that ... [is] solicited, encouraged, guided, and directed' (p. 97). The language evokes populist images of democracy that entails local involvement in schools and the arriving of consensus about the 'goals' guiding and judging individual schools. The school and classrooms as communities of learning are sites that recalibrate the political aspirations of the individual with the new assemblies of communities as *the social*. The citizen home is transnational, simultaneously belonging to the nation that criss-cross changing conditions of cultural interconnectedness and mobility in contemporary international and global relations.

The casting out into unliveable spaces: The child left behind

The citizen as an unfinished cosmopolitan does not stand as independent from qualities and characteristics, which it is differenced and divided from. The other who is-not-yet-cosmopolitan and a lifelong learner and is classified as the child at-risk, disadvantaged, ethnic, and immigrant. These human kinds become the object of policy and research; populations that are placed inbetween and outside spaces of those who can pursue 'happiness'. The recognition of inclusion is ordered and classified by being different. The gesture of the hope of inclusion is coupled with distinctions that divide. The double gestures circulate in the 'reason' that orders efforts of 'interculturalism', multiculturalism, and urban, for example. The latter are signified through distinctions and differentiations about the kind of child who is 'left behind', a phrase used in U.S. reforms and research to express the commitment to an equitable and just society by focusing on programs to include those populations that have been excluded.

Policy, research and the enactments of classroom recognise particular kinds of people for inclusion, yet differentiated and divided from what are unspoken cultural theses about the modes of living that constitute the unity and harmony of the society. One such cultural thesis to constitute the social harmony discussed earlier is the lifelong learner who inhabits the Knowledge Society. Silently travelling to differentiate and divide the child who requires remediation and rescue, the lifelong learner becomes the 'other' that 'the at-risk' child is not. The dangerous populations are individualised and psychologised as different and abjected as belonging to unliveable space of moral disorder.

The child not in the space of 'all children': The urban child left behind

The cultural territory of the child to be rescued and redeemed so as to embody the qualities of citizenship is a particular kind of human, what can be signified in the US as *the urban child*. Whereas The Social Question at the turn of the twentieth century gave focus to the populations of the city who were characterised as constituting the moral disorder to be rectified, today's Social Question addresses youth as socially and psychologically troubled. No longer do the psychologies of schooling talk about children's 'fatigue', as was talked about in the early twentieth century. Differences today are discussed through the seemingly instrumental and psychological language of 'low expectations', low self-esteem, family dysfunctions and different learning styles. Embedded in the distinctions of 'lows' and dysfunction are a continuum of values about what is esteem, functionality and the organisation of the self in society. The categories of the 'urban child' and immigrant live in the social and psychological spaces that are simultaneously an in-between place of rescue and exclusion because 'their' qualities are different from those that constitute the citizen *qua* lifelong learner..

It is significant that the category of the urban child has little to do with geographical place. It is a cultural space and entails a cultural thesis about difference and divisions. I say this as the notion of urban can refer to the 'urbane' and cosmopolitan who lives in the city and where there is great wealth. Children who live in the high-rise apartments and brownstones of American cities appear as urbane and not urban. The child of urban education, in contrast, is a political designation of populations targeted for social inventions. Urban signifies spaces of poverty and racial segregation. The distinctions of urban education is not restricted to 'the inner city' as it serves children who live in suburbia and rural areas (Popkewitz, 1998b).

The expertise of science, again as was its performance at the turn of the century in *The Social Question*, is a strategy of changing the conditions of urban life by changing the urban child, and the interventions are expressed as processes of designing classrooms (and children) in the service of a democratic ideal. The sentiment of design is today ordered as processes to enable collaboration, participation, flexibility and multiple solutions that are taken as what constitutes democratic processes. The notions of socialisation and acculturation of the Settlement House for immigrants now become problems of pedagogy and learning theories. The theory of democracy is procedural and psychological. It is argued, for example, that school decisions are best made at the site where problems arise. Designing learning environments, for example, allow local authorities, parents and teachers to yield better results through participation.

The object of design research is to provide a finer-tuned relation between the conditions of schooling and the self-government of people. The word *re-engineer* is used to talk about the mode of living in which the teacher and child continually 'innovate' through principles homologous with unfinished cosmopolitanism. The National Research Council's (2002) commissioned report for the implementation of U.S. Congressional legislation, *No Child Left Behind* (2002), is to identify 'rigorous' design procedures and replication through the technologies of research. The warrant of this report is for a democratic, inclusive society. The use of rigorous research is in designing an individuality bound to 'the nation's commitment to improve the education of all children requires continuing efforts to improve its research capacity' (National Research Council, 2002, p. 21).

The design of research is the political in the sense that design procedures order and classify the everyday activities of classrooms as a system inscribed as a harmonious and consensual set of relations. Flexibility and continual assessment give order and tidiness to the 'things' and the people to be changed. One's life is made into an event of planning with a coterie of experts to assist in that planning (Berger et al., 1974). The working of the open system is bounded by the ordering and classifications of psychological theories of learning, motivation, communication, and individualisation that are to change 'the metacognition of the child and the teacher' (Kelly, 2003, pp. 3, 5). The science of complexity is ironically the desire towards certainty—to 'lose the credibility gap' and the incompleteness of knowledge. The openness of the design process is a closed-loop system that is driven by its own internal logic.

Ironically, the certainty that bounds the system is not certain. The qualities of the present are somewhat like Deleuze and Guattari's (1987) rhizome, an assembly of heterogeneous components and a multiplicity that functions with variation, expansion and offshoots. The lifelong learner is a mode of living in varied communities that move at different rates of time and space. The normative assertions about democracy and an inclusive society embodied in designing people are the micro-governing of life which have multiple dimensions of time—time of a regulated life, time of living in different communities where there are processes of continuous innovation, and the comprehension associated with the Internet and multi tasking. The child at-risk is classified as living outside the multiplicities and variations that become described in linguistic differences of family interactions or quantity of vocabulary.

Reclaiming the birthright and American exceptionalism

The pedagogical production of the transnational citizen is framed as the moral and ethical imperatives of designing the citizen that embodies the subjectivities designed for globalisation. Teacher education reforms, for example, are presented as fulfilling obligations of democracy resulting from changes in America's populations, of renewing the competitiveness of the nation in a global economy and of promoting hospitality to the Other. *What Matters Most: Teaching for America's Futuree*, a foundational report in developing national teacher standards in the first decades of the twenty-first century, for example, invokes the exceptionalism of the nation in the promise of the reorganisation of teacher preparation programs (National Commission on Teaching and America's Future, 1996). The soul of the nation and the soul of the teacher are made the same. They articulate the salvation theme of redemption that is simultaneous individual and collective.

> We must reclaim *the soul* [italics added] of America. And to do so, we need an education system that helps people forge shared values, to understand and respect other perspectives, to learn and work at high levels of competence, to take risks an persevere again the odds, to work comfortably with people from diverse backgrounds, and to continue to learn throughout life. (p. 12)

The reclaiming of the collective soul re-memorialises the optimism of prior nineteenth century American exceptionalism to correct the past by providing for progress. 'Reclaiming the soul of America' is a narrative of loss and the hope of redemption. That hope is expressed as a commitment to fulfil the dream of a democratic society. That dream is to forge consensus and harmony. Teacher education is to generate collective values in learning communities whose mode of living 'respects others', 'takes risks' and works with 'diverse people' by making an individual who makes choices in which there is no choice not 'to continue to learn throughout life.'

The dream, however, engenders fears and processes of abjection. The school where 'all children learn' is a comparative injunctive about fears of *the child left behind*; the child who is not able to or does not realise the dream of the nation. The 1996 teacher education reform report asserts that there is a national urgency (National Commission on Teaching and America's future, 1996, p. 3) to act on those who threaten the future and form its dangers and dangerous populations. The fears about the child are expressed in pedagogical discourses about those children whose low literacy produced welfare, crime, and a non-productive worker. The conclusion is that

> We cannot afford the continued expansion of prison populations, public assistance programs, and unemployment
> (National Commission on Teaching and America's future, 1996, p. 12)

While no longer evoking the early twentieth century Social Question, the moral disorders of the city still occupy reforms to (re)vision that Question. The Social Question is transmogrified into the optimism of the new American exceptionalism placed in harm's way through the illiterate, the criminal, and 'growing number whose first language is not English, many others with learning differences, and others with learning disabilities—teachers need access to the growing knowledge that exists about how to teach these learners effectively' (National Commission on Teaching and America's future, 1996, p. 8).

The second report of the National Commission on Teaching and America's Future (2003), *No Dream Denied: A Pledge to America's Children*, memorialised the nation as providing the unity of the whole that signifies what is natural to *all* children as their 'educational birthright' that is scaled with the constitutional rights of the citizen. The birthright is, on one layer, bound to *being* a lifelong learner in 'a culture of continuous learning.' The hope of community and lifelong learning is to reclaim as the enlightenment's political realisation in its republic.

The *all* in the standards reforms, teacher education, and research that circulate in the U.S and European Union documents express ideas that *all* children learn, *all* children have high achievement, and so on are taken as the broad political commitment that schools serve all segments of society equally. The signifying of *all* children is an iteration of fears of the unity that 'all' implies, of not providing the correct strategies to include, and the fears that cast out the dangers and dangerous qualities of those whose characteristics and capabilities are different. The distinctions and categories enunciate cultural theses about the unfinished cosmopolitan and its Others within the same phenomenon. The enunciation of hope and abjection embodied in the phrase of 'all children learn' recognises, divides, and abjects. The double gestures of hope and fear function to qualify and disqualify individuals for participation.

Designing the child as the global citizen, cosmopolitanism and processes of abjection

I started this chapter with the statement that the citizen is not born but made. The focus was on the technologies that are put into play in making the child as the future citizen. I focused on the system of reason that generate principles about who the child is and should be. I called this a history of the present, considering the conditions that make the objects of reflection and action intelligible and possible. While Enlightenment commitments to human agency, freedom, and empowerment travel into the present through conceptions of the citizen, the concrete practices in which these commitments are enacted are never merely about the subject but a method of making the subject calculable and administrable.

This approach on systems of reason embodies certain theoretical and political assumptions that I briefly mention as I discuss it further elsewhere (Popkewitz, 2008). It recognises that ideas are social practices, entering or looping into the making of programs, theories and narratives about people. This 'new' materialism entails making the objects of schooling as historical eventsthrough which principles are generated to think about kinds of people, to act on particular populations, and as cultural thesis for people to act for themselves.

To explore the systems of reason historically, I argued that I argued that particular elements of Enlightenment notions of the cosmopolitan order what is said, talked about and acted on in schooling from at least the turn of the twentieth century to the present. Cosmopolitanism traverses pedagogical projects as the hope of society is placed in the growth and development of the child. The political of schooling lies in that distinctions and principles through which the hope of 'the reasoned' cosmopolitan child. These principles embody a comparative style of thought. The comparative differentiations perform as double gestures in which hope embodies the fears of the dangers and dangerous populations to the future. Embedded in the qualities and characteristics of the cosmopolitan child are distinctions and divisions that serve to exclude and abject in the impulse to create an inclusionary society.

Science is historically a cultural 'actor' in the governing discussed and the production of who is, should be, and who does not 'fit'. The double gestures of the social and education sciences move across policy, pedagogical practices and the sciences of education. Dual qualities are generated in the classifications, distinctions and calculations to order and plan (design) changing the world by changing people. It is the paradox of sciences of education. They express being in service of the ideals of democracy through planning to change the conditions of people that change people. The enunciations of planning people are continually placed in transcendental categories of humanity and values of a cosmopolitanism whose universalism differentiates its notion of humanity from others.

The principles of dividing and abjecting that traverse contemporary social policy and its reform sciences in education are part of a particular orthodoxy of modernity and its assembly of the Enlightenment, but not itself a necessary conclusion of the Enlightenment's insertion of reason and rationality as a condition of life and change (see, e.g., Foucault, 1984).

This leads to a final point about the certainty that silently is embodied in the search for 'useful' and practical knowledge for changing people. Where there are declarations of useful or practical knowledge, such claims need to be scrutinised for the principles they generate about the kinds of persons invented to embody what is classified as useful and practical. To declare 'useful' knowledge does not escape the historical inscriptions of the particular comparative style of reason in contemporary research. Difference is established through giving ontological status to the identities of human kinds, such as the lifelong learner who is the embodied citizen and its other—the immigrant, or the at-risk child and family. Where science claims itself the arbiter of the democratic schooling, such sentiments, while important to the present, need to be scrutinised to understand the limits in the inscriptions of the particular calculated 'people' included and excluded.

References

Bush, G. W., (2001) *No child left behind*, Washington, DC: Department of Education, US Government Printing Office.

Cooley, C. H., (1909) *Social organization: A study of the larger mind*, New York: Charles Scribner's Sons.

Cruikshank, B., (1999) *The will to empower: Democratic citizens and the other subjects*, Ithaca, NY: Cornell University.

Deleuze, G., and Guattari, F., (1987) *A thousand plateaus: Capitalism and schizophrenia*. Translated by Massumi, B., Minneapolis: University of Minnesota Press.

Dewey, J., (1929) *The sources of a science of education*, New York: Horace Liveright.

Drost, W. H., (1967) *David Snedden and education for social efficiency*, Madison: University of Wisconsin Press.

Ferguson, R. A., (1997) *The American enlightenment, 1750-1820*, Cambridge: Harvard University Press.

Foucault, M., (1979) Governmentality, *Ideology and Consciousness*, 6: 5-22.

Foucault, M., (1984) What is the enlightenment? Was ist Auflärlung?, in Rabinow P., (ed.) *The Foucault reader*, New York: Pantheon Books, 32-51.

Kelly, A., (2003) Research as design, *Educational Researcher*, 32(1), 3-4.

Lagemann, E. C., (2000) *An elusive science: The troubling history of education research*, Chicago: University of Chicago Press.

Lilla, M., (2007) The politics of God, *The New York Times Magazine*, pp. 28-35, 50, 54-55.

Lybarger, M., (1987) Need as ideology: Social workers, social settlements, and the social studies, in Popkewitz, T., (ed.) *The formation of the school subjects: The struggles for creating an American Institution*, New York: Falmer Press, 176-189.

Martin, G. H., (1895) *New standards of patriotic citizenship*. Paper presented at the National Educational Association, St. Paul, MN.

McKnight, D., (2003) *Schooling, the puritan imperative, and the molding of an American national identity. Education's "errand into the wilderness"*, Mahwah, NJ: Lawrence Erlbaum Associates.

McMahan, D., (2001) *Enemies of the enlightenment. The French counter: Enlightenment and the making of modernity*, Oxford, UK: Oxford University Press.

Meyer, J., (1986) The politics of educational crisis in the United States, in Cummings, W. et al., (eds.) *Educational politics in crisis*, New York: Praeger, 44-58.

National Commission on Teaching and America's Future (2003) *No dream denied: A pledge to America's children*, Washington, DC: Author.

National Commission on Teaching and America's Future (1996) *What matters most: Teaching for America's future*, Washington, DC: National Commission on Teaching and America's Future.

National Research Council (2002) *Scientific research in education*, Washington, DC: Center for Education, Division of Behavioral and Social Sciences and Education, Committee on Scientific Principles for Education Research, National Research Council.

Nye, D. E., (1999) *American technological sublime*, Cambridge, MA: MIT Press.

Nye, D. E., (2003) *America as second creation: Technology and narratives of new beginnings*, Cambridge, MA: MIT Press.

Popkewitz, T., (2008) *Cosmopolitanism and the age of school reform: Science, education, and making society by making the child*, New York: Routledge.

Popkewitz, T., (1998a) Dewey, Vygotsky, and the social administration of the individual: Constructivist pedagogy as systems of ideas in historical spaces, *American Educational Research Journal,* 35(4): 535-570.

Popkewitz, T., (1998b) *Struggling for the soul: The politics of schooling and the construction of the teacher,* New York: Teachers College Press.

Popkewitz, T. and Martin, C., (forthcoming 2013) 'Now we are European!' How does it get that way?, in Nóvoa, A. and Lawn, M., (eds), *Rethinking the European Educational Space.*

Rancière, J., (2004) *The flesh of words: The politics of writing.* Translated by Mandell, C., Stanford, CA: Stanford University Press.

Rodgers, D. T., (1998) *Atlantic crossings: Social politics in a progressive age,* Cambridge, MA: Belknap Press of Harvard University Press.

Ross, D., (1972) *G. Stanley Hall: The psychologist as prophet,* Chicago: The University of Chicago Press.

Simon, M., and Masschelein, J., (2006) The governmentalization of learning and the assemblage of a learning apparatus. Paper presented at the *Foucault and Adult Education/Adult Learning Conference,* 8-10 February 2006, Sweden: Linköping University.

Thorndike, E. L., (1909/1962) Darwin's contribution to psychology, in Joncich, G. M., (ed.) *Psychology and the science of education: Selected writings of Edward L. Thorndike,* New York: Bureau of Publications, Teachers College, Columbia University, 37-47.

Thorndike, E. L., (1912/1962) Education. A first book, in Joncich, G. M., (ed.) *Psychology and the science of education. Selected writings of Edward L. Thorndike,* New York: Bureau of Publications, Teachers College, Columbia University, 69-83, 141-147.

Tröhler, D., (2006) *Max Weber and the Protestant Ethic in America (unpublished paper).* Zurich, Switzerland: Pestalozzianum Research Institute for the History of Education, University of Zurich.

U.S. Government Printing Office (1874) *A statement of the theory of education in the United States of America as approved by many leading educators,* Washington, DC: Author.

Wagner, P., Weiss, C. H., Wittrock, B., and Wollman, H., (eds.) (1991) *Social sciences and modern states: National experiences and theoretical crossroads.* Cambridge: Cambridge University Press.

Wald, P., (1995) *Constituting Americans: Cultural anxiety and narrative form.* Durham, NC: Duke University.

Ward, F. L., (1883) *Dynamic sociology, or applied social science, as based upon statistical sociology and the less complex sciences,* New York: D. Appleton and Co.

Wiebe, R. H., (1995) *Self-rule: A cultural history of American democracy,* Chicago, IL: University of Chicago Press.

Wittrock, B., Wagner, P., and Wollman, H., (1991) Social science and the modern state: Policy knowledge and political institutions in Western Europe and the United States, in P. Wagner, C. Weiss, B. Wittrock and H. Wollmann (eds.) *Social sciences and modern states: National experiences and theoretical crossroads,* Cambridge, UK: Cambridge University Press, 28-85.

Wood, G. S., (1991) *The radicalism of the American revolution,* New York: Vintage Books.

Chapter 5

Spaces for influence

Dennis Beach, Lisbeth Lundahl and Elisabet Öhrn

As pointed out by Gordon and Lahelma (2002, p. 4) young people in educational institutions are often looked upon 'as adults-to-be' who need to be raised and educated in order to become citizens in the fully socialised sense of that term, who are able to exercise their rights, duties and responsibilities in acceptable ways. However, at the same time these young people also have democratic rights that have to be respected in the schools they go to. They have to be allowed and encouraged to 'act out citizenship in everyday life' in school in the present tense (also Gordon, 2006, p. 3). In previous research these two different dimensions are typically separated into two research fields. The first focuses on the content of education. The second looks at young people's actions to influence school and how these are responded to. We have considered both of these dimensions in the present chapter based on a recently completed three-year ethnographic project in three upper-secondary schools in Sweden[12]. Two academic and two vocational programmes have been involved in this research along with two classes of students from the so-called Individual Programme at a third school[13]. Questions concerning the values and understandings of citizenship and democracy that are expressed in school and how education is organised with respect to teaching and learning about citizenship and exercising influence have been in focus. Together with a theme relating to the reproduction of hierarchical relations between academic and vocational learning they frame the coming presentation.

Research about teaching and democracy

With respect to the teaching of democratic values, international research has shown that some changes have occurred in recent years. One is to the very meaning of democracy, which is said to be changing and to increasingly refer to

12 Active citizenship? On democratic education in the upper secondary school, funded by The Swedish Research Council (no 2006-2694).
13 This programme can be of varying length and should generally be tailored to meet the needs of students who are not eligible or prepared to attend one of the 3-year national and/or special programmes in the country. The proportion of students attending the Individual Programme averages out at between seven to nine per cent, but with large local variations.

economic de-regulation and the workings of a free market and efforts to maintain individual freedom and free spaces for 'unregulated business manoeuvres in a free-market economy' (Apple and Beane, 2007, p. 150). This shift has been suggested to be an outcome of a contemporary neo-liberal turn that emphasises individual freedom of choice and individual rights at the expense of collective justice and equality and through it there has been a shift in focus from collective responsibility in society to an emphasis on individual choice.

The shift to neo-liberalism is also reflected in what is taught. What we can see is that much less attention is paid to political criticism and reflection and the main issues stressed in teaching nowadays are the individual's rights as an autonomic actor in relation to the State and the communication of factual knowledge (Dovemark, 2004). Issues related to more fundamental democratic issues such as the unequal distribution of rights in society, the situation of subordinate groups and struggles against oppressive practices, both in and outside schools as institutions, are far less common (Öhrn, 1998). A shift in the valency of democracy and democratic values is also reflected in schools and their curricula and interactions in the way democracy is lived out and practiced (Gordon et al., 2003). Even here individual responsibility and freedom of choice in the curriculum take precedence.

The effects of these changes, in what is taught about democracy and how democracy is lived out in school practices, are not yet fully accounted for in research. However there are some signs and suggestions concerning some possible negative outcomes, such as the significant variations in terms of knowledge about democracy, political decision-making and political influence (Swedish National Agency for Education, 2003). These cause concern, as does the reduced involvement in political parties and electoral participation by young people in recent years and increased experiences of powerlessness in relation to politics (Demokratiutredningen, 2000).

In relation to the above, some studies have occasionally suggested that girls in Swedish secondary schools have developed greater social and moral understanding than boys (e.g. Svingby, 1993) and, hence, that there is a greater need to develop teaching for boys in these respects (Swedish National Agency for Education, 1999). However, there is as yet no research that unequivocally supports the idea that schooling promotes the development of democratic values amongst girls better than it does for boys, or indeed that boys in general act in less democratic ways than girls do (Öhrn, 2001). If anything, contemporary research rather suggests that democracy issues have a weak position in general.

In this respect, upper secondary school with its differently gendered and classed programmes that prepare students for various careers and further education as differently positioned subjects with regard to democratic participation and challenges provides an interesting context for studying young people's democratic education and initiatives.

The study

A major aim of our research was to address the lack of knowledge about schooling and democracy, both in terms of teaching about democracy and in terms of the living out of democratic values of involvement and influence in curriculum interactions and decision-making processes on the part of the students. We hold that these issues are particularly important in the present era. Young people are on average spending a much longer period of time in formal education, and this further underlines the importance of the ways in which democratic issues are treated there.

Students from differently gendered and classed upper secondary programmes were involved in the research and standard ethnographic methods of participant observation and informant interviewing were adopted. In the following chapter, we attempt to highlight some issues we noted in an earlier attempt to synthesise research findings (Beach et al., 2011), from the investigations in five upper-secondary programmes involved: Natural Science (Hjelmér, 2011a), Child and Recreaction (Hjelmér, 2011b), Social Science (Rosvall 2011a), Vehicle (Rosvall, 2011b) and Individual (Dovemark, 2011). We will here attempt to draw together and discuss the results in respect of four central themes: (1) teaching students to influence, (2) student initiatives to exert influence and (3) the reproduction of hierarchical relations and (4) representations and relations of academic and vocational learning.

Teaching students to influence

One common finding regarding student influence in school was that the investigated programmes generally showed few instances of formalised teaching about how students can exercise influence as individuals and groups in school and everyday life. Instead, teaching about democracy was rather more factual and objective and concerned the principles of representative democracy and its procedures in various countries; particularly those in the EU. This focus coincides with that of national textbooks (Bronäs, 2003) and means that the forms of influence that are typically used by youth without voting rights are seldom addressed.

A second finding was related to the kind of representative democracy that is usually present in schools in the form of student councils, where democratic action can be conducted, reflected over and learned from, and that is meant to be a forum of influence. However, we found that this kind of formal arrangement appears to attract little student interest and to have little effect on school decisions at the upper-secondary school level. This is also reflected on in other research (e.g. Davies, 2002). It is well known that such formal student bodies are not powerful means for students to exert influence even in the earlier school years, and that the students there might be disciplined and supervised through their participation in what appears to be participatory processes but really are not. This does not imply that there is no democratic value in organisations such as these school councils. As was shown in Öhrn (2001), these councils can provide significant opportunities to communicate with teachers and they also offer potential spaces for criticism of school that students might choose to use without needing to fight their way into negotiations. In addition, they may also help the development of certain formal democratic techniques and competences (Rönnlund, 2010). Nevertheless, as stated above, according to our study these activities do not seem to be developed at the upper secondary level.

This led to a third general finding, which was that there are exceptions to the above. Assistance with and direct teaching about how to organise actions and influence things were provided in some instances. This was manifested on various occasions but occurred most particularly when students had already initiated a specific action. One example was when the students on the Vehicle Programme researched reacted against the lack of substitute maths teachers and the amount of teacher-free lesson time on the programme (Rosvall, 2011b). This example can be contrasted with another example, which occurred when the students in the Natural Science class tried to influence the pace and content of their maths teaching (Hjelmér, 2011a).

The outcomes from these two student initiated events were quite different. In the second example, senior staff responded to the student initiative quickly but the problem was in a sense taken over and then redefined by them with the help of the teachers on the programme. The formal authority in other words took over responsibility for the problem and for dealing with it, but when this was done the problem also became defined as a different one to the one that was initially voiced.

In the first example the students on the Vehicle programme were able to own their dispute, which is quite the opposite of the above. Indeed, in contrast to the above they had difficulty in getting their issue formally recognised and responded to at all. However, they did eventually get some assistance from their class teacher in this respect. This teacher had extensive experience of trade union work outside school, which he suggested might have enabled him to teach the students about practical strategies of influence, and he was able to emphasise the importance of collective action and the advantages of formal meeting protocols to back up requests. He taught them therefore how to organise their protest and pursue their interests collectively in a democratic fashion. Teachers usually lack significant experience of such work and of collective actions in the workplace. This may be one reason why they seem to be passive and ill equipped for teaching students about, and promoting, democratic structures in school.

In addition to the above there appeared to be a particular pattern related to what students were able to influence in school and what they were not. What we found was that students in most of the classes were invited to influence administrative aspects of teaching and the forms of educational communication. They could also influence the order of studying certain content and timing of tests and presentations. However, they were less often given opportunity to influence the selection of content and how school performances were to be assessed and by whom. This was particularly obvious in some cases where student options for voicing criticism and suggesting changes were extremely curtailed and at times even challenged, as with the science class example above. Differences were most apparent with respect to the status of the various subjects, programmes and groups of students. For instance, the subjects and programmes that were the most amenable to student influence at the level of content were either the least prestigious ones or were in programmes that were considered to be outside the academic mainstream of the school (cf. Beach and Dovemark, 2007) or the main core or character subjects relating to a strongly framed content area in vocational education. This aspect is discussed at greater length below.

Student initiatives to exert influence

A central question in the investigation thus became what students could influence in their education and in what kind of contexts. However, another important question was whether students act collectively or individually and how the schools and the teachers respond. When analysing the findings we noticed that, with only some few exceptions, because of the highly individualised characteristics of schooling today, responses are often individual and that a collective approach to exerting influence has not been adopted in most cases. As suggested above collective actions tended to occur in relation to non-teaching matters.

Another important finding was that it was only very rarely that the collective actions initiated by students resulted in more than very marginal changes. Context, again, proved to be important. As suggested in Beach (2008) in academic subjects students generally favoured the use of strong forms of external control and visible pedagogy by teachers as this led to an uncomplicated delivery of what students felt was correct knowledge that might crop up in examinations and influence grading. This kind of situation fits well with the academic programmes and subject contexts of the present study and also some parts of vocational studies, as mentioned above. It applied particularly but not only to the natural sciences. In these contexts, there was little attempt to influence formal content, except when the pace was felt to be so fast that it was impossible to keep up. Otherwise both there and in the Social Science class, students were offered few if any opportunities to influence content. Moreover, although they contended in interviews that there were things they were uncomfortable with and would like to change students took few or no initiatives to try to do so.

The attempts to influence the teaching of mathematics by the Natural Science class, and the final outcome of those attempts, are quite significant here. These students tried to collectively and formally influence the pace, level of difficulty, choice of textbook and grading in mathematics. But they did so without success. The following seems to have been important:

- The problem was taken over by the institutional representatives;
- These representatives quickly employed individualising technologies and effectively closed ranks by saying that the subject was not amenable to the requested reduction of pace;
- They added that this would dilute content in the programme and that the problem was not the way mathematics was taught, or the qualities of the illustrative materials used, but rather in the individual learning difficulties of some of the students, who were slowing others down and perhaps should be on another programme.

As suggested earlier things were different in the Vehicle class maths example. But there were some similarities in terms of power relations and the exercise of power. In the Vehicle class, repeated cancellations of mathematics lessons due to the teacher's illness led to collective protests from the students, but no compensatory measures were taken. When student absenteeism rose in maths lessons, the situation was primarily explained by staff in terms of student lack of interest in academic content generally and in mathematics specifically. This reduction of the problem is also one that brings it down to the level of individual differences. It has been seen and discussed before as an aspect of the political and ideological ecology of school mathematics (Beach, 1999a; Beach and Dovemark, 2007). Henderson and Hudson (2010) speak of mathematics fundamentalism in this context and of mathematics as a content that is unshakable and extremely difficult to influence by either the students or the teachers. The underlying causes of the problems collectively identified by students are transformed from teaching-related factors to suggested deficiencies and difficulties for certain individuals who, it was both directly and indirectly suggested, perhaps lacked the metal for maths at this level (Beach, 1999a/b).

These similarities in the ways protests were responded to in the programmes must not overshadow important differences. In the Natural Science class, the proposals of the students were rejected with the argument that it was impossible to lower the standards of teaching. In the Vehicle class the school accepted that students did not get the teaching they were entitled to at the level they desired. But this was, it was added, primarily because they were said to not need it or were unable to benefit much from it. In the Science Programme, the students gave in to the demands. In the Vehicle class, the students gave up trying to get a stronger instructional response from the school. The outcomes were similar, but the processes behind them were not.

The locus of interest away from academic teaching was even clearer in relation to the highly individualised and fragmented study situation of the Individual Programme. Here, as well as in the Child and Recreation Programme class we researched, health and well-being were the most prominent factors behind efforts to exert influence and most examples of influence were developed around daily negotiations initiated by a few students. These students acted as individuals who were trying to reduce the length of lessons (by getting extra breaks or extending scheduled ones). Their aim was to reduce workload on the basis of a claimed tiredness. Their efforts received support from a small but vociferous group, even though the outcome usually applied to everyone in the class.

There were also occasions when students on the Individual Programme initiated collective actions. Again, however, these concerned other aspects than teaching. For example, a group of girls took an initiative to counteract sexual harassment, which many girls in the programme said they had to endure on a regular basis during their school time.

The reproduction of hierarchical relations

A clear social hierarchy between programmes that corresponds to academic status and social class markers has been reported previously in research in Sweden (Johansson, 2009). This is evident in talk and action from both students and teachers and can be seen in the responses constructed in relation to efforts to exert influence discussed above. However, this hierarchy is visible also in other ways, such as in the differences between the physical environments of the programs, including the newness and quality of buildings and their proximity to the informational centre of the school. The locations of student council meetings at the schools we researched provide examples. These were situated closer to the academic programme quarters in the involved schools. These students were, according to interview data, expected to be more interested in school, more able to provide a positive input in a forum such as the school council and more willing to take part more often in such activities, than the vocational students. In one of the schools, the school information screens were also centrally placed in the main hallway of the school's main building, which was not normally used by vocational students as their activities were based in a separate location.

Such indications of status differences seem to carry over into and affect student experiences, emotions and feelings. As the Individual Programme students regularly pointed out, they felt they were on the margins of the school and they regularly described themselves as less able and/or less interested in obtaining high marks than other students, and of being belittled by the teachers. Comments about ritualism, recalcitrance and an absence of a clear sense of the purpose to their role in school were also common.

We can bring these two lines of reasoning and their empirical foundations together. Academically oriented students are often physically, subjectively and even emotionally placed at the centre of the school. They are talked about by teachers (and themselves) as being in school to obtain good marks in important subjects that can be exchanged for a good future education and a good job or career. The students of the vocational (in our study, particularly the Childhood and Recreation Programme) and even more so the Individual Programme are placed outside the centre and are often talked about as being less interested, less involved, less committed and less bright (Johansson, 2009).

We are tentatively suggesting that a pattern emerges of how the hierarchy between subjects represents relationships not only between the subjects, but also, and more importantly, between fields of practice (vocational and academic). Moreover, there are two further interesting points here. These are, first, that the students' desires to avoid instruction in the vocational programmes is heeded more than their demands for deeper subject matter and a more demanding academic education; and second, that students from the vocational programmes have most scope for influencing their education, but again, largely in terms of diluting academic demands and avoiding lessons and teaching (see also Beach, 1999b). The relationship is not just about subject content; it also reflects (and reinforces) divisions of labour, social class, social fields and class power (Bernstein, 2000).

Representations and relations of academic and vocational learning

The amount, content and scope of core academic subjects such as Swedish, English, mathematics and history in vocational education and training has been a recurrent and controversial issue in Swedish education politics and is now once again being subjected to change through the 2009 upper-secondary education reform, implemented from July, 2011 (Lundahl et al., 2010). This is a so-called re-traditionalisation reform, which will, *inter alia*, lead to a reduction of the time allotted to academic subjects in vocational education and training, and conversely create more space for vocational subjects. Knowledge will be more strongly classified; the boundaries between different subjects and teacher categories will be sharper again, and the vocational programmes will no longer provide general eligibility to higher education. Moreover, the contents of core academic subjects are also to be adjusted in line with the main orientation of the vocational programmes (e.g. 'industrial Swedish' will be taught in the Industry Programme). The change is mainly motivated by an alleged need asserted by the present government to focus on vocational preparation and employability; but at least as apparent are assumptions that vocational students from less academic backgrounds, backgrounds with less economic and cultural capital, have less interest in, motivation for and need of general academic knowledge than other students do (Lundahl et al., 2010).

Our research allows us to question such assumptions, not least those concerning the lack of theoretical interest amongst students who choose vocational programs. Indeed these assumptions seem to be as often refuted as confirmed by student actions and the conclusions thus seem to rest entirely on foundations that are socially constructed elements of a dominant discourse about social belonging, social origins and intellectual ability. Overall our studies show that there is no distinction between students from vocational programmes and others in regard to interests in and desires for a good education. This is in line with lower secondary school research showing students generally to be highly concerned about the quality of their teaching and that they act to improve it (Öhrn, 2004, 2005). Moreover, the proportion of students applying to vocational programmes decreased considerably in autumn 2011 when these programmes no longer provided sufficient content in core academic subjects to guarantee eligibility to higher education. Finally, if there is a dividing line with respect to subjectively expressed interests in a theoretical or practical education, our research suggests it is between programmes that have clear orientation toward the future with respect to specific occupations in the labour market and those that do not. In the material we have examined, this is manifested in differences between the Natural Science and Vehicle Programmes on the one hand and the Child and Recreation and Individual Programmes on the other.

The Vehicle Programme differs from the other two non-academic programmes by offering an education that targets a distinct set of occupations. It might be argued that this clarity also makes it easier for students to identify and request competences from the school that are needed for their future vocational life and career, and to be more compliant and committed to valued parts of their education and training. We note, for instance, that Vehicle Programme students were both more strongly committed to parts of their education such as vehicle mechanics, and also strongly critical of the mathematics teaching they received because it was not sufficiently demanding. Like the Natural Science students, they requested maths instruction that provided them with the means to cope with assumed future assignments and challenges. Similar demands and actions from students related to their future careers and studies were not seen in the classes of programmes with weaker identities and labour market connections; primarily the Child and Recreation and Individual programmes but also to some degree the Social Science Programme.

Final comments

Recent investigations of schooling processes in Scandinavia have highlighted a neo-liberal turn and the development of increasingly individualised learning (Gordon et al., 2003). Our research confirms this turn in its descriptions of student involvement in and influence on their education in today's upper-secondary school system. It is apparent that the schools and teachers favoured students' individual voices and choices at the expense of collective student influence in all the studied cases. This has consequences for the relationship of schooling to democracy described by Gordon and Lahelma (2002) and presented at the beginning of the present chapter. The students had a certain freedom of action when it came to sequencing their reading, the timing of tests and choice of text material in individual work. This can be seen as a way of fostering the self-governing, performance-oriented persons that post-industrial Sweden is commonly supposed to require (cf. Dovemark, 2004; Lindblad et al., 2002; Österlind, 1998). Such an understanding of citizenship and democracy may partly explain the relative scarcity of collective actions and their lack of success in school as well as add to the reduced political involvement noted recently among young adults in Sweden compared with previous decades.

In our investigation joint initiatives from the students to influence the level, content and methods of their education seem to receive very little support or encouragement from teachers and other adults in the school, particularly if and when these actions constitute a threat to strong classification and framing of upper secondary education. Thus it seems that the defence of teachers' knowledge-based superiority, particularly in subjects within a vertical discourse, still constitutes one of the greatest obstacles for students' initiation and carrying through of actions aiming to change aspects of education. We have also hinted at the possible value of having adults in school who are able to support such efforts for change.

References

Apple, M. W. and Beane J. A., (2007) Lessons from democratic schools, in Apple, M.W. and Beane, J. A., (eds.) *Democratic schools. Lessons in powerful education*, Portsmouth: Heinemann.

Beach, D., (1999a) Matematikutbildningens politik och ideology. [The policy and ideology of mathematics], *Nämnaren*, 26(3): 56-61.

Beach, D., (1999b) Om demokrati, reproduktion och förnyelse i dagens gymnasieskola. [Democracy, reproduction and renewal in upper-secondary school], *Pedagogisk forskning i Sverige (Pedagogical Research in Sweden)*, 4(4): 349-365.

Beach, D., (2008) The paradoxes of student learning preferences, *Ethnography and Education*, 3(2): 145-159.

Beach, D. and Dovemark, M., (2007) *Education and the commodity problem: Ethnographic investigations of creativity and performativity in Swedish schools*, London: the Tufnell Press.

Beach, D., Lundahl, L., and Öhrn, E., (2011) Synthesis, in Öhrn, E., Lundahl, L. and Beach, D., (eds.) *Young people's influence and democratic education. Ethnographic studies in upper secondary schools,* London: Tufnell.

Bernstein, B., (2000) *Pedagogy, symbolic control and identity: Theory, research, critique,* rev. ed., Lanham, Maryland: Rowman and Littlefield.

Bronäs, A., (2003) Demokratins ansikte [The face of democracy], in Jonsson, B. and Roth, K., (eds.) *Demokrati och lärande. Om valfrihet, gemenskap och övervägande i skola och samhälle,* Lund: Studentlitteratur.

Davies, L., (2002) Pupil voice in Europe, in Schweisfurth, M., Davies, L. and Harber, C., (eds.) *Learning democracy and citizenship: international experiences,* Oxford: Symposium Books.

Demokratiutredningen, (2000) *En uthållig demokrati! Politik för folkstyrelse på 2000-talet: Demokratiutredningens betänkande. [A sustainable democracy!],* SOU 2000:1, Stockholm: Fritzes offentliga publikationer.

Dovemark, M., (2004) *Ansvar—flexibilitet—valfrihet: En etnografisk studie om en skola i förändring. [Responsibility—flexibility—freedom of choice: An ethnographic study of a school in transition, in Swedish],* Thesis (PhD), University of Gothenburg.

Dovemark, M. (2011) Can this be called democracy?, in Öhrn, E., Lundahl, L. and Beach, D., (eds.) *Young people's influence and democratic education. Ethnographic studies in upper secondary schools,* London: the Tufnell Press.

Gordon, T., (2006) Girls in education: Citizenship, agency and emotions, *Gender and Education,* 18 (1): 1-15.

Gordon, T. and Lahelma, E., (2002) Becoming an adult: Possibilities and limitations—dreams and fears, *Young,* 10(2): 2-18.

Gordon, T., Lahelma, E. and Beach, D., (2003) Introduction. Marketisation of democratic education: Ethnographic insights, in Beach, D., Gordon, T. and Lahelma, E., (eds.) *Democratic education: Ethnographic challenges,* London: the Tufnell Press.

Henderson, S. and Hudson, B., (2010) What is subject content knowledge in mathematics?, *The 2010 Teacher Education Policy in Europe Conference,* Sept 30-Oct 2, Tallinn, Estonia.

Hjelmér, C., (2011a) Collective actions in the Natural Science Programme, in Öhrn, E., Lundahl, L. and Beach, D., (eds.) *Young people's influence and democratic education. Ethnographic studies in upper secondary schools,* London: the Tufnell Press.

Hjelmér, C., (2011b) Negotiations in the Child and Recreation Programme, in Öhrn, E., Lundahl, L. and Beach, D., (eds.) *Young people's influence and democratic education. Ethnographic studies in upper secondary schools,* London: the Tufnell Press.

Johansson, M., (2009) *Anpassning och motstånd: En etnografisk studie av gymnasieelevers institutionella identitetsskapande. [Adaption and resistance: An ethnographic investigation of the development of institutional identities amongst upper secondary school pupils, in Swedish],* Thesis (PhD), University of Gothenburg.

Lindblad, S., Lundahl, L., Lindgren, J. and Zackari, G., (2002) Educating for the New Sweden, *Scandinavian Journal of Educational Research,* 46(3): 283-303.

Lundahl, L., Arreman, I. E., Lundström, U. and Rönnberg, L., (2010) Setting things right? Swedish upper secondary school reform in a 40-year perspective, *European Journal of Education,* 45(1): 46-59.

Rosvall, P-Å., (2011a) Pedagogic practice and influence in a Social Science class, in Öhrn, E., Lundahl, L. and Beach, D., (eds.) *Young people's influence and democratic education. Ethnographic studies in upper secondary schools,* London: the Tufnell Press.

Rosvall, P-Å., (2011b) Pedagogic practice and influence in a Vehicle Programme class, in Öhrn, E., Lundahl, L. and Beach, D., (eds.) *Young people's influence and democratic education. Ethnographic studies in upper secondary schools*, London: the Tufnell Press.

Rönnlund, M., (2010) Student participation in activities with influential outcomes: issues of gender, individuality and collective thinking in Swedish secondary schools, *European Educational Research Journal*, 9(2): 208-219.

Svingby, G., (1993) *Manligt eller omoget? [Male or immature?]*, Stockholm: Utbildnings-departementet (Department of Education).

Swedish National Agency for Education (1999) *Läroplanerna i praktiken. [Curriculum in practice]*, Stockholm: Statens skolverk.

Swedish National Agency for Education (2003) *Ung i demokratin: Gymnasieelevers kunskaper och attityder i demokrati- och samhällsfrågor. [Young people in democracy: Knowledge and attitudes among upper secondary students]*, Stockholm: Skolverket, www.skolverket.se/publikationer?id=1180 [Accessed 16 December 2010].

Öhrn, E., (1998) Gender and power in school: On girls' open resistance, *Social Psychology of Education*, 1(4): 341-357.

Öhrn, E., (2001) Marginalisation of democratic values: A gendered practice of schooling?, *International Journal of Inclusive Education*, 5(2/3): 319-328.

Öhrn, E., (2004) Young people as political actors in school, *The European Conference for Educational Research*, 22-25 September, University of Crete, Greece.

Öhrn, E., (2005) *Att göra skillnad. En studie av ungdomar som politiska aktörer i skolans vardag. [To make a difference. A study of young people as political actors in schools]*, Göteborg: Department of Education, University of Gothenburg.

Österlind, E., (1998) *Disciplinering via frihet: Elevers planering av sitt eget arbete. [Disciplining via Freedom: Independent work and student planning]*, Thesis (PhD), Uppsala University.

Chapter 6

Changing discourses of employability: From the meritocratic to the enterprise discourse of abilities? A review of the current and emerging research on abilities

Katri Komulainen, Hannu Räty, Maija Korhonen, Päivi Siivonen, Riitta Kärkkäinen and Kati Kasanen

Topical change in the discourses of abilities

Employability has now emerged as a novel discourse that has replaced the previous way of describing the workforce in Europe. Instead of speaking about a shortage of employment, policy has started to speak about a lack of employability, and citizens have come to be described as employable or not employable and thus in need of employability skills (Fejes, 2010). We suggest that interpretations of abilities are at the core of reshaping employability discourses. Therefore, in this chapter we explore the socio-psychological dynamics pertaining to the encounter between the two representations of employability, namely the discourses of meritocratic and enterprise abilities. We review the current and emerging research on abilities and reflect on what kind of conceptions of intelligence and abilities are embedded in the discourses of employability and how they form the social identities and related social differences, such as gender and class, of different groups. We suggest that the current and potentially contradictory intersection of discourses of employability could be a fruitful focal point for future research. The research on education and social differences conducted by Tuula Gordon and Elina Lahelma has greatly inspired and influenced our current and emerging studies and ideas.

Discourses of ability play an important role in the formation of various symbolic orders in society, yet they have rarely been examined from a socio-psychological perspective. In our previous studies (Räty and Snellman, 1998), we have addressed interpretations of intelligence, which are constitutive of all systems of education as they encapsulate definitions of who are entitled and to what kind of education and related occupational positions. For the speaker, the interpretation of a person's abilities is a subjectively conclusive description of his/her individuality, masking the potential social connections of the interpretation. Importantly, judgments of abilities are also construed in relation to the predominant institutional representations of intelligence endorsed by school and social groups. It seems that the traditional meritocratic, individualised, differential, and verbal-cognitive, i.e., academic, notion of intelligence is quite resistant to any change, and it represents an important symbolic distinction used by social groups in constructing their identities.

Moreover, there is a need for socio-psychological research on the discourses of abilities outside of formal education, especially in working life, where the meritocratic notion of intelligence might be challenged. As Bourdieu (2005) argues, the education and labour market can be viewed as operating in separate and competitive fields, within which there exist struggles for the definition of 'proper' abilities of employability. However, current neo-liberal market society (Miller and Rose, 2008) creates a situation with a significant amount of tensions: apart from the predominant meritocratic discourse of intelligence, a new discourse of enterprise abilities has emerged. This new discursive reframing of employability tends to emphasise non-academic abilities, which have so far been undervalued in formal education, such as innovativeness, flexibility, risk-taking, having initiative, and social and communicative competencies. The discursive shift in employability, from an individual getting a job to a definition that places at its core the individual acquisition of a set of attributes and abilities that makes one appealing to employers, is neo-liberal in its emphasis on the individual project of the self (Boden and Nedeva, 2010). Individuals are, then, invited to (re)consider their own abilities in a situation that is characterised by the encounter of (at least) two partly different ability discourses.

We suggest that it would be fruitful to place the magnifying glass of research at this particular crossroads and examine the ways in which adults in different social positions and relations to work and education negotiate their skills and construe their *ability selves*. With this concept, we refer to an individual's interpretation of his/her own abilities and other internal properties, which orientate him/her towards education, work, and an occupation. It is vital to explore one's ability self according to the ways by which it is lived through and narratively constructed in life history interviews (Komulainen, 1999; Siivonen, 2010) and also in terms of the extent to which a person sees his/her abilities as malleable or fixed. The empirical anchors (the material) of one's ability self are his/her life experiences, which s/he has dealt with in different contexts of evaluation, particularly in education and work. Two modes of evaluation can be distinguished: interpersonal (normative comparison) and intrapersonal or temporal (Kärkkäinen et al., 2008). Further, it is useful to analyse the constructions of ability selves according to their contents (cognitive versus other kinds of capability), emphasis (profiling), and evaluation (as positive or negative). By scrutinising prototypical elements, we may well talk about ability selves at the group level, too. For instance, the 'ideology of natural giftedness' can be seen to represent the core features of ability selves among middle-class parents (Räty and Kasanen, in press).

The meritocratic discourse of abilities

As to the meritocratic discourse of abilities, we refer to the representation of intelligence endorsed by schools. Historically, the discourse of abilities upheld by schools was scientifically styled by the psychometric concept of intelligence (Danziger, 1990). This resonance entails the ranking of students according to the normal distribution—or the 'cosmic rule', as Sir Francis Galton called it—expressed in such categories as 'bright', 'mediocre' and 'poor'; the definition of intelligence as a mainly cognitive capacity, with an implied distinction between theoretical and practical skills and related school subjects; and the implicit distinction drawn between male and female abilities and the corresponding school subjects.

Objectified through everyday practices, this discourse seems to represent relative continuity in school organisation from basic to adult education. Despite all criticism, it has maintained its central place because the routines and principles of schools make diversity among children an issue that can be conveniently addressed through a differential notion of intelligence (Räty and Snellman, 1998). This is one important reason why educational reforms have failed to challenge conventional notions of intelligence (Hart, 1998). Accordingly, as individuals construe their ability selves, they are invited to reflect on the central question: Where do I locate myself in the hierarchy of cognitive-verbal versus other abilities?

In previous research, we studied individualised but socially constructed interpretations of personal abilities and educational potential. What did we find? First, one of our major findings was that school mediates the meritocratic discourse of abilities to children. While participating in daily school practices, especially differential routines, the child quite quickly adopts the way, endorsed by a school, of assessing competencies as an internal phenomenon of the individual (Kasanen and Räty, 2002; Kasanen et al., 2003). In the course of schooling, the child also learns the normative way of judging his/her achievements, which tends to almost completely displace the intrapersonal way of judgment and significantly affects the formation of the child's academic self-concept (Kärkkäinen et al., 2008). The child's educability is based on the assessment of his/her individual abilities and subsequent academic achievements which makes it a functional part of the differentially individualising interpretative system of the school. It is a naturalising process that represents, in Bourdieu's (1985) terms, an 'alchemistic transformation' occurring in school, in which original social differences are transformed into natural individual differences.

Second, the meritocratic discourse of abilities produces groups' social identities and related distinctions. Parents' educational position seems to measure their social distance from school and its hegemonic representation of intelligence. Our cross-sectional and longitudinal studies consistently demonstrated that parental judgments of their child's academic proficiencies and abilities are related to the child's gender and the parents' education; moreover, these judgments already surfaced during the child's preschool stage (Räty et al., 1999, 2006b). In light of these results, the 'ideology of natural giftedness' may well be regarded as the hegemonic representation of intelligence that connects a school (teachers) and highly educated parents (Räty et al., 2006b). Highly educated people's educational attitudes that emphasise the child's individuality reflect the fact that members of dominant groups tend to consider themselves as individuals with a fair amount of intrapersonal distinctiveness (Gordon, 1992; Lorenzi-Cioldi and Clémence, 2003). The introduction of a novel discourse of abilities may pose a problem of identity, as practical-social skills can be a threat to social contrasts that favour the middle class in terms of 'higher' (i.e. cognitive-verbal) skills.

Third, what is adopted in schools contributes to later life. Parents' own school recollections have numerous and even predictive connections with their perceptions of their child's schooling (Räty, 2010). More importantly, our previous studies on adults' educational life histories indicated that adult students reflected on themselves and their abilities through the predominant meritocratic discourse of abilities and the categories it includes (Komulainen, 1999; Siivonen, 2010). The differential conception of ability (normative comparison) turned out to be a basis for negative self-examination, especially for general upper secondary school adult students and students studying social work who experienced a lack of previous education or who had interrupted their education at some point. A low level or lack of previous education was taken as proof that the students did not have the abilities valued by school, and the blame for the lack of those abilities was put on the students themselves. In upper secondary school of general adult education, our studies demonstrated that it is still important to document one's intelligence through the grading system and formal qualifications. Paradoxically, then, it turned out that proving one's ability and competence as a student and learner through formal qualifications was more important than the principles of lifelong learning.

However, through an emphasis on essentialist femininity and/or working class values, the female students in the fields of social work questioned the significance of continuing education and theoretical abilities as the measure of the moral value of the self (Komulainen, 1999; Käyhkö, 2006). Instead of focusing on individuality and intelligence, the women construed 'a caring self', which underlined the abilities attached to caring and emphasised its status in the hierarchy of abilities (cf. Skeggs, 1997). Thus, even though the hegemonic discourse of meritocratic abilities represents the relative continuity of the school system, it is challenged by the abilities and values associated with femininity, the working class, and the discourse of lifelong learning.

The discourse of enterprise abilities

Conceptions of abilities arising from the neo-liberalisation of education and the labour market place emphasis on the functional importance of abilities that have so far been devalued in formal education, for example, generic and interpersonal skills (communication and teamwork capabilities), personal attributes (resilience, commitment, risk-taking ability, and creativity), and transferable or flexible skills (Boden and Nedeva, 2010; Brown et al., 2003). These kinds of entrepreneur-like properties and motivations are regarded as essential capital in the neo-liberal market society characterised by free competition, constant changes, and uncertainty. Compared with cognitive and verbal abilities, for example, these may be somewhat less measurable but equally subordinated to evaluation and ranking.

Enterprising skills are also seen as important because of changes in careers: static careers have been substituted with new boundless ones and with protean careers emphasising the individual's self-directed and opportunity-seeking behaviour (Arthur and Rosseau, 1996; Hall and Mirvis, 1996). Performing in the protean careers compares eminently with entrepreneurship: everyone is held responsible for her/his career and employment. Employees have an obligation to develop their personal potential and to have the capacity to market their know-how and flexibly navigate from one task to another (Sinisalo and Komulainen,

2008). When abilities are regarded as personal properties that have an exchange value in the labour market, individuals must constantly redefine themselves to be suitable for the jobs (Urciuoli, 2008). Accordingly, when individuals construe and negotiate their ability selves, they have to reflect on the central question of 'Who am I really?' instead of articulating 'What do I formally know?'

Along with changes in the forms of careers, bureau professionalism has been challenged in the neo-liberal era, and there are attempts to replace it with a new managerial regime. The new managerial regime increases emphasis on the individual as opposed to collective relations with the employee, and stresses the need to motivate people to produce quality and strive for excellence themselves (Gewirtz and Ball, 2000). The new managerial regime in education emphasises the instrumental purposes of schooling and is frequently articulated within the lexicon of enterprise, excellence, quality, and effectiveness (Gordon et al., 2003).

In recent research (Korhonen et al., 2012), we explored how Finnish comprehensive school teachers construct and negotiate the aims of entrepreneurship education promoted by the Finnish Ministry of Education (see Finnish Ministry of Education, 2009). We explored how they evaluate their pupils' abilities from the point of view of enterprising and entrepreneurial skills, as well as what the ideal abilities are in the context of entrepreneurship education. In addition, we looked at the new task of educating enterprising citizens that the Finnish school system now faces by analysing the kinds of narratives of enterprising selves described by ninth grade girls and boys in their entries to the annual Finnish writing competition *Good Enterprise!* (Komulainen et al., 2009).

Our results show that teachers used a logic that intertwined with the school system's conventional understandings about ability to evaluate the pupils' potential to become entrepreneurs (Korhonen et al., 2011). The notion of an academically competent pupil was not questioned as the basis of evaluating the pupils' abilities: instead, it was utilised as a discursive *contrast* to which the talents of 'the entrepreneur type' of pupils were compared. Further, the teachers saw entrepreneurial potential particularly in those boys who were seen as socially talented, bold, easy-going, risk-taking, creative, and/or competent in practical skills. Because the qualities of the 'good student' were particularly associated with girls (Lahelma, 2005), they were excluded from the categories of the entrepreneurial type of pupil.

In their narratives, pupils constructed the middle-class version of the self, where the person is not contingent on external affects but is an autonomous self-governing individual. However, the boys' narrated selves matched the culturally valued representations of the 'proper', autonomous and risk-taking entrepreneurial individual more closely than the self-representations of girls did. To sum up, we suggest that the traditional gender hierarchy seems to persist within the discourse of enterprise abilities, although the value of academic competence and theoretical abilities is challenged, implying a general process of *particularisation*—the new element tends to change the meaning of the familiar one (Moscovici, 1988).

Notions of intelligence and abilities reflect one's chances in society

Despite their differences, the discourses of meritocratic and enterprise abilities also have common features. They share a logic according to which abilities are individual, internal characteristics, and hence abilities are considered in isolation from social positions and contexts. Simultaneously, the notion of the autonomous and naturally gifted individual remains unquestioned (Oyserman and Markus, 1998). In both discourses, the individual's abilities are naturalised and objectified. As Urciuoli (2008, p. 224) notes, 'all these aspects of social action and personhood are skills insofar as they are divorced from their users' everyday social context and recast, entextualised, inculcated, and assessed by experts for the work applications'.

The new skills replicate those associated with being a consultant, having the capability to move smoothly from one task to another, which is seen to reflect an individual's general internal potential (Sennett, 2006). Actually, this particular view dates back to the very first scientific models of human intelligence, especially to those proposed by Spearman, which highlight the importance of general and context-free intelligence, the g-factor instead of specific abilities. According to Sennett (2006), the judgment of one's internal potential is far more personal than that of performance. To claim that an individual lacks potential is much harsher and even more consequential than to say that this time he/she has failed.

Interestingly enough, many modern scientific models of human intelligence seem to reflect changes in society. For instance, theories of emotional intelligence stress the significance of social skills (Mayer and Salovey, 1997). This is also seen in the influential theories developed by Gardner (1995) and Sternberg (1999) where practical and interpersonal skills are brought side by side with cognitive and problem-solving skills. In addition, Dweck's (1999) theory of subjective conceptions of intelligence is interesting in its attempt to demonstrate that the endorsement of the conventional static notion of intelligence has many negative effects on learning. In contrast, the adoption of the incremental notion of intelligence is associated with effort where mistakes and failures are not seen as lack of intelligence but rather as enriching challenges for further learning and developing skills. The first conception seems to concur with the conventional meritocratic notion of abilities, while the second conception relates to some of the major ideals of the notion of enterprise abilities. Scientific theories of intelligence are not disconnected from society, and social (interest) groups forcefully use and transform them from their own points of view (Moscovici, 1988). As Tuddenham (1964) once put it, the ultimate yardsticks of human intelligence are to be found in the requirements posed by society and culture.

Focusing future research—the study of gendered and classed ability selves

We suggest that the current and potentially contradictory intersection of discourses of meritocratic and enterprising abilities could be a fruitful focal point for future research. The emergence of the discourse of enterprising ability is a transformational process that brings into play not only a new set of interpretations of ability, intelligence, and skills but also a new set of values and a new moral environment of education and working life. We suggest that in this process, it may even generate new subjectivities (Gewirtz and Ball, 2000). We want to emphasise that there is no simple or absolute process of change at work. In people's interpretations, the new language of abilities still encompasses aspects of the established discourse of meritocratic abilities. Moreover, people bring with them into this transformation their life histories, including their experiences and memories of ability selves and their social positioning—age, gender, class, level of academic attainment—which mean that a straightforward totalising fit with the emerging discourse of enterprising abilities is a delusion. On the contrary, these social differences structure and differentiate people's experiences and their interpretations of ability selves.

Evidently, there is a need for a methodological approach that recognises the constitutive force of discourses of employability, and in particular, of discursive practices, and at the same time recognises that people are capable of exercising choice in relation to these practices. Through analysing life histories from the point of view of discursive and narrative social psychology, it is possible to explore how women and men have adopted representations of abilities, which include some people and exclude others; how they have participated in the various discursive practices through which meanings are allocated to these representations; how they position themselves in terms of these constructions and story lines of abilities; and how they elaborate different subject positions in the context of discourses of employability and negotiate their ability selves in relation to these discourses, which contain significant gender- and social class related distinctions. By analysing life histories, it is possible to trace the trajectories through which adults have learned and lived the discourses of meritocratic abilities which have positioned them in such categories as 'bright', 'mediocre' or 'poor', theoretical or practical (see Lahelma, 2009), or in positions such as autonomous/dependent, innovative/ordinary, risk-taking/cautious, proactive and creative/stuck in old patterns of thinking, flexible/unflexible (Hartshorn and Sear, 2005).

Most research on employability has ignored gender differences (Smetherham, 2003) and has taken class as a given position. We suggest, however, that not only the hegemonic discourse of meritocratic ability but also the emerging discourse can be regarded as a classed and gendered system of knowledge and evaluation which governs—enabling or limiting—the adults' access to certain subject positions of *able selves*. Thus the subject position of the *able self* is not equally available to all. Both the ideal *able self* constructed within the discourse of meritocratic ability, and the risk-taking, enterprising, mobile, individualistic self with its particular personality package, require access to the right resources to produce itself (cf. Skeggs, 2004, p. 176).

Moreover, we wish to expand the present research of employability by adopting a positional conflict theory approach through which we contextualise adults' educational and occupational life histories, career transitions and the formation of their abilities (Brown et al., 2003). This approach challenges the idea of employability as simply to do with finding a job. It focuses on the duality of employability by giving consideration to both the rigging of the market for credentials and the ranking of individuals in the labour market on the basis of social and cultural capital (Boden and Nedeva, 2010). On the one hand, employability and related notions of abilities are considered to be connected to the demand for certain kinds of labour. A complex mixture of social, personal, organisational, institutional, economic, and political factors mediates any particular individual's employability and the meaning and value of her/his abilities. On the other hand, employability is a social construct that is closely related to and informed by an individual's social identities, such as gender and class, and his/her life history and self-concept. In sum, this theory highlights ranking in the labour market, power play and positional differences among individuals, both between and within the classes and genders. The interest lies in the ways in which individuals use various cultural resources and mobilise forms of capital to gain positional advantages in the labour market (Tomlinson, 2008).

Sociological research on employability has so far mainly concentrated on the occupational life chances of young graduates and on the overall processes of how the self is packaged by labour market entrants. For young people, the transition as such is likely to generate worry talk and calls for training in practical professional skills during the course of their formal education. Accordingly, it would be equally important to explore, in socio-psychological terms, the ways in which people who are more or less settled in their jobs perceive their situation in terms of abilities and related requirements.

To recapitulate, we suggest that it would be important to explore the socio-psychological dynamics of the encounter between the discourses of meritocratic and enterprise abilities in the context of changes in discourses of employability. Does this change contribute to individuals' ability negotiations, whom does it concern in particular, and in what ways do people deal with the change? How, for example, is one's ability self negotiated and interpreted: what sorts of ability categorisations have been adopted and how have they been lived and experienced, what sorts of criteria are used to evaluate one's ability self and what kinds of possibilities do individuals see for the development of their abilities? Do women and men come in touch with the encounter of the two discourses of abilities, and in what ways do they deal with these particular incidences socio-psychologically? For instance, how is the new anchored in established categorisations and valuations, and how does the new change the interpretations of established categories? In what ways do the narrative environments of multifaceted social contexts, such as universities, professional organisations, and workplaces, structure peoples' interpretations? How do gender and social class and their intersections contribute to the (re)construction of one's ability self and related social identity?

By looking at the encounter between the two major discourses of abilities in their relations to the changes in the discourses of employability, we may acquire new research findings in two main domains. First, by exploring life history narratives as to the meaning-making processes of abilities in different social contexts, knowledge can be obtained about the 'grass-roots level' socio-psychological dynamics of present social changes. Second, by investigating the highly individualised ability issue, so dear to our society and culture, a host of important social dependencies and contents of that discussion can be explicated. Analysing ability negotiations may well provide an important and fairly novel perspective on the social reproduction of education, too. This also offers the possibility of promoting critical reflection and emancipation in relation to often unquestioned beliefs of abilities.

References

Arthur, M., and Rosseau, D., (1996) The boundaryless career as a new employment principle, in Arthur, M. and Rosseau D., (eds.) *The boundaryless career*, New York: Oxford University Press.

Boden, R., and Nedeva, M., (2010) Employing discourse: Universities and graduate 'employability', *Journal of Education Policy*, 25(1): 37-54.

Bourdieu, P., (1985) *Sosiologian kysymyksiä. [Questions of sociology]*, Tampere: Vastapaino.

Bourdieu, P., (2005) *The social structures of the economy*, Cambridge: Polity Press.

Brown, P., Hesketh, A., and Williams, S., (2003) Employability in knowledge-driven society, *Journal of Education and Work,* 16(2): 107-126.

Danziger, K., (1990) *Constructing the subject: Historical origins of psychological research*, Cambridge: Cambridge University Press.

Dweck, C., (1999) *Self-theories*, Howe: Taylor and Francis.

Fejes, A., (2010) Discourses on employability: Constituting the responsible citizen, *Studies in Continuing Education*, 32(2): 89-102.

Finnish Ministry of Education (2009) *Guidelines for entrepreneurship education*, Helsinki: Publications of Ministry of Education 2009:9, www.minedu.fi/export/sites/default/OPM/Julkaisut/2009/liitteet/opm09.pdf [Accessed May 2012].

Gardner, H., (1995) Reflections of multiple intelligences, *Phi Delta Kappan*, 77: 200-208.

Gewirtz, S. and Ball, S., (2000) From 'welfarism' to 'new managerialism': Shifting discourses of school headship in the education marketplace, *Discourse: Studies in the Cultural Politics of Education*, 21(3): 253-268.

Gordon, T., (1992) Citizens and Others: Gender, democracy and education, *International Studies in Sociology of Education*, 2(1): 43-55.

Gordon, T., Lahelma, E. and Beach, D., (2003) Marketisation of democratic education: Ethnographic insights, in Beach, D., Gordon, T. and Lahelma, E., (eds.) *Democratic education: Ethnographic challenges*, London: Tufnell Press.

Hall, D., and Mirvis, P., (1996) The new protean career: Psychological success and the path with a heart, in Hall, D. T., (ed.) *The career is dead: Long live the career: A relational approach to careers*, San Francisco, CA: Jossy-Bass.

Hart, S., (1998) A sorry tail: Ability, pedagogy and educational reform, *British Journal of Educational Studies*, 46: 153-168.

Hartshorn, C., and Sear, L., (2005) Employability and enterprise: Evidence from the North East, *Urban Studies*, 42(2): 271-283.

Kasanen, K. and Räty H., (2002) 'You be sure now to be honest in your assessment': Teaching and learning self-assessment, *Social Psychology of Education*, 21: 1-16.

Kasanen, K., Räty, H., and Snellman, L., (2003) Learning the class test, *European Journal of Psychology of Education*, 18: 43-58.

Komulainen, K., (1999) A course of one's own: The rhetorical self in educational life stories by women, *Nordic Journal of Women's Studies*, 7: 123-137.

Komulainen, K., Korhonen, M., and Räty, H., (2009) Risk taking abilities for everyone? Finnish entrepreneurship education and the enterprising selves imagined by pupils, *Gender and Education*, 21(6): 631-649.

Korhonen, M., Komulainen, K., and Räty, H., (2012) 'Not everyone is cut out to be the entrepreneur type': How Finnish school teachers construct the meaning of entrepreneurship education and the related abilities of the pupils, *Scandinavian Journal of Educational Research*, 56(1): 1-19.

Kärkkäinen, R., Räty, H., and Kasanen, K., (2008) Children's notions of the malleability of their academic competencies, *Social Psychology of Education*, 11: 445-458.

Kärkkäinen, R., Räty, H., and Kasanen, K., (2009) Parents' perceptions of their child's resilience and competence, *European Journal of Psychology of Education*, 24: 405-419.

Käyhkö, M., (2006) *Siivoojaksi oppimassa: Etnografinen tutkimus työläistytöistä puhdistuspalvelualan koulutuksessa. [Learning to be a cleaner: Ethnographic research on working-class girls in cleaning services education]*, Joensuu: Joensuun Yliopistopaino.

Lahelma, E., (2005) School grades and other resources: The 'failing boys' discourse revisited, *NORA, Nordic Journal of Women's Studies*, 13(2): 78-89.

Lahelma, E., (2009) Dichotomized metaphors and young people's educational routes, *European Educational Research Journal*, 8(4): 497-507.

Lorenzi-Cioldi, F., and Clémence, A., (2003) Group processes and the construction of social representation, in Hogg M. A. and Tindale R. S (eds.) *Blackwell handbook of social psychology: Group processes,* Malden: Blackwell Publishing.

Mayer, J., and Salovey, P., (1997) What is emotional intelligence?, in Salovay, P. and Slyter, S. (eds.) *Emotional development and emotional intelligent: Educational implication,* New York: Basic Books.

Miller, P., and Rose, N., (2008) *Governing the present,* Cambridge, UK: Polity Press.

Moscovici, S., (1988) Notes towards a description of social representations, *European Journal of Social Psychology*, 18: 211-250.

Oyserman, D., and Markus, H., (1998) Self as social representations, in Flick, U. (ed.) *The psychology of the social,* Cambridge, UK: Cambridge University Press.

Räty, H., (2010) Do parents' own school memories contribute to their satisfaction with their child's school?, *Educational Studies*, 36: 581-584.

Räty, H., and Kasanen, K., (in press) Parents' perceptions of their child's academic competencies construe their educational reality: Findings from a 9-year longitudinal study. *Journal of Applied Social Psychology.*

Räty, H., Kasanen, K., and Honkalampi, K., (2006a) Three years later: A follow-up study of parents' assessments of their children's competencies, *Journal of Applied Social Psychology*, 36: 2079-2099.

Räty, H., Kasanen, K., and Kärkkäinen, R., (2006b) School subjects as social categorizations, *Social Psychology of Education*, 9: 5-25.

Räty, H., and Snellman, L., (1998) Social representations of educability, *Social Psychology of Education*, 1: 359-373.

Räty, H., Snellman, L., and Vainikainen, A., (1999) Parents' assessment of their children's abilities, *European Journal of Psychology of Education*, 14: 423-437.

Sennett, R., (2006) *The culture of new capitalism*, New Haven: University of Yale.

Sinisalo, P., and Komulainen, K., (2008) The creation of coherence in the transitional career: A narrative case study of the woman entrepreneur, *International Journal for Educational and Vocational Guidance*, 8(1): 35-48.

Siivonen, P., (2010) From a 'student' to a lifelong 'consumer' of education? Constructions of educability in adult students' narrative life histories, *Research in Educational Sciences* 47, Helsinki: Finnish Educational Research Association.

Skeggs, B., (1997) *Formations of class and gender: Becoming respectable*, London: Sage.

Skeggs, B, (2004) *Class, self, culture*, London: Routledge.

Smetherham, C., (2003) *The employability of first class graduates: The labour market outcomes*, Saarbrücken: VDM Verlag.

Sternberg, R., (1999) Successful intelligence, *Trends in Cognitive Science*, 3: 436-442.

Tomlinson, M., (2008) 'The degree is not enough': Students' perceptions of the role of higher education credentials for graduate work and employability, *British Journal of Sociology of Education*, 29(1): 49-61.

Tuddenham, A., (1964) The nature and measurement of intelligence, in Postman, L., (ed.) *Psychology in the making*, New York: Alfred a Knopf.

Urciuoli, B., (2008) Skills and selves in the work place, *American Ethnologist*, 35: 211-228.

Part 3: Transitions

Chapter 7

The expansion of higher education in the UK: Winners and losers

Janet Holland and Rachel Thomson

Nam: What do you think do you think education is more important or being happy with life?
Int: I think happy is pretty important ...
Nam: Providing okay that you've got a decent full time job that you enjoy that has average income of 11,000 a year ... which is not a lot but you're happy with it, and or ... you can go to uni having a stressful time you know, all this debt and shit, you know—what would you prefer ...?
Happy in life you see, a lot of people do that, they work full time ... they quit education you see but that's a stupid thing to do, because you know you'll never make a lot of money. There's a part of me that says yeah education is good and another part of me says enjoy life while you can you see.   (Nam[14], 20, 2003)

Nam expresses the ambivalence that many of the working class young people in the Inventing Adulthood study felt towards education. His parents, migrants from south east Asia, wanted for him the good education they had not had; he wanted to have fun. He suspected that university might offer someone like him stress and debt, but perhaps also the promise of a well-paid job. In this chapter we examine the expansion of UK higher education (HE) in the late twentieth early twenty-first centuries, exploring how the lives of young people have been affected. Our account is based on the Inventing Adulthood Study (IA)[15], which has followed 121 people growing up in five sites, urban and rural, disadvantaged and affluent, north and south in England and in Northern Ireland as they moved through their teens and twenties from 1996-2010. The

14 Pseudonyms are used for the young people.
15 Funder ESRC: Youth Values 1996-1999 (L129251020); Inventing Adulthoods 1999-2002 (L134251008); Youth Transitions 2002-2007; Families and Social Capital ESRC Research Group; Making the Long View 2007-2012. Core team: Sheila Henderson, Janet Holland, Sheena McGrellis, Sue Sharpe and Rachel Thomson. (www.lsbu.ac.uk/inventingadulthoods).

study generated a wealth of material in up to six biographical interviews, with additional methods—lifelines, questionnaires, focus groups and memory books (Thomson and Holland, 2005). In 2009/10 we revisited participants in the Northern Irish research site[16] and hope to re-interview in all sites. With largely digital transcripts and audio, this expanding dataset provides a unique window on most aspects of growing up through an important period of social change in the UK.

Our initial access to the young people was through schools located in distinct and socio-economically varied localities, providing different conditions for life. We followed them through their final year examinations and post-16 decisions into further and higher education. During the period there have been many changes in education policy in the UK, and a change of government. The New Labour government (1997-2010) oversaw the development of Education Action Zones, Excellence in Cities[17], and the introduction of Education Maintenance Allowances (EMA), which provided a modest weekly payment for low-income young people over the statutory school leaving age of sixteen and in full time education. These policies targeted poorer or potentially socially excluded groups to facilitate the expansion of numbers of students in higher education. The inner city school in our study grasped every opportunity for working class young people to get into further and higher education, including mentoring, scholarships, and being part of the EMA pilot study. The school on the disadvantaged northern estate also made great efforts, and in each case we saw a number of the young people going to university 'against the odds'. Often they would go to a local university, a new university, or by route of a college of further education. Even if they had an opportunity to go to a more elite old university, the social and experiential (and often physical) distance to be bridged between that type of educational establishment and their home and community, and the fear of loss of support from family and friends often led young people to take more local options (Reynolds 2007; Tolley and Rundle 2006).

We write at a moment of policy change and the possibility that the expansion of HE has halted, reframing a story of the democratisation of university to one of a 'lucky generation' of working class kids who got in 'just in time'. In this chapter we draw on the experiences of the young people in our study, focusing on the sites vulnerable to social exclusion and subject to the tranche of policies

16 Funders Joseph Rowntree Foundation, report McGrellis www.jrf.org.uk.
17 Launched March 1999 to raise standards and promote inclusion in inner cities, included Learning Mentors, Learning Support Units, provision for Gifted and Talented pupils, and construction of city Learning Centres.

mentioned here. Before moving on to explore their experiences we contextualise this moment in policy-making within a broader review of education policy in relation to higher education in the UK.

Education policy in the UK: twentieth century expansion

The education system in the UK underwent considerable change in the late twentieth century. A post-war political consensus based on commitment to full employment, the welfare state, and general support for a reforming education policy began to fall apart at the end of the 1960s, and the economic recession of 1971-73 was the final blow. The period had seen an extension of education through the tri-partite school system introduced in 1944, which created grammar, technical and secondary modern schools. This system reproduced the hierarchical class structure of the UK, but provided opportunities for a minority of working class young people to gain a secondary and occasionally a tertiary education. Means-tested grants, and provision of full fees were introduced in 1960, and in1963 the Robbins Report successfully urged immediate expansion of higher education to enable access for all those with ability and qualifications. This led to a rise in university entrants of 150 per cent by 1989 followed by ongoing expansion of higher education. In 1938, the proportion of the eighteen year-old population entering university was two per cent; in 1948 it was 3.7 per cent; by 1996 the figure had jumped to 33 per cent. Under the New Labour government it rose to 47 per cent in 2009-10 (BIS, 2011)[18].

Given an overall drop in education spending after 1979 (Conservative government), such a massive expansion of higher education required a range of policy measures. A two-pronged approach was employed, with a squeeze on capital expenditure and the physical fabric of schools, and a total change in the funding of higher education, as part of a process of 'marketisation'. In 1988, polytechnics and some colleges of higher education were removed from local education authority (LEA) control and constituted as competing corporations resourced through a new funding body. Between 1989 and 1992, polytechnics alone accounted for 50 per cent of the growth in student numbers. In 1992, funding was linked to student numbers, and the binary divide between polytechnics (vocational) and universities (academic research and scholarship) was removed so that polytechnics became universities and could award degrees.

---

18 This figure included gender, social class and ethnicity gaps of varying complexity identified by Broecke and Hamed (2008), from analyses of UK Longitudinal Cohort statistics.

In a third prong, benefits and grants were removed from students throughout the 1980s, and in 1990, maintenance grants were frozen and student loans introduced.

Following this trend, the New Labour government passed the *Teaching and Higher Education Act 1998* which included new and expanded arrangements for loans, abolished maintenance grants and introduced tuition fees for undergraduates. Subsequently, the government proposed to deal with the under-funding of universities by enabling them to charge top-up fees of up to £3,000 a year, and despite considerable opposition, this measure was put in place in 2005. These policies raise the spectre of student debt, and government policies for financing universities in general seemed to be at odds with their plans to widen access to families who might see university as beyond their reach, or had no previous experience of university education, like many of our young people (Chitty, 2009; Mizen, 2004). The Conservative/Liberal Democrat coalition government that took over in 2010 allowed universities to charge up to £9,000 against great opposition.

Claire Callender and colleagues have demonstrated in a series of research projects into student finance that government policies of raising student fees had a detrimental effect on poorer students from lower class backgrounds. Fear of debt deters them, and if they do get to university, they are increasingly reliant on paid work to augment their income. Those most dependent and working the longest hours come from the poorest families, and this has a detrimental effect on their education. The main beneficiaries of the change from grants to loans were wealthier students (Callender and Wilkinson, 2003; Callender and Jackson, 2008).

Egerton and Halsey (1993) conclude their study of access to higher education over the twentieth century by identifying three major features: it was a period of considerable expansion; there was a significant reduction in gender inequality; but there has been no reduction in relative social class inequality. There is a general consensus that expanding HE has benefited less bright wealthier, middle class young people, rather than the brighter working class, and that the situation on working class access to education has worsened in more recent years (Metcalf, 1997; Machin and Blanden, 2004). Machin (2003) reports that in 1991-92, thirteen per cent of children from the lowest social class went to university but by the end of the decade, after the introduction of tuition fees and abolition of the student grant, the figure dropped to seven per cent. Over the same period, participation by children from the professional classes increased from fifty-five to seventy-two per cent. There is also evidence that class and ethnicity influence the sector of HE that young people enter, mapping onto the hierarchy of HE institutions (Brown and Lauder, 2009). For example, figures for 1998 indicate that minority groups were disproportionately entering the new rather than elite universities: students of Caribbean origin were over-represented by forty-three per cent, Asians by 162 per cent and Africans by 223 per cent in this sector.

So there is good and bad news on expansion of higher education in the UK. The situation has been improving for young women, and for middle-class young people. Despite government policies designed to improve the situation, access is currently declining for working class young people, and amongst those from different ethnic groups there is variability (Perry and Francis, 2010).

Inventing adulthoods: Education and ambivalence

'Traditional' educational transitions were enjoyed by a few of the young people in the Inventing Adulthoods study, particularly in the middle class, on a privileged path to professional careers. Others followed less traditional and less supported working class routes into further and higher education. Those who failed to secure a sense of competence and recognition in education might follow several routes: they could seek accelerated adulthood by leaving school and entering work as soon as possible, they could focus on the domestic domain, start a steady relationship and 'settle down', or they might want to have fun and pursue leisure. But one route has become increasingly common and featured in different ways in our group: a struggle to maintain a connection with education, building a portfolio of vocational courses, which might lead nowhere, whilst also working in dead end jobs—a yo-yo transition (Du Bois-Reymond and Lopez Blasco, 2003, p. 23).

Balancing education and study with other aspects of life was another important theme, and young people drew on various resources to manage this. They talked about not risking educational attainment in order to pursue serious relationships, getting the balance right between study and social life. Work and education appeared sometimes to be competing rather than complementary goals, and the allure of an independent income was strong. A pattern of postponing the demands of intimate relationships and the pursuit of a particular type of femininity also emerged in young women's accounts, particularly related to desires for social mobility through education. They needed to avoid the bonding social capital (Putnam, 2000) that could bind them to community; to leave their locality in order to achieve this aim; to get out in order to get on.

The pattern of combining education and work that the young people had pursued through school continued into further and higher education. Sometimes the motivation was similar: to have their own money and not burden their parents—linking to the resources of the domestic sphere and family. In other instances the work they did enhanced their educational route. Edward and Francis, for example, took vacation placements that complemented their work ambitions, and could lead to an actual career.

Our research sites were chosen to reflect socio-economic diversity, and of the seventy young people interviewed for a fourth time at age 18-24 in 2002, twenty (29%) were at university. Of these, nine were working class, eight of these young women, most the first in their family to go to university, perhaps reflecting the expansion of higher education and improved access for young women. Many of the young people in the study placed a high value on education as a good in itself. Others saw it as a means to an end—a good job and reasonable income. Carol, a middle-class young woman in Northern Ireland, had a great social time; she 'didn't really enjoy the academic side of school'. Her approach was highly instrumental; she was 'at university to get a good job', not particularly enjoying her course:

> I'm not there to enjoy it, if you know what I mean, which I don't know if that's a good or bad thing … if I was financially secure and not have to go and work academically, I would jump at the chance. … I'm interested in what I'm doing at the moment, but I wouldn't say I'm ecstatic.
>
> (Carol, 22, 2003)

Nat, a middle class young man in the leafy suburb, was similarly instrumental, with his choice of course providing a backup:

> But computing is basically—and I knew what it would be when I chose the course—it would be a backup if I never realised what I wanted to do, or found something. So I suppose that's what it will be in the end—a back up—not my first.
>
> (Nat, 21, 2003)

Samuel left university after a year because 'It's about who you know not what you've done', and by then he had developed the skills, contacts and social capital he needed for his planned future in the entertainment world.

There were very few who thought that education had little impact or meaning in their life. A group of young men in a pupil referral unit, excluded from school for behavioural reasons, all subscribed to education as one of the most important things in life despite the fact that it was clearly not working for them. A number in the study felt that university was not necessarily a good route for them, or that they and others could do just as well in work and earnings without it. Some were ambivalent about the value of education, and others felt they personally had made the wrong choices, either of university, or of specific subjects.

Edward in the leafy suburb developed the argument about university not being for everybody in the context of a critique of government policy:

> Because of this misguided emphasis on qualifications as pieces of paper, there's a feeling that you have to go to university if you want to get ahead in life, and people who aren't temperamentally suited to university life are deciding to go through three years of something they don't enjoy and ending up with a debt—or in less satisfying jobs than they could be doing otherwise. … People are being forced to do things in order to meet government targets rather than because it's likely to do them or society any good at all, and that's a mistake.　　　　(Edward, 20, 2002)

The detrimental effect of fees was certainly apparent for the working class young people who were attempting to pursue further and higher education. Maisie, who grew up on the disadvantaged northern estate, identifies the gap between government rhetoric and the actualities of struggling to get a university degree with little or no support. She explains that it is a 'struggle', 'really hard' adding 'I don't think normal people are supposed to go to university, the way they work it out'. (Maisie, 20, 2003)

Although narratives of social mobility and improvement have been accepted tropes of educational discourse, little attention has been paid to the emotional labour and loss of belonging demanded by such policy imperatives. As fees rise (in England) and the burden of educational inclusion is shifted to students, the costs of participation are increasingly evident. In the following section, we explore the stories of two academically able working class young women from our most disadvantaged site in order to illustrate the emotional landscape of educational policy. The young women, Lauren and Maureen were friends when we first met them—yet over the years their paths diverged as they responded differently to the pull of community and the push of self improvement in changing economic times.

Two trajectories into further and higher education

Lauren and Maureen both grew up in a large physically isolated and economically disadvantaged housing estate on the outskirts of a Northern city. An area with a reputation for violence and gangs, it has many of the characteristics of social exclusion and a history of policy responses to that situation. Levels of unemployment and crime are high; health is poor. Much of the employment in the area is relatively low paid and unskilled. In the research period, the young people's school was declared a 'failing school', despite the obvious commitment of teaching staff.

When first met in 1999, unlike the rest in this site, two young women expressed a desire for social mobility demonstrated by professional ambitions. Each saw education as a route out of the estate. Over the course of our interviews, they engaged in contrasting strategies to pursue these ambitions, and faced different obstacles. Both stories present a situated balance between individual and wider resources, and access to support and social capital (Thomson et al., 2003). They demonstrate that for young people from economically deprived backgrounds, individual resources of ability and ambition do not necessarily translate into educational and occupational success (Brown and Lauder, 2009). Community-oriented values and investments can militate against social and geographical mobility. Social mobility has exacting emotional costs (Walkerdine et al., 2001) as we illustrate through Maureen's acceptance and Lauren's rejection of the imperative that you need to get out of a disadvantaged community in order to get on.

Lauren

Lauren was seen as bright and academically able in her school. Her highest professional ambition, at sixteen, was to be a psychologist, and she saw education including university as the pathway to this ambition. Lauren was also strongly attached to her family and community, giving her considerable support. Like all the young people on this site, and most in the study, Lauren worked throughout her education. Her father provided his 'princess' with material support and contacts for work. Her mother gave emotional and practical support, intervening at key moments to alter Lauren's trajectory. A critical moment occurred before Lauren's first interview in 1998 (aged fourteen), when her beloved grandmother died. Illness, accidents and bereavement played a part in her story, quite typical for young people in this site. Her grandmother had provided a strong value base for Lauren, and was part of a rich vein of adult female culture on which she drew to construct her own identity. Just prior to an interview in 1999 Lauren went through 'a bad patch'. She had been in a relationship with a 'bad boy' who had been committed to prison, and had been drawn into the criminal and drug culture of the estate. She came close to the dominant form of femininity in the locality (involving early pregnancy), and was slipping back in her schoolwork. Her mother intervened and helped her get back on track. For Lauren her mother was her 'saviour' who 'sat me down and had a chat about it all, she put me right really.' Lauren reasserted herself as a good pupil, did very well in her final examinations and went on to college to do four Advanced level courses (required qualifications for university entry).

But after a few months at college Lauren lost confidence and became very stressed. Her mother intervened once more, suggesting that perhaps she was not a 'paperwork' but a more practical person and should give up college, steering her towards training and work in hair and beauty. Lauren was interviewed for the study mere days after the decision to drop out had been made (in 2001), and was clearly in a state of great uncertainty. Her interviewer commented that 'A sense of instability and chaos, linked to rapidity of change underpinned all Lauren's interviews'. Lauren had considerable personal resources to draw on, being able with a strong work ethic and a desire to succeed through her own efforts. Despite having a different boyfriend at each interview and being linked into the community through this, she was determinedly avoiding the more usual female route through early pregnancy, and planned to have children 'in ten years time'. She had considerable resources to draw on in her family and community, but these bonds pulled her back to more limited horizons. At this point it was looking increasingly less likely that Lauren would realise her academic potential and pursue the university route.

Between 2001 and 2004 there was considerable contact with Lauren, although an interview in 2002 was called off through illness. At an interview in 2004 when she was nineteen, things had changed again; Lauren had reinvested in education and was in the second year of a Nursing Diploma at university.

Lauren: Yeah well I'm at uni now.
Int: You're at uni?

Lauren: Even though I didn't finish me A Levels, but training to be a nurse instead. So I've always wanted to do it really deep down I think.

Lauren related this choice to caring for her grandmother. But cliffhangers persisted in this new educational route and she was awaiting exam results, which would dictate her future:

So um if we fail it this time, we get a re-sit, if we fail the re-sit you're off the course. … So I don't know what's gonna happen. (Lauren, 19, 2004)

Although not interviewed since 2004, her researcher still maintained contact with Lauren. We have learned that she took a break in her course to have a baby girl in 2006. She broke up with her boyfriend when the baby was just a few days old. Her parents also split up during her nursing course, but she reports that her mother remains a key source of support. Despite setbacks including medical problems and postnatal depression, Lauren returned to her course and qualified as a nurse in 2007. She currently has a job in a private hospital, and lives in her own house with her child, no longer allowing any partners to live with her. She describes herself as taking responsibility for herself and her daughter.

As with many young people from her background, Lauren struggled to get onto, and maintain an educational route. Her passage demonstrates the interplay of personal resourcefulness and a range of material and less tangible resources that are at play in individual biographies. Lauren's account is historically located, contingent on the provision of new routes into nursing, itself transformed into a degree subject. The fact that two of her friends also pursued training for nursing suggests the extent to which Lauren's strategy exists within the confines of the possible in her locality.

Maureen

Although close friends, Maureen's attitude towards the local community was very different from Lauren's, communicating the view that she had to get out in order to get on. Maureen's parents had separated when she was six, and she regarded her two-homes style of living, in which she had a bedroom and family life with both her mother and partner, and her father and partner, as a positive resource. The homes were in less disadvantaged areas on the estate, and the physical separation helped Maureen to maintain her emotional separation from the community. Although both mother and father had grown up locally, they were socially mobile within that locality. Her mother has been a consistent support for Maureen, and both father and mother motivated her to want to leave the estate and pursue education. Her strategy was to sever connections with the community, including a break up with Lauren engineered by her mother when both were sixteen. Lauren and Maureen each pursued their different routes, one drawn back into the community, the other totally rejecting all ties, and coincidentally arrived at the same (nearby) university.

The researcher reflected that Maureen's 'take on the future has not changed throughout the study: she has always seen education as her key route to an adult life beyond her local world with university always part of it. She has never been clear on the detail of her career, but a profession has always been assumed'. Maureen's determination and self-confidence increased over time with increasing evidence of her academic ability. One strategy was to defer the physicality and pleasures associated with the teenage life to achieve her educational and occupational ends. Her mother intervened to ensure that Maureen did not get involved in dangerous local leisure worlds, in order that she should avoid risks of low aspirations, sex, crime and related pitfalls. At sixteen (2001), Maureen talked about 'having to wait to do anything with me life beyond education' and of having little space for fun, boys, pubs and clubs, whilst these were things that she would have liked to pursue. One of the costs was the need to defer active heterosexuality and womanhood until they held less of a threat to her desired future.

We missed an interview with Maureen in 2002 but caught up in 2004 when she was in the second year of a law degree. At this point she was uncertain what she would do with her degree, but getting away from the estate was still a prime motivator. Since the previous interview in 2001 she had fallen out with her mother and left home with her sister. Although her mother retracted the next day, the young women had gone to stay with their father and stepmother until the university term began. Maureen experienced growing feelings of independence whilst at university, the first year in halls, the second in a shared flat with girlfriends, including her sister. The interviewer commented 'She is now a confident young woman ensconced in her student lifestyle' and evidently enjoying some of the pleasures she had eschewed earlier in her education. She has broken bonds with her mother, but her father provides financial support, although she is one of the few on her course who have worked throughout.'She seem to be making her own way now, supported by the "friends for life" that she has made at university' (Researcher, 2004). The only information available to us about Maureen subsequently was that in 2008 she was living with her boyfriend's parents in an affluent suburb of the city.

Both Lauren and Maureen are caught up in the expansion of higher education that was taking place during the study, and their stories illustrate how social mobility can be lived and resisted, with the ties of belonging to family and community existing in tension with the kinds of bridging social capital that facilitate more mobile subjects willing and able to negotiate access to new resources and modes of interdependency. Both of the young women had ability and considerable support from their families, and yet still their route could be fraught. Lauren seemed to have worked out a way of balancing the pull of community, with a less high achieving path through education, ultimately gaining a qualification and her desired profession alongside a version of independent working motherhood echoed in the matrifocal patterns of local gender relations (Thomson, 2000). Maureen's journey of social mobility may have been serendipitously enabled by the existence of two parental homes, necessitating more ambivalent identifications and loyalties. The forging of strong peer relations with other students through shared housing as well the existence of a travelling companion in the form of her sister provide a scaffold of support and opportunity that Maureen is able and willing to realise. These case studies help us see beyond broad classifications of social class in order to discern more subtle and contingent forces which position young people in relation to a range of less tangible emotional and strategic resources—expressed and experienced through modalities of belonging, disappointment and desire.

Conclusion

During the course of our research, we were able to trace simultaneous processes through which higher education was democratised, while at the same time recalibrating so that new forms of distinction and privilege could be created within an expanded field of participation. The expansion of higher education has mainly benefited the middle class (which has also expanded) but the working class young people in our group who have made it into HE are mainly young women. Although many have resources of material, social and cultural capital, particularly in the middle class, others have fought against the odds in their attempts to follow an educational route. Successive governments have had contradictory goals with respect to dealing with the gap in educational attainment between different social class groups, and stalling social mobility in the UK. On the one hand, they pursue policies designed to increase access to university for those previously excluded, and on the other, place often insurmountable obstacles in their way, for example, by increasing the cost of accessing higher education. On the one hand, they argue for social capital as a glue to bind communities together, or seek a 'big society' where voluntarism will help alleviate the problems of disadvantage, and on the other, decry the loss of or advocate social mobility on a very individualistic basis, which as we have seen, can require abandoning community and often family ties. But for the young people in our study, family can be the major resource to enable them to find a way through the complexities of inventing adulthood. As Nam observed at the beginning of this chapter, the costs of improving oneself can be high and the rewards uncertain.

References

BIS (Department for Business Innovation and Skills) (2011) *Participation rates in higher education: Academic years 2006/2007-2009/2010*. http://stats.bis.gov.uk/he/ Participation_Rates_in_HE_2009-10.pdf [Accessed 10 May 2012].

Broecke, S. and Hamed, J., (2008) *Gender gaps in higher education participation: An analysis of the relationship between prior attainment and young participation by gender, socio-economic class and ethnicity*, DIUS Research Report 08 14. http://www. bis.gov.uk/assets/biscore/corporate/migratedd/publications/d/dius_rr_08_14.pdf [Accessed 10 May 2012].

Brown, C., and Lauder, H., (2009) *Social class and education: changes and challenges*, Education Department, University of Bath.

Callender, C., and Jackson, J., (2008) Does fear of debt constrain choice of university and subject of study?, *Studies in Higher Education*, 33(4): 405-429.

Callender, C., and Wilkinson, D., (2003) *Student income and expenditure survey*, Research Report 487, DfES, Nottingham.

Chitty, C., (2009) *Education policy in Britain*, Houndsmill: Palgrave Macmillan.

Du Bois-Reymond, M., and Lopez Blasco, A., (2003) Yo-yo transitions and misleading trajectories: towards integrated transition policies for young adults in Europe', in Lopez Blasco, A., McNeish W., and Walther. A., (eds.) *Young people and contradictions of inclusion: Towards integrated transition policies in Europe*, Bristol: The Policy Press.

Egerton, M., and Halsey, A.H., (1993) *Trends in social class and gender in access to higher education in Britain*, Oxford Review of Education, 19: 183-196.

Metcalf, H., (1997) *Class and higher education: the participation of young people from lower social classes*, London: CIHE in conjunction with PSI.

Machin, S., (2003) Unto them that hath, *CentrePiece*, 8(1): 5-9.

Machin, S. and Blanden, J., (2004) Educational inequality and the expansion of UK higher education, *Scottish Journal of Political Economy*, 51: 230-249.

Mizen, P., (2004) *The changing state of youth*, Houndmills: Palgrave.

Perry, E. and Francis, B., (2010) *The social class gap for educational achievement: A review of the literature*, http://www.thersa.org/__data/assets/pdf_file/0019/367003/RSA-Social-Justice-paper.pdf [Accessed 10 May 2012].

Putnam, R. D., (2000) *Bowling alone: The collapse and revival of American community*, New York: Simon and Schuster.

Reynolds, T., (2007) Friendship networks, social capital and ethnic identity: Researching the perspectives of Caribbean young people in Britain, *Journal of Youth Studies*, 10(4): 383-398.

Thomson, R., (2000) Dream on: The logic of sexual practice, *Journal of Youth Studies*, 4(4): 407-427.

Thomson, R., Henderson, S. Holland, J., (2003) Making the most of what you've got? Resources, values and inequalities in young people's transitions to adulthood, *Educational Review*, 55(1): 33-46.

Thomson, R. and Holland, J., (2005) 'Thanks for the memory': Memory books as a methodological resource in biographical research, *Qualitative Research*, 5(2): 201-219.

Tolley, J. and Rundle, J., (2006) *A review of Black and minority ethnic participation in HE*. Prepared for The National BME Education strategy Group. http://www.aimhigher.ac.uk/sites/practitioner/resources/Conf%20Summary%20report%20final%20(2).pdf [Accessed 10 May 2012].

Walkerdine, V., Lucey, H., and Melody, J., (2001) *Growing up girl: Psychosocial explorations of gender and class*, Basingstoke: Palgrave.

Chapter 8

Fast-track youth and education—exploring meanings of adulthood and gender

Sinikka Aapola-Kari

In today's late modern societies the phase of youth is multidimensional, and transitions towards adulthood are partial and gradual. Definitions of age vary in different life spheres (see Aapola, 2002; Westerberg, 2005). Here, the focus is on young people who have gained 'adult' social statuses in at least one life-sphere—education, the family, sports or work-life—at an early age. They include young mothers, young people who have lived alone since teenage or who finished their education faster than usual, and successful young athletes and artists. They have been on a kind of 'fast-track' to adulthood, but whether they have actually intended to 'grow up early' will be explored. They can be defined as 'transgressors of cultural age orders'; they have departed from the standard models of the life-course (see Aapola, 2002; Du Bois-Reymond, 1998). The focus here is on their educational paths and their views on adulthood.

The main theoretical starting-points in this study[19] are recent debates of age and life-course (e.g. Rantamaa, 2003), youth studies and feminist educational research, inspired by Tuula Gordon and Elina Lahelma's research on young people's lives (e.g. Gordon et al., 2005; Gordon and Lahelma, 2002, 2004; Lahelma and Gordon, 2008).

A high average level of education and a generally positive attitude towards a prolonged education characterises the Finnish society; the society also supports young people's education strongly by offering free schooling even at the university level. There are also subsidies for young people living alone; however, parents' income is taken into account when these subsidies are calculated for those below the age of eighteen. In Finland young people, particularly young women, tend to move out of the parental home earlier than in most other European countries (Salonen, 2005).

---

19 My research project *Young People Transgressing Cultural Age Orders* was part of a larger research programme *Many Routes to Adulthood—Changing Cultural Age Orders in Finland* that I directed. It was funded by the University of Helsinki research foundations in 2005-07. (See Aapola, 2005; Aapola-Kari, 2006; 2007.)

Data and analysis

The study is based on a small, theoretical sample, selected for its assumed relevance. The data consists of biographical interviews with three young men and seven women, between twenty-one to twenty-nine years old. They lived in the bigger cities of southern Finland. Some of them worked, others studied, and some were just entering military service. Most lived alone, but some still lived with their parents, while others were cohabiting or dating. They were mainly heterosexual, but some were bi- or homosexual. All were white ethnic Finns.

The interviewees were 'hand-picked' through personal networks. Some interviewees suggested a friend to be interviewed. Many of these young people were quite visible in their social environments, as they had, for example, won medals in international championships. One of them had finished his doctorate unusually early. In order to secure their anonymity, minor details in the quotes have been altered. The interview themes varied, but we always discussed their life narratives, education, work, family, romantic relationships and meanings of adulthood.

The analysis was inspired by a critical discourse analytical framework (see Fairclough, 1992; Aapola, 1999), where interviews are seen as sites where general cultural discourses and evaluations are displayed.

Most of the young people came from middle-class families, with relatively highly educated parents. Some of their parents had divorced, and one parent had died when the interviewee was little. Most had received much familial support, but some had had considerable difficulties with their parents. The role of the family is central in young people's educational processes. (See also Lahelma and Gordon, 2008; Thomson et al., 2003; Walkerdine et al., 2001)

Growing up in today's society

Today's Western societies are characterised by the prolongation of youth. Young people are expected to spend a lengthy period studying, switching between temporary jobs and romantic liaisons. However, recent Finnish governments have encouraged more speedy transitions for youth through education into work in the name of global competition. Still, growing numbers of young people have dropped out of education and employment. (See Aapola et al., 2004; Järvinen, 2003.)

Adulthood has become more obscure (see Hoikkala, 1993; Wyn and White, 1997). It is difficult for young people to reach signposts traditionally linked with adulthood, such as permanent jobs and sufficient income. Educational paths have lengthened, the labour market has become unstable, and young people postpone having children. There are fewer taken-for-granted landmarks in the life-course (Aapola and Ketokivi, 2005). 'Fast-track' youth represent the individualisation of the life-course. Their relationship to education is central in their progress towards adulthood.

Two educational routes

The interviewees with experiences of early adulthood had diverse experiences, but their educational routes can be divided in two: either they had chosen an 'academic' prolonged educational route via general upper secondary education to higher education, or the practical, vocational route with an early labour-market entry, either directly from comprehensive school or via a short vocational training. This model is often used to divide educational choices in Finland (see Brunila et al., 2011). These two routes are not mutually exclusive; some of the interviewees continued their studies later, although they had dropped out of school as teenagers. This division is used to clarify factors effecting young people's educational choices: their own gendered ambitions, the available study choices, and the family's significance. (See also Lahelma and Gordon, 2008; Tolonen, this book.) The academic route is described first, then the vocational path.

The academic route

About half of the interviewees were university students. For them, continuing to upper secondary school and thereon to university was self-evident, as their professional interests required an academic education. Their parents were usually also highly educated and encouraged their children's studies. By coincidence, all of them had attended a specialised school, with an emphasis in performing arts, sports or natural science, or alternatively they had attended upper secondary school by taking evening classes. About ten per cent of all upper secondary schools in Finland have a specialisation (Järvinen, 2003). Their over-representation in the data reflects the fact that young people with special talents are more likely to enter these schools.

The 'academic' interviewees described their studies very positively. School offered a rewarding social community, a possibility to concentrate on one's special interests and to regulate one's study pace. For some, special school was their 'salvation' from a socially difficult situation, after feeling out of place in comprehensive school. The special school meant a 'new start' for them, both academically and socially.

Young man, early twenties, recently graduated from a school specialising in performing arts:

> I am very happy that I went to this special upper secondary school, because the friendship circle there was extremely close, really close. It was like a family ... we would always listen to each other. So we were like more than friends to each other.[20]

The specialised schools give entry points for the students' activities in their specialty, offering an opportunity even for students whose overall grades would be too low for other schools. Some of the interviewees had clear ambitions and wanted to develop their talent. The specialised schools appear as sites where students can concentrate on their special interests in a safe study environment with rewarding social ties. Some of the interviewees had moved away from their hometown to enter the desired specialised school. Some lived in boarding schools or stayed with relatives; some lived alone.

Young man, early twenties, who specialised in natural sciences:

> it [the school] was directed to this group of people which I felt I wanted to belong to. ... And so I thought well only the best of all the students who are interested in this subject are going to be there [at the school].

The specialised schools also provided a kind of social 'buoyancy' for their students; they entered a small elite group, which developed a positive group identity easily. By contrast, the evening classes attended by some interviewees only meant increased individualisation in organising their studies, and loose relationships with other students.

The interviewees on the academic route had 'special talents'; they were either academically or artistically gifted, and their family and school had nurtured their talent from an early age. Having talent can be a big bonus in school: it brings positive attention from teachers and can sometimes mean participation in special educational programs. Not surprisingly, most of these interviewees described their educational route as unproblematic and linear. They had used

---

20 Original interviews were in Finnish. The translations into English were made by the author.

the schooling system to their advantage. For them, education meant support and encouragement, positive challenges and rewards. Many excelled in school in general, not only in their special field.

Often they had developed an early sense of their particular talent and had clear vocational goals, which enabled them to make strategic educational choices: they had 'aligned ambitions' (see Schneider and Stevenson, 1999). The schools and families played a major role in the formation of the students' ambitions. (See also Tolonen, 2008a/b.)

Young woman, early twenties, university student, writer:

> A: Well, I have written half-seriously since I was about thirteen. At that time I thought for the first time that this would be a really good thing. … I attended a writing school for children and youth from thirteen to sixteen years of age. We used to write stuff, do all sorts of practices, get feedback, do projects. That was actually when I first started to get training in writing.
>
> Q: How did you know to go there?
>
> A: Actually it was my Finnish teacher who suggested that me and my friend go there. She had read our essays and she thought that we might be interested. And then I continued on to an upper secondary school specialising in performing arts, and they also had courses in writing, and I took them all.
>
> Q: At what age did you think that you would become a writer?
>
> A: Well yeah! I think I was about nine years old when I first thought that I would become a writer. And probably at around fourteen to fifteen years I started to really think that it could hopefully be true one day.

These interviewees felt they had their 'foot in the door' in their professional career, with one exception: a young woman who had international sports success had attended a school specialised in sports. However, her vocational aspirations lay elsewhere. For her sports was only a hobby—albeit a serious one—and a source of self-confidence.

The type of positive support that is directed to students with special talents is not available to other students. However, a special talent is not always only a blessing. It can actually lead to social problems and frustration at school. In one case the interviewee had been bullied severely in comprehensive school, and he had to change schools. Some of the students had psychological problems.

However, even these young people gradually got into higher education, encouraged by a teacher or their parents. They believed university would be different, the right place for them. They sped up their studies in order to get to university as quickly as possible.

Young woman, mid-twenties, university student:

> When I entered upper secondary school, it was pretty clear what I would like to do, and I was in a terrible hurry to get out of school. After I had been (at school) for a few weeks, I decided to change from day school to evening-school, because you could read through stuff more independently there. ... And then I did it [the whole exam] in, perhaps one and a half years or two years. (In average, it takes three years—SA-K)—It was really fast, because I desperately wanted to get to university. ... But perhaps it was not a good solution emotionally, going through school so quickly. And going to the evening school was not so good either, because ... all my buddies were in day school, and my daily rhythm was totally different. And it meant also ... being alone a lot, and somehow narrowing my life. And perhaps being a bit isolated too.

Evening classes enabled this young woman to study fast, but as a result her social life suffered. Later, she entered university, and her social world improved. She continued to keep up a fast study pace even then, but gradually realised that she actually wanted to prolong her studies as she enjoyed them.

'School of life'

Half of the interviewees did not want to prolong their studies. They attended a short vocational training, started working straight after school or stayed at home with a child. I call this route 'the school of life', because the most important learning environments were outside of the formal school system. Many of these interviewees had lived independently from a young age, and most had experienced considerable difficulties in their personal lives. They had a controversial relationship with formal school, and their academic success was modest.

Surprisingly, all my cases in vocational education were young women, although more young men in Finland choose vocational education. These young women had moved from their childhood homes at fifteen to sixteen years of age and had not returned. They had relatively middle-class backgrounds, but some had serious problems at home, resulting from a parent's death or illness, alcohol abuse, divorce and/or conflicts with (step-)parents. This affected their education negatively. Some had experienced psychological problems, but at the time of the interview, these had been overcome. Some had established a stable life with a steady job, their own apartment, sometimes also a family. Some were less established in their lives, and even considered moving abroad.

This group emphasised their practical abilities. They wanted to prove how skilful and responsible they had been in their jobs and other tasks. They did not really value vocational training, it was just a necessary gateway to the labour-market. One of them had actually finished the upper secondary school with a specialisation in home economics, and had enjoyed its practicality. However, after that she had not attended education, and her jobs were not related to her specialisation. The interviewees spoke enthusiastically about their experiences at work, and positioned themselves as equal to more experienced adults.

Young woman, early twenties, working in services:

> In a way I have never wanted to study, I have always been like a handy– a handyman.

Young woman, early twenties, working in sales:

> I, like, I am more like a practical person, I do things. When I was (studying) ... I had an internship at an old people's ward, and it was so lovely, it was absolutely wonderful, I just enjoyed myself there so much. I could do things, but in the ... school ... I was really good at practical things, in practical subjects, and the only thing that bugged me was anatomy. ... I took the anatomy course three times and never passed it. But the practical things there were just lovely, and ... in the hospital, it was so great to work there. In principle, if I (could choose) something, ... I would go to the old people's ward. ... I am not at all a reading person, or like an exam-, grinder.

This interviewee had a frustrating experience with vocational training: her failure in an exam closed her route to a caring vocation, although she thought she would have been good at it. The interviewees talked enthusiastically about their positive experiences of taking care of practical matters and their dislike of theoretical studies. Practical internships gave them positive experiences not available at school. (See Schneider and Stevenson, 1999.)

The risk of unemployment and social marginalisation is high for a young person without an upper secondary level education (see Komonen, 2001), which was the situation for some of the interviewees. It is not surprising, therefore, that even interviewees with a vocational diploma and a secure job, talked about returning to school later. Life-long schooling is an obligation more than a choice in today's society, and young people are strongly encouraged into upper secondary education in Finland. (Brunila et al., 2011; Komonen, 2001.)

Educational routes and growing up

The meanings of adulthood in relation to different educational backgrounds have not been thoroughly explored in earlier research. Here, some tentative differences can be discerned. The interviewees defined adulthood generally through two kinds of criteria, 'external' and 'internal'. The external criteria were institutional or material landmarks, such as finishing education, getting a job and living alone. The 'internal' criteria consisted of psychological steps: becoming responsible for one's own life, taking care of a child, and becoming emotionally independent from parents. The general criteria for adulthood did not differ between the two educational groups. However, their views concerning their own relation to adulthood differed depending on the kind of signposts they had reached (Westerberg, 2004).

A young man, early twenties, entering military service:

Q: Do you consider yourself an adult?
A: I don't see myself as an adult at all yet. ... probably, an adult means that you have sort of life-experience, and an ability to take responsibility for things. And maturity, to a degree.
Q: Don't you think you have any of these qualities?
A: Well they're not, I don't think these are the sort of things that you either have or you haven't got, but rather like. I would not say that I have quite reached that stage yet, even if it sounds like scientology [laughs]. ... Well. I don't think of myself as such a responsible person yet, that I could for example start a family and take responsibility for kids. No way!

Living alone was important: those still living with their parents did not consider themselves adults, while those living independently were likely to do so. Additionally, those who were close to finishing their studies were more likely to consider themselves adults than those who had just started their studies. Growing up was identified as being a gradual, individual process. Autonomy was a central criterion for adulthood, and it was associated with both emotional and financial independence.

Young woman, mid-twenties, university student:

> A: I do think of myself as an adult. I don't quite know when that happened but. Yes, I do see myself as an adult.
> Q: Can you mention any ... criteria that you associate with adulthood?
> A: I think taking care of one's own things, taking care of one's own life, independence that you can in a way at least in principle take care of all your own stuff alone. To make your own decisions.
> Q: Can you say since what age you have ... taken responsibility for your own matters?
> A: Well probably from when I moved away from home, when I was nineteen years old. But I have to say that it has been like that for the past couple of years, really last year. The first year was a little bit like practicing. Whenever there was a problem I called home for advice; how should I do this, I cannot do this!

Adulthood raised uncertainties, and the interviewees set high demands on maturity (see Lahelma and Gordon, 2008; Thomson et al., 2003). For them, reaching a signpost linked to adulthood in one field of life was not proof of adult status in general. For example, finishing a degree early was not sufficient to qualify as an adult.

Young woman, early twenties, university student:

> Q: What do you think of yourself at the moment, do you think you are an adult?
> A: I think that in relation to some issues I am an adult, but in relation to others I am not. I feel that in, like, intellectual matters I am really an adult and ... my peer group are other adults with whom I can talk about these matters ... But in emotional matters, I feel I am not so very adult. Sometimes I feel I have a child's emotional life.
> Q: What would it be then, feeling like an adult?

A: I think that adulthood would perhaps be about standing on your own two feet, emotionally speaking. … Many of my young friends think that financial independence is such a huge thing, that they want to, like, prove their own adulthood to themselves by not asking their parents for money even if they don't have any money. But I have never felt that such matters question my adulthood at all. But instead this standing on your own feet emotionally is more important.

Those who lived alone at an early age associated adulthood with independence. Some had to take financial responsibility for themselves, even if their parents had given them some money. This had sometimes led to serious difficulties. Usually they had been in paid work from an early age. Almost all of them defined themselves adults, and thought they were more mature than other young people, because they had coped with difficult situations. It had been a question of honor for them to make ends meet; they did not want to ask for money from their parents. A child's financial independence is culturally valued and encouraged in Finland (see Hoikkala, 1993).

The interviewees defined adulthood positively, but for some it carried negative connotations. They felt they had been forced to grow up, and had not received enough parental care.

Young woman, early twenties, working in sales:

Q: Well then, would you say that at the moment you are an adult?
A: Well, yes, at least in some matters. … In money matters I am an adult. And in relation to work I am an adult. Emotionally I am not even close … I feel that I have been pushed into the world of adults at such a young age, as a child really. And I can say that in principle, I turned into an adult overnight, when I moved into that apartment alone, nobody took care of me in principle; I became an adult at that stage. And then for a while I used to play at being a child when I went home, I was like a child there, a daddy's girl. I cannot explain it, but now I feel I am at the right age for the moment. But when I was fifteen, I had to be older than I actually was, I had to be an adult, but now I can be young. … I would like to go back, and stay that way for a little while, before people expect me to become an adult according to the standard, because … I skipped so much in between.

This interviewee refers to the idea of a normal biography (see Hoikkala, 1993), which takes its course from childhood to adulthood gradually. Her own life has deviated from this model, as she lived alone at an early age. She thought she had not experienced an important life stage, youth. Her independence had been forced on her too early.

The link between education and growing up is not linear. Academic success and a vocational route can both sustain a young person's early sense of adulthood. The schooling system supports and encourages young people with academic or artistic talent (see Järvinen, 2003). Their ways of growing up, through education, are easily accepted. By contrast, young people with a more practical orientation often have to look for rewarding learning environments and agentic positions elsewhere.

Gendered processes of growing up

Gender definitions are linked to processes of growing up. Girls are often expected to mature earlier than boys (see Aapola, 1999). Representations of adult womanhood emphasise subdued and controlled conduct, postponement of one's own needs and taking care of others. It is no wonder that in Tuula Gordon and Elina Lahelma's study (2004), eighteen-year old girls hesitated to define themselves as adults. In my study, even a mother of several children in her late twenties was surprisingly reluctant to embrace the adult status:

Young woman, late twenties, university student:

A: Well, I don't feel exactly like a middle-aged person either. Perhaps I could define myself a young adult. … Perhaps it is associated with that I haven't finished my studies yet, this line of study I am doing now. So I am a student. And I feel that somehow … I don't like … I don't feel young, but I don't experience myself as a real adult either. Perhaps I am like … Well, I don't really think about myself on the basis of age.

She suggests there are different levels in adulthood, and only the highest stage is associated with 'real adulthood'. Her current student status undermines her adulthood even though she could easily claim it as a mother.

The interviewees did not see gender differences in connection to young people's processes of growing up, although we discussed this topic. However, their own experiences seem to suggest otherwise, although generalisations cannot be drawn. The young women who had moved early away from their childhood homes were expected to take care of themselves: they had to prepare their own meals and manage their budgets. One of them had been very short of money during her first year of living alone, after receiving large telephone bills, and her father refused to give her more. She even went hungry for days. Later she saw this as a valuable lesson. (Cf. Tolonen 2005.)

The young women expressed a strong desire to cope alone, even if it was difficult. Only one of them moved back to her childhood home for a short time. They embraced the idea of independent adulthood. Still, growing up had not been easy, and meanings of adulthood were ambiguous for them. (See also Gordon and Lahelma, 2002, 2004; Gordon et al., 2005.) They expressed a strong sense of individual achievement, perhaps in opposition to traditional gender expectations according to which a woman's individuality is always questionable.

By contrast, the young men who studied in other towns stayed either in boarding schools or with relatives. They did not mention financial problems or heavy responsibilities, just having felt lonely sometimes. Their parents expected them to move back home when they finished school, and they complied. One could conclude that (young) male individuality is not so easily threatened by someone else taking care of them.

Discussion

We started with a question whether young people's early achievements transport them to early adulthood. The answer is not simple. Their routes to adulthood seemed gradual and uncertain. Few embraced the adult status, despite their achievements. In today's society, adulthood is linked with many institutional and personal conditions. Success in one sphere of life is not sufficient for achieving general adult status.

The interviewees claimed they had not deliberately wanted to be adults early, although their life-course could easily be interpreted otherwise. After all, they had made important decisions about their vocational futures, started families, or sped up their studies. For them, these decisions had other meanings, such as escaping dismal family conditions, wanting to develop their talent further or acquiring new social contacts. Their criteria for adulthood were numerous: finishing their studies, getting a permanent job, starting a family and emotional independence. In today's society, however, a degree does not guarantee a permanent job, families may break down, and one's social position may be redefined any time. This was very clear to the interviewees. (See Wyn and White, 1997).

The two educational routes—academic and 'school of life'—were connected to slightly different definitions of adulthood. A prolonged youth linked with lengthy studies has become normative for Western middle-class young people. They often get both financial and mental support from their families (see Merenluoto, 2005; Walkerdine et al., 2001). The student's status does not coincide with the adult status, but the students in my study were not very concerned about it; they enjoyed their studies both socially and intellectually. Growing up was linked to a valued educational process. They thought they would become adults after graduation or when they found employment. In general, they were content in the socially valued student role.

The 'school-of-life' young people emphasised their practical skills and autonomy. For them, growing up was related to living alone, being financially independent and responsible for themselves. Adulthood was achieved through surviving difficulties, often at a considerable cost. They were more willing to consider themselves adults than their academic peers. For them, adulthood was associated more with external criteria, leading an independent life, than with emotional criteria (see Westerberg, 2004). They emphasised their agency and responsibility at work, and considered themselves more mature and grown-up than their peers.

Adulthood gains different meanings depending on the young person's life situation, and it is measured by both material and psychological criteria. Adulthood seems like a continuum, along which a young person can progress towards 'real adulthood'. Even then, adult status can be threatened: parenthood, educational success or independent residence is not sufficient to secure it. Adulthood is for many young people like a mirage: it seems to escape no matter how far they advance.

References

Aapola, S., (1999) *Murrosikä ja sukupuoli. Julkiset ja yksityiset ikämäärittelyt. [Adolescence and gender. Public and private formulations of age.]*, Finnish Literature Society 763, Youth Research Society/Youth Research Network, Publication 9. Helsinki: Finnish Literature Society.]

Aapola, S., (2002) Exploring dimensions of age in young people's lives. A discourse analytical approach, *Time and Society*, 11(2/3): 295-314.

Aapola, S., Gonick, M. and Harris, A., (2004) *Young femininity. Girlhood, power and social change*, Houndmills: Palgrave.

Aapola, S. and Ketokivi, K., (2005) Aikuistumisen ehdot 2000-luvun yhteiskunnassa [Terms of adulthood in the twenty-first century society], in Aapola, S. and Ketokivi, K., (eds.) *Polkuja ja poikkeamia—Aikuisuutta etsimässä. [Paths and diversions—Looking for Adulthood]*, Publication 56. Helsinki: Youth Research Society/Youth Research Network.

Aapola-Kari, S., (2007) Celebrated but amusing? An intersectional analysis of children's and young people's media portraits, in Fornäs, J., and Fredriksson, M., (eds.) *Inter: A European cultural studies: Proceedings* from the Conference *in Sweden 11–13 June 2007.* http://www.ep.liu.se/ecp/025/ [Accessed 12 November 2010].

Brunila, K., Kurki, T., Lahelma, E., Lehtonen, J., Mietola, R. and Palmu, T., (2011) Multiple transitions: Educational policies and young people's post-compulsory choices, *Scandinavian Journal of Educational Research*, 55(3): 307-324.

Du Bois-Reymond, M., (1998) 'I don't want to commit myself yet': Young people's life concepts, *Journal of Youth Studies*, 1(1): 63-79.

Fairclough, N., (1992) *Discourse and social change*, Cambridge: Polity Press.

Gordon, T., Holland, J., Lahelma, E. and Thomson, R., (2005) Imagining gendered adulthood: Anxiety, ambivalence, avoidance and anticipation, *European Journal of Womens' Studies*, 12(1): 83-103.

Gordon, T., and Lahelma, E., (2004) Who wants to be a woman? Young women's reflections on transitions to adulthood, *Feminist review*, 78(1): 80-98.

Gordon, T., and Lahelma, E. (2002) Becoming an adult: Possibilities and limitations—dreams and fears, *Young*, 10(2): 2-18.

Hoikkala, T., (1993) *Kataoako kasvatus, himmeneekö aikuisuus? Aikuistumisen puhe ja kulttuurimallit. [Does upbringing disappear, does adulthood dim? Discourses of growing up]*, Helsinki: Gaudeamus.

Järvinen, T., (2003) *Urheilijoita, taiteilijoita ja IB-nuoria. Lukioiden erikoistuminen ja koulukasvatuksen murros. [Athletes, artists and IB-youth. The specialization of gymnasiums and the breach of school education.]*, Publication 37. Helsinki: Youth Research Society/Youth Research Network].

Komonen, K., (2001) *Koulutusyhteiskunnan marginaalissa? Ammatillisen koulutuksen keskeyttäneiden nuorten yhteiskunnallinen osallisuus. [In the margins of education society? Social participation of young drop-outs from vocational schooling]*, Joensuun yliopiston yhteiskuntatieteellisiä julkaisuja nro 47, Joensuu: Joensuun yliopisto.

Lahelma, E. and Gordon, T., (2008) Resources and (in(ter))dependence: Young people' reflections on parents, *Young*, 16(2): 209-226.

Merenluoto, S., (2005) *Nopeasti maisteriksi.—Tutkimus nopeasta valmistumisesta ja valmistujasta. [Quickly to a Master's degree—A study about speedy graduation]*, Turun yliopiston kasvatustieteiden tiedekunnan julkaisuja A:204, Turku: Turun yliopisto.

Rantamaa, P., (2001) Ikä ja sen merkitykset. [Age and its meanings], in Sankari, A. and Jyrkämä, J., (eds.) *Lapsuudesta vanhuuteen.* [From childhood to old age], Tampere: Vastapaino.

Salonen, R., (2005) Milloin omaan kotiin? Aikuistumisen vastuu Suomessa ja Espanjassa- [When to move to one's own home? The responsibility of growing up in Finland and in Spain], in Aapola, S. and Ketokivi, K. (eds.) (see above.)

Schneider, B. and Stevenson, D., (1999) *The ambitious generation. America's teenagers, motivated but directionless*, New York: Yale University Press.

Thomson, R., Hendersson, S., and Holland, J., (2003) Making the most of what you've got: Resources, values and inequalities in young people's transitions to adulthood, *Educational Review*, 55(1): 33-46.

Tolonen, T., (2005) Sosiaalinen tausta, paikallisuus ja sukupuoli nuorten koulutussiirtymissä. [Social background, locality and gender in youth educational transitions], in Aapola, S. and Ketokivi. K. (see above), 33-65.

Tolonen, T., (2008a) Success, coping and social exclusion in transitions of young Finns, *Journal of Youth Studies*, 11(2), 233-249.

Tolonen, T., (2008b) Menestys, pärjääminen ja syrjäytyminen—Nuorten elämäntyylit ja luokkaerot. [Success, coping and marginalization—Young people's life-styles and class-differences], in Tolonen, T., (ed) *Yhteiskuntaluokka ja sukupuoli*. [Social class and gender], Tampere: Vastapaino, Helsinki: Youth Research Society/Youth Research Network, 226-254.

Walkerdine V., Lucey H., and Melody J., (2001) *Growing up girl: Psychosocial explorations of gender and class*, New York: New York University Press.

Westerberg, A., (2004) Forever young? Young people's conceptions of adulthood—the Swedish case, *Journal of Youth Studies*, 7(1), 35-53.

Wyn, J., and White, R., (1997) *Rethinking youth*, London: Sage.

Chapter 9

Classed and gendered meanings of marginalisation in young people's transitions

Tarja Tolonen

This chapter examines young people's different ways of dealing with the risk of marginalisation. The text is based on interviews of young people conducted in different locations in Finland. I will present four selective cases of young people, who claim to be in a situation of marginalisation, and reflect their various ways of understanding marginalisation. I also analyse the different forms of capital related to these situations. In so doing, my intention is to link the young peoples' stories of transition to new theories of social class, in which gender can also be connected to. Young people from various social backgrounds were found in the situation of marginality. The study took place in different locations in Finland. It was conducted in the context of transition studies; transitions are broadly understood to refer to education, adulthood, locality, family and leisure (see Gordon, 2006; Gordon and Lahelma, 2002, 2003a/b; Lahelma and Gordon, 2008; Gordon et al., 2005, 2008).

Here I claim that young people in the study had unequal resources and various ways of coping with marginality depending on their family background.

Social class as reflexive play

From early 1990s, the analysis of social class has been more or less left aside, while new paradigms, such as late modernism, have significantly influenced social science as well as youth studies. In British as well as Finnish sociology, the silence about 'the old dinosaur', social class, almost lasted to the new millennium (see Skeggs, 1997, 2004; Tolonen, 2008c). In the sociology of youth, this meant that individuality was highlighted and social and cultural interpretations of youth cultural matters were criticised (cf. Muggleton, 2005).

This study is conducted in the light of new theories of social class to highlight the importance of studying young people's resources and resourcefullness.

In this chapter, I use social class and gender as tools of analysis, referring to new studies of social class, which rely on Pierre Bourdieu's analysis. Class is not understood as a stable position in the labour market or education, but rather as 'a reflexive play' through which people acquire capital, build up identifications and value for themselves (see Devine and Savage, 2005; MacDonald and Shirldrick, 2007; Skeggs, 1997, 2004).

In this text, young people are described as being 'working-class' or 'middle-class'. They are described as belonging to one of the two classes on the basis of their parents' occupations (mentioned in the interviews), and education and social, cultural and material resources they have,but in addition young people's reflections towards education, work and leisure[21] are highlighted. One's class position is changing and ambivalent, and also the labour market is changing (see also Nayak, 2006; Savage et al., 2001). Thus class in not understood as a stable and unchanged structure.

Identifications are seen to develop not through consciousness, but through cultural distinctions (see Devine and Savage, 2005, p. 14). The social, cultural and economic resources/capital of different individuals may vary, and relates to their families and social and cultural locations and fields as well as to other differences such as gender and ethnicity (Bourdieu, 1997, pp. 47-54; Skeggs, 1997, p. 8, 2004). In this research, class is seen as intertwining with gender and ethnicity. According to Anthias, different intersecting categories and differences (economic, ethnic or gender) may reinforce each other to strengthen hierarchies in societies, but she claims that these categories can also be contradictory; subjects can be positioned differentially within these divisions. (Anthias, 2005, pp. 31-32, 36-37.)

In the next section, I concentrate on positions and lifestyles of marginalisation. This lifestyle is distinquished out of several lifestyles found in the research (see later). By *lifestyle* I refer to being in the *habit of doing* something (see Bourdieu, 1990 on *habitus*; Jokinen, 2004).

I present four selective cases of young people (out of seven who claim to be in a situation of marginalisation), and reflect their various ways of understanding marginalisation. I also analyse the different forms of capital (see Bourdieu, 1977)[22] related to these situations. In so doing, my intention is to link the

---

21 Many studies show that in Finland about half of the people consider themselves as middle-class or lower middle-class, and about twenty per cent as working class. Usually these differences are seen to be economical, educational and more rarely, political (Erola, 2010; Kahma, 2010).

22 When referring to young people's different resources, I pursue Bourdieu's notions of capital (1997). Bourdieu distinguishes four forms of capital: social, cultural, economic and symbolic (Bourdieu, 1997, pp. 47-51). I use the notion of capital in particular way in the context of youth studies (see critique of the term capital in Skeggs, 2004;

cont. over

stories of young people to new theories of social class, in which gender can be connected to.

Marginalisation, coping and success as a method

The data used here is based on several projects,[23] involving cooperation with Docent Tuula Gordon. It consists of interviews with sixty-one young people from different parts of Finland—twenty-nine girls and thirty-two boys between seventeen and twenty-three years of age—and explores their social and spatial transitions. The young people were mainly from a middle class or working class background (according to the information they provided in the interviews).

The interviews were life-historical (Gordon and Lahelma, 2003a) in the sense that they followed the interviewees' life experiences. The interviews took place in quiet rooms in schools, in cafeterias, libraries or youth houses. All interviews in both studies were voluntary, and followed principles of research ethics, requesting research permissions of institutions and young people.

The themes of the interviews concentrated on transitions of various kinds: for example education and work, moving away from home, transitions in social life (see Gordon and Lahelma, 2003a/b). In addition, the interviewees were asked to describe their notions of, and tell stories of success, coping and social exclusion, and to indicate if and how the terms might refer to their or other people's life situations (see MacDonald et al., 2005; Savage et al., 2001). I used the terms success, coping and marginalisation as *tools for reflecting* their life situation and way of determining *value of work and education.* Young people told stories (for example of success or marginalisation) and attached values to themselves and others included in their stories.

The analysis of the research themes was made by reading though the data (interviews and field notes) and making mark of the research themes. A summary was made of each interview, and included information on the research themes and current life situations of the respondents. I organised information on the

22 cont/
   Tolonen, 2007, 2008a). In this analysis, I use *cultural capital* in the meaning of acquiring educational (institutional form of) capital, and in acquiring *symbolic capital* (the 'right kind of lifestyle', morals and taste valued in society). *Social capital* is understood as the networks and social relations one has and can rely on. *Economic capital* refers to attaining economic assets and to parents' assets, as mentioned by the young people in the interviews.

23 The research projects: *Social and Spatial Transitions in Young People's Life Course* (2001-2003) (Academy of Finland); *Agency and Power in Young People's Lives: Boundaries and Limitations* (2002-2006) (led by Tuula Gordon, University of Helsinki).

interviewees and research themes into a matrix; such as information on family relations, education and future plans, moving or staying, friends and networks, and their leisure practices.

From sixty-one interviewees,[24] seven young people described themselves as being socially excluded in multiple ways at the time of their interview (family, education, illness, money). Young people thought someone was in the margin if s/he did not have friends or money, if they abused substances, or if they stayed in a place that offered no employment. Through a method of discussions on the subjects of marginalisation, coping and success in the interviews, I found several lifestyles based on the valuation of *education and work*. I have named them: 1) a lifestyle with the risk of marginalisation; 2) a working-class lifestyle stressing coping in life and finding a steady job in which education was valued as mean to get a better job; 3) a distinctive working-class lifestyle valuing ambition in work; 4) a middle-class lifestyle emphasising cultural capital, ambition and fulfilling work. (See Tolonen, 2008a/b). In this chapter, I concentrate on *lifestyle with the risk of marginalisation*, in which young people had a special relationship to *education and work*; these were seen through the lense of positions one hoped to gain. All seven interviewees were out of school and work at the time of the interview. All young people in this position saw themselves as heading towards an 'ordinary life', that is to have a job, to finish their secondary school diploma, and possibly to have a home and a family of their own. In the next section, I will argue through four cases that there were various classed and gendered ways of dealing with the lifestyle of marginalisation.

Lifestyle with the risk of marginalisation

Almost in all sixty one interviews young people 'knew' what it meant to be marginalised: primarily this was taken to mean that someone was socially marginalised, that is, without friends. Some also referred to other forms of marginalisation, such as being poor, drinking too much or being ill. Seven of the sixty-one young people described themselves as being marginalised at the time of the interviews, and an additional few described themselves as recovering from such a situation. For the seven young people who called themselves marginalised,

24 Over a third of the sixty-one young people, twenty-four out of sixty-one, described themselves as coping. They lived in various life situations: some were students while others were recovering from family crises. Seventeen young people described themselves as being successful at the moment. This category included most of the university students and some college students. Eight young people either refused to describe themselves through the terms success, coping or marginalisation, or gave an answer that was not clear enough to be coded.

this meant quite different things: for example, economic dependency on others, social exclusion from others, or a previous or present addiction to drugs or alcohol. Some interpreted this as meaning the difficult life situation (such as unemployment or illness) of their family instead of themselves. So the life situations or life styles as well as the reasons and ways of describing oneself as being marginalised varied a great deal among the interviewees. It was clear that the meanings of being ordinary, successful or marginalised varied and depended on who was speaking, and that positions of 'me' and 'them' were different. Here is one example of how one young woman described success as being distant to her life.

> *Tarja*: What do you think, what kind of people are successful ones ... ?
> *Kirsi*[25]: I guess those big persons in leading positions (at work).
> *Tarja*: What kind, women or men?
> *Kirsi*: Men and women, who walk there with the fur coats...

Kirsi, came from a working-class family, and her parents were divorced and lived far from each other and from her. Her parents had had lots of social problems, and she had not met them for a while. She was seventeen years old, and had dropped out of education. At the time of the interview, she was looking for a job, but this was quite difficult to find since she was expecting to give birth quite soon. Kirsi received social security benefits and did not have much money to spend. She was low on economic capital (no fur coats) as well as cultural capital—meaning education here (no leading position at work). From the point of her lifestyle, with little money (and economic capital), it is very telling that she saw 'success' as being distant to herself. Success was somewhere 'out there' where some other people used clothes too expensive for her taste.

Kirsi was pregnant and had no relatives to turn to. She was not a single mother, but felt alone since her boyfriend worked in another town because work was difficult to find in her hometown. On the other hand, she did not long for money but for social support. She valued social capital, that is, close relationships with her relatives, more than economic capital, as has been mentioned by other young women from a working-class background (see Kelhä, 2009; Walkerdine et al., 2001). Becoming a mother was the most important theme in her interview, and seeking closer contact with her distant mother and father was at the top of her

25 All the names presented here are pseudonyms to protect the identity of the interviewee.

agenda at the time of the interview. She seemed to think one way of out of her difficult situation of low social support was to develop a closer relationship to her parents again.

Another young woman, *Riitta*, was a twenty-one–year-old from 'ordinary working-class family', as she said. At the time of the interview, she was unemployed and pregnant: she was to become a single mother soon. She positioned herself as 'used to be marginalised', and she described her current situation being better than it used to be; earlier she had used substances too much and had not finished her education. She also saw her life as moving toward a better situation because she had left the drug abusing father of the child she was expecting. Her parents were there to support her.

Riitta: I want to have this baby, and after that want to finish my compulsory education. And if I have the energy, I want to be a vet.
Tarja: Now you have your baby on your mind, what do you think, how will it affect your life situation in the future?
Riitta: Oh, it has changed everything completely. I had big problems in my life. Everything has changed now.
Tarja: How was it before then, do you want to tell anything from your past?
Riitta: Well it was then, I had this period of drugs … Since last autumn, I have been off the drugs. I was just about to go to rehab, and then I realised I was pregnant. Now I go to this clinic … I have even stopped smoking cigarettes.

At the moment, Riitta was primarily thinking about the coming baby. In addition, she wanted to finish her education in future. She knew she wanted to have a better future, but had slightly ambivalent feelings if she should move or not out of her hometown with a high youth unemployment rate. On one hand, she wanted to move from her hometown to receive education (and gain cultural capital), but on the other hand, she wanted to stay close to her parents so that they could help her to raise her child and she would have social support (social capital) (see Skeggs, 1997; Walkerdine et al., 2001). In Riitta's mind the baby would ensure her life staying on the right track (see also Kelhä, 2009).

Mikko, a seventee-year-old young man, saw himself at risk of marginalisation because he was dependent on social security. He was from a middle-class family. According to Mikko, his parents had an academic education and careers and his family was a rather wealthy one. Mikko had moved away from home due to conflicts with his father about his choice of education, and at the time of the interview he lived alone.

> *Tarja*: What does marginalisation mean?
> *Mikko*: It means, I mean, I myself live on social benefits. I know the meaning of money. I also know how easy it is to get marginalised. I know many young people like that.
> *Tarja*: How would you describe, how are they marginalised?
> *Mikko*: They have just dropped out of their tracks. They didn't manage to continue their education any more. That is simply the way it started. Their parents have kicked their ass because [they] did not want to look; there are those even in this [name] prosperous little town. The parents kicked them out because they didn't want to see this lazy young person in their house anymore. Then they moved into a cheap rental apartment, and the days go by being lazy and sleeping and enjoying money from the social system.

Mikko's middle-class position was ambivalent. He was low on economic capital but was on his way to accumulating cultural capital in a field chosen by him. Mikko saw his situation as one of living on the dole, but viewed this as temporary. In his mind he was in a marginalised position but this was not a life style for him. He wanted to move on with his life. With his determination to pursue his desired educational path, I assume he approached his life as a *middle-class* project or project of one's own life—he knew what he wanted and how to gain it—through specific education (see Tolonen, 2008b).

Mikko's *valuation of himself* (see Skeggs, 2004) as someone who wanted to succeed in life was evident also in his valuation of others—he assumed moral distance to other young people enjoying social benefits:

> *Tarja*: What do think of that (i.e. to be dependent on social security)?
> *Mikko*: Well that kind of life cannot be absolutely unacceptable. I only accept my social benefits because I study. I could not live with it otherwise, because of my moral codes. I couldn't live in this society without working. … Being successful means that you are able to have a career; the money comes with it. That is the fact in this society. One can't overrule that.

I see Mikko as a middle-class young man whose moral codes oblige him to continue his life and do not allow him to stay, not even economically, in a marginal position. His reflections on his present situation and his future plans clearly reflected middle-class values of his parents, who also had academic careers (see more Tolonen 2008b).

Jukka, a twenty-two year old working-class man, described coming from a hard-working family and he claimed he carried these values with him, even if it did not show in his current actions. According to Jukka's interview his both parents were working and they had some vocational education. I have interviewed Jukka twice—first time in 1995, in the context of an ethnographic research at school (Tolonen, 2001). In the first interview he claimed that he had had a happy childhood, and that he had succeeded well in school. Everything started gradually changing when he was about twelve years and his parents divorced.

> *Jukka*: ... I have always been good at drawing. I had a nine [ten is the best mark] in arts ... and also in maths. ... Now it is about five. ... Then my parents divorced; I suppose that has had quite an effect on me. ... When my dad is not at home, no-one can tell me off how to live my life. My mom is like, she takes care of us, but there is no discipline; she can't tell us how things should be done.

During his school time, his cultural capital remained the same while the social capital and emotional balance of the family, support and discipline seemed to have been changed (cf. Coleman, 1988). He seemed to blame his parents and was not willing to take responsibility for his actions in 1995 and after. Instead, he started to create 'subcultural social capital' (Tolonen, 2008a), that is, social relations valued within youth cultures. These kinds of social relations are highly valued and useful within youth cultures in comprehensive school (cf. Bullen and Kenway, 2004). However, in the long run, this created problems for him. He left school with quite poor marks. His social relations did not lead him find work—instead, they helped him to take part in illegal activities, such as using drugs, and supported him to stay unemployed.

> *Tarja*: We met last time (1995) when you were in secondary school. How is your life now (in 2002)?
> *Jukka*: Well, there won't be enough tape if I tell you everything.

Tarja: I've got another one there ... (laughs)

Jukka: I don't know. After the secondary school, my life went in quite a bad way, until that finished when I had trouble with the law and I had to do community service (instead of going to juvenile detention—TT) for forty hours. On the last day of 1998, that was finished. In 1999, I went into the army and completed my training as a medical servant there. Since then, I have tried to find a job. This year I was in my second job, but only for two days because I didn't like it there.

When I met with Jukka, he was on medication to reduce his drug use; his father supported him with this goal. He was also striving to find a job, 'a real working-class job' involving manual work; however, he doubted that he would able to maintain a job, due to his weak physical condition. He dreamt of ordinary family life and thought he would be quite a responsible father, if he ever had children. At this point, Jukka's life existed in the margins of working life and he was low on the economic and cultural capital demanded in the labour market. He had friends and his father supporting him, and with this social capital he wished 'to make it back to normal life someday' (cf. MacDonald et al., 2005; Strandell et al., 2002).

To compare the strategies of the young people one can say they were gendered and classed: the young working-class women, Kirsi and Riitta, saw motherhood and some kind of future education as their way out of marginalised positions. Jukka, a working-class boy, struggled with his substance use, while dreaming of ordinary work of any kind. He also dreamt of a becoming a parent like Kirsi and Riitta, but for him this position was not available at the moment.

Mikko's way out of his current position was clearly a middle-class one. He had made a clear choice about his educational route—even at the cost of disagreeing with his father about his education (see Paju, 2011), this leading him to live alone with currently low economic capital.

Social class and gender as a means to understand and act

Above, I have analysed four out of seven cases of young people who described themselves as being in marginalised positions at the time of the interview (some other cases are analysed elsewhere, see Tolonen 2005a/b, 2007, 2008a/b). I have shown the importance of class and gender for them. I do not expect that their life situations, lifestyles and class positions will stay unchanged (Tolonen, 2008a; see also Gordon and Lahelma, 2002, 2003b; Skeggs, 2004).

The future will show what kinds of educational and family life routes are possible for Kirsi, Riitta, Mikko and Jukka. Their ways of making educational choices, valuing themselves and different forms of capital were connected to social class and gender. The working-class young men and women seemed to want security and steady jobs in their life; also early parenthood was a useful strategy to achieve this. For girls, early parenthood was accepted and normal, and they were offered support (social capital) provided by several generations of women. (See Kelhä, 2009; Skeggs, 1997; Walkerdine et al., 2001). Rather than valuing primarily economic and cultural capital, working-class young people pursued social capital as an important solution and resource in their lives.

For more middle-class youth, the choice of not just any route, but a specific educational route, was their primary ambition (see Paju, 2011; Tolonen, 2008b; Walkerdine et al., 2001). This was also taking place when they occupied marginalised position like Mikko in this chapter. Possible economic success followed from making the right choices in education.

The purpose of this chapter was to show the importance of class in contemporary Finnish society and to document the ways class provides a framework for understanding one's life situation, as well as one's relationship to education and work. I have teased out classed and gendered meanings of education and work by talking about success, coping and marginality with the young people in interviews. My purpose has not been to classify the young people as successful, coping or marginalised. On the contrary, I have tried to show how the meanings of these terms are relative, that is, they depend on who is talking and from what position. Secondly, my purpose has been to demonstrate that the cultural, social and economic resources different individuals have, **provide meaning to** the terms above, and help young people to deal with practical matters related to their current life situation. My aim has been reflect on the stories of young people through new theories of social class and their interconnections with analyses of gender.

Individuals have the power to change the course of their life, but some things in life are also repeated in habitual (as well as gendered) ways (see Bourdieu, 1997; Skeggs, 1997). Young people act as individuals, but as stated above, they are able to 'read' local structures, cultures and different life chances and local unemployment situations, and form 'realistic' expectations of their chances in the labour market (see Clarke et al., 1986/1976, p. 49) as well as their expected self-value in it in the frame of social class and gender (see also Skeggs, 2004).

References

Anthias, F., (2005) Social stratification and social inequality: Models of intersectionality and identity, in Devine, F., Savage, M., Scott, J., and Crompton, R., (eds.) *Rethinking class, cultures, identities and lifestyles*, London: Palgrave MacMillan.

Bourdieu, P., (1990) *The logic of practice*, Stanford, CA: Stanford University Press.

Bourdieu, P., (1997) The forms of capital, in Halsey, A. H., Lauder, H., Brown, P., and Stuart Wells, A., (eds.) *Education, culture, economy, society,* Oxford: Oxford University Press.

Bourdieu, P., (1998) *Distinction. The social critique of the judgement of taste,* London: Routledge.

Bullen, E., and Kenway, J., (2004) Subcultural capital and female 'underclass'? A feminist response to underclass discourse, *Journal of Youth Studies*, 7(2): 141-153.

Clarke, J., Hall, S., Jefferson, T., and Roberts, B., (1986, first printed 1976) Subcultures, cultures and class. A theoretical overview, in Hall, S., and Jefferson, T., (eds) *Resistance through rituals. Youth subcultures in post-war Britain*, London: Hutchinson.

Coleman, J. S., (1988) Social capital in the creation of human capital, *American Journal of Sociology*, 94: S95-S120.

Devine, F., and Savage, M., (2005) The cultural turn, sociology and class analysis, in Devine, F., Savage, M., Scott, J., and Crompton, R., (eds) *Rethinking class, cultures, identities and lifestyles*, London: Palgrave MacMillan, 1-23.

Erola, J., (2010) Luokkarakenne ja luokkiin samastuminen Suomessa. [Of class identifications in Finland], in Erola, J., (ed) *Luokaton Suomi? Yhteiskuntaluokat 2000-luvun Suomessa. [Classless Finland? Social Classes in Finland in the 2000s]*, Helsinki: Gaudemus.

Gordon, T., (2006) Girls in education: Citizenship, agency and emotions, *Gender and Education*, 18(1): 1-15.

Gordon, T., and Lahelma, E., (2002) Becoming an adult: Possibilities and limitations, dreams and fears, *Young,* 10(2): 2-18.

Gordon, T., and Lahelma, E., (2003a) From ethnography to lifehistory, *International Journal of Social Research Methodology*, 6(3): 245-254.

Gordon, T., and Lahelma, E., (2003b) Home as a physical, social and mental space: Young people's reflections on leaving home, *Journal of Youth Studies*, 6(4): 377-390.

Gordon, T., Holland, J., Lahelma, E., and Tolonen, T., (2005) Gazing with intent: Ethnographic practice in classrooms, *Qualitative Research*, 2005 5(1):113-131.

Gordon, T., Holland, J., Lahelma, E., and Thomson, R., (2008) Young female citizens in education: emotions, resources and agency, *Pedagogy, Culture and Society,* 16(2): 177-191.

Jokinen, E., (2004) Kodin työt, tavat, tasa-arvo ja rento refleksiivisyys, in Jokinen, E., Kaskisaari, M., and Husso, M., (eds.) *Ruumis töihin! Käsite ja käytäntö*. [Body, concepts and practises], Tampere: Vastapaino.

Kelhä, M., (2009) *Vääränikäisiä äitejä? Ikä ja äitiyden yhteiskunnalliset ehdot. [Wrong-aged mothers? Age and social conditions of motherhood]*, Research Reports 223/2009. Department of Education. Helsinki: University Press.

Lahelma, E., and Gordon, T., (2008) Resources and (in(ter))dependence: Young people's reflections on parents, *Young,* 16(2): 209-226.

MacDonald, R., Shildrick, T., Webster, C., and Simpson, D., (2005) Growing up in poor neighbourhoods: The significance of class and place in the extended transition of 'socially excluded' young adults, *Sociology*, 39(5): 873-891.

MacDonald, R., and Shildrick, T., (2007) Street corner society: Leisure careers, youth (sub)culture and social exclusion, *Leisure Studies*, 29(3): 339-355.

Muggleton, D., (2005) From classnessness to clubculture. A genealogy of post-war British youth cultural analysis, *Young*, 13(2): 205-219.

Nayak, A., (2006) Displaced masculinities: Chavs, youth and class in the post-industrial city, *Sociology*, 40(5): 813-831.

Paju, P. (2011) *Koulua on käytävä. Etnografinen tutkimus koululuokasta sosiaalisena tilana. [An ethnographic study of a school class as social space]*, Publication no 115, Helsinki: Youth Research Society/Youth Research Network.

Savage, M., Bagnall, G., and Longhurst, B., (2001) Ordinary, ambivalent and defensive: Class identities in the Northwest of England, *Sociology*, 35(4): 875-892.

Skeggs, B., (1997) *Formations of class and gender. Becoming respectable*, London: Sage.

Skeggs, B., (2004) *Class, self, culture*, London and New York: Routledge.

Strandell, H., Julkunen, I., and Lamminen, K., (2002): "Ku ois vaan sellane normaali elämä!" elämänkulku marginaalista katsoen. [I wish I had a normal life! Lifecourse looking from marginal position], in Juhila, K., Forsberg, H., and Roivainen, I., (eds.) *Marginaalit ja sosiaalityö. [Marginality and social work]*, Jyväskylä: SoPhi, University of Jyväskylä.

Tolonen, T., (2001) *Nuorten kulttuurit koulussa. Ääni, tila ja sukupuolten arkiset järjestykset. [Youth cultures at school]*, Helsinki: Gaudeamus, Helsinki: Youth Research Society/ Youth Research Network.

Tolonen, T., (2005a) Locality and gendered capital of working-class youth, *Young*, 13(4): 343-361.

Tolonen, T., (2005b) Sosiaalinen tausta, paikallisuus ja sukupuoli nuorten koulutussiirtymissä. [Social class, locality and gender in youth transitions], in Aapola, S., and Ketokivi, K. (eds.) *Polkuja ja poikkeamia—aikuisuutta etsimässä. [Searching for adulthood]* Helsinki: Nuorisotutkimusverkosto, Youth Research Network.

Tolonen, T., (2007) Social and cultural capital meets youth research, in Bynner, J., and Helve, H., (eds.) *Capitals, Identities and Cultures of Young People*, Tuffnel Press, London.

Tolonen, T., (2008a) Success, coping and social exclusion in transitions of young Finns, *Journal of Youth Studies*, 11(2): 233-249.

Tolonen, T., (2008b) Menestys, pärjääminen ja syrjäytyminen—Nuorten elämäntyylit ja luokkaerot. [Youth lifestyles and class differences], in Tolonen, T., (ed.) *Yhteiskuntaluokka ja sukupuoli. [Social class and gender]*, Tampere: Vastapaino, Helsinki: Nuorisotutkimusverkosto/Youth Research Network.

Tolonen, T., (2008c) Yhteiskuntaluokka: menneisyyden dinosauruksen luiden kolinaa? [Social class as the dinosaur of the past?], in Tolonen, T., (ed.): *Yhteiskuntaluokka ja sukupuoli. [Social class and gender]*, Tampere: Vastapaino, Helsinki: Youth Research Society/Youth Research Network.

Walkerdine, V., Lucey, H. and Melody, J., (2001) *Growing up girl. Psychosocial explorations of gender and class*, Hampshire: Palgrave.

Chapter 10

Value and values: Injustice, investment, judgement and caring

Beverley Skeggs

We lost everything, families, houses, whole streets went. You have no idea and you never will. I sometimes wonder how we got through. I was sent to the countryside. I don't want to talk about it ... but then I went into the army. I was only young and we were sent to barracks in Newcastle and we starved. We had to steal food and we couldn't get warm. Then we were sent out (reference to WW2). We were in no condition to fight. Just fodder really. And we did it all for what? Look at the state of the country now. We fought to have a decent life, a decent country, decent people. Now we just have greed and everybody else sharing the spills. We're all fighting each other for the meagre crumbs left over when the fat cats have taken their chunk. It's disgusting. We nearly died to now be treated like dirt. Like we don't matter. We helped rebuild this country. Our labour, our sweat, our families and for what ... ?

(Ken, Middlesbrough, 2006)

Ken addresses matters of value through life, death, investment, national belonging, class inequalities and morality, issues that will frame this paper about how those excluded from the traditional means for economic and symbolic value accrual understand and generate their own value.

Part of the difficulty in understanding value is that it slips between understandings of value (economic, symbolic) and values (cultural, moral). This slippage has been recently intensified by nation states' attempts to produce 'subjects of value': that is the accruing, self-interested individual promoted by the World Bank and the International Monetary Fund (IMF) to ease the transition from Eastern communism to Western capitalism. Likewise the Chinese government is promoting and rewarding suzhi—the 'quality person' in order to develop a market in consumption (including education), generating an urban middle class which relies on the labour of the rural working class. Most theories of the self in the last decade have extensively documented how the Western subject must constantly accrue value to itself (beyond the economic, through cultural activities and social networks, etc.), making itself into a 'project' (Foucault, 1988) such as the 'enterprising self' (du Gay, 1986), through the 'self-work ethic' (Heelas, 2002).[26] Even an understanding of the self-produced in conditions not of its own making, such as Bourdieu's (2000) *habitus*, rely on ideas about self-interest and/or 'playing the game'. If the good and proper subject of capitalism is one that repeatedly adds value to itself, what about those who do not have access to the forms of exchange in which value accumulation is made possible? What about the working class who are excluded from the key sites for value accrual and are constantly devalued symbolically as undeserving and unworthy in government rhetoric and popular culture?

In most theories of value, the working class and working class women in particular are conceptualised as:

a. *Exploited*, in the traditional (Marxist) exchange of one's labour power in capitalist social relations in order to produce surplus value.

b. In Bourdieu's analysis as *negative capital*, as lack, deficit, a void of value (Boyne, 2002), capital that cannot be converted or legitimated. Women, in particular exist as sentimental repositories for the difficulties of necessity, often suffering (for instance, as they are represented in Weight of the World), (McRobbie, 2002), or as carriers of men's symbolic power, as bearers of taste (Lovell, 2000).

c. As the *symbolic constitutive limit* of proper personhood in the system of the legitimate dominant symbolic, coming to stand for all that is abject, figured through excess in the UK as 'chavs' (Skeggs, 2005; Tyler, 2008), or literal waste (trash in the US (Hartigan, 1997), the 'no quality' subject of China (Anagnost, 2004).

d. As *essentialised through gender*, as carriers of moral value generated through the psychological pre-disposition to care through biological reproduction (Gilligan, 1982).

Apart from the former, which is relatively straightforward, the others all present particular problems for understanding value, in b and c as always negative, and in d essentialised with no class analysis. These latter three theoretical understandings of value do not have any explanatory power for all the research

26 See Skeggs, B., (2004). Exchange value and affect: Bourdieu and the self, in *Feminism after Bourdieu*. L. Adkins and B. Skeggs. Oxford, Blackwell., for a description of how all these different selves work within a normative national frame. See Skeggs, B., (2004) *Class, Self, Culture*, for an extended critique of the idea of the self.

projects in which I've been involved where people are daily engaged in value practices that enable the symbolically devalued to live with value. In the chapter, I will draw on some of these research projects which were: a longitudinal ethnography of white working class women in the North of England during 1980- mid 1990s, published as *Formations of Class and Gender* (1997) (FCG) which showed how over eleven years how white working class women claimed and performed respectability as a defence against what they considered to be repeated devaluation. In *Class, Self, Culture* (2004) (CSC), I detail how a new subject of value is coming into effect in the West, one that has to accrue value to itself to display its legitimacy in public. This is a study of middle class formation. *Contingencies of Value: What Matters* (CoV) was a small project with ex-offenders and elderly people in London in 2006 which, in contrast to CSC, investigated how those who are outside of the traditional fields for exchange, generate value for themselves.[27] *Making Class and Self through Televised Ethical Scenarios*[28] 2005-2008 (MCS) was an empirical project on the moral economy of reality TV. It did not begin as a study of value but ended with a restatement of the workings of ideology through practices of investment and accrual.

If we take the models of value above, we can firstly apply traditional understanding of extraction of surplus value. The working class groups with whom I've worked have all been subject to exploitation in its traditional forms. In FCG, women were being trained on 'caring courses' into providing 'free' care through voluntary or family care to compensate for cuts in the welfare state. They also provided domestic labour to middle class families in order that these families could 'enterprise themselves up' into future-accruing subjects of value. The elderly women in the *Contingencies of Value* project (CoV) had worked in factories throughout their lives, and the men in this project had all experienced unemployment.

CSC demonstrated how cultural mechanisms also work as a form of exploitation, whereby culture operates as a form of property in which some people's dispositions, affects and cultural practices can be extracted from them

---

27 Published in parts as Skeggs, B., (2011) Imagining personhood differently: Person value and autonomist working class social relations, Sociological Review, 59(3): 579-594. Skeggs, B., (2012) "Struggles for value": Value practices, injustice and affect, British Journal of Sociology, forthcoming.

28 (ESRC funded) (2005-2008) with Helen Wood and Nancy Thumin. Published in parts as Skeggs, B., (2009) The moral economy of person production: The class relations of self-performance on "reality" television, Sociological Review, 57(4): 626-644, Skeggs, B., (2010) The value of relationships: Affective scenes and emotional performances, Feminist Legal Studies, 18(1): 29-51.

and turned into economic value by others (Skeggs, 2004a). For instance, the criminality of working class men is deployed as a form of glamour in fictional films, yet the men whose criminality has been appropriated are likely to end up imprisoned (what I've identified as a process of 'affect stripping'). Likewise, sexuality can be marketed in a way that detaches the pathological value associations from one group (working class women) to attach to another group where new configurations are produced by its location with other forms of cultural capital that enable its value to increase (the *Sex in the City* value relocation process). Contemporary class relations are lived through these different processes of exploitation, which work through affect, culture and morality, alongside economic exploitation.

For the purposes of this chapter, the research projects have been amalgamated to develop an overall framework. The impetus for this move was generated from recognising the regularity and repetition of themes across all the projects. Three interlocking themes emerged, all premised and generated from the material conditions lived: Firstly, values generated through an understanding of in/justice and fairness produced through knowledge of unfair inheritances, the prior investment of labour in the nation, and the precarity of economic life. These understandings led to articulated feelings of bitterness, anger and resentment but also fed into debates about the ethic of care. Secondly, opposition to greed, selfishness and instrumentalism was made known and contrasted to value practices of labour, loyalty, care, affection and attention. Thirdly, friendship, pleasure and humour were key to all research projects, revealing these practices to be survival mechanisms as well as critique of pretension.

Injustice: 'Accident of birth'

The initial injustice that all groups noticed was the 'accident of birth' which fed their sense of injustice and inequality:

I'm not ashamed of, you know what I mean? It's an incident of birth, where I'm come from or who I am is an accident of birth.
(John, CoV, 2006)

Why should then my sons, 'cause they happen to be born in... from my background ... why should they have to work three times harder than anyone else? [Inaudible 14.58] why should his opportunities be limited just by the fact of where he was born? (Jack, CoV, 2006)

They feel that the 'accident of birth' establishes very different conditions to those who do not have to worry about the same things. The elderly 'Ladies' (their term) of the CoV project emphasise the extra stress, emotional cost, effort and labour and sheer struggle that goes into generating what appear to be the same 'deeds' from this accident of birth:

> For me not having to worry about everything now is the main thing. Not going to bed and wondering how you're going to cope, not having to pretend that everything is ok when it isn't, not having to show that you're alright when you're not.   (Florrie, CoV, 2006)

Ruby from the television project (MCS) discusses why appearing on reality television is an opportunity structure:

> Before you're struggling, ducking and diving, and then you get an opportunity through Reality TV and then all of a sudden you're able to provide for yourself, provide for your family and not go to bed and ... you know what I mean ... And not wake up in the morning and think, 'Oh God, where is this going to come from, where am I going to get that from?' Reality TV does that.   (Ruby, MC, 2007)

This is a different ontology, one of insecurity, not security. The sheer precariousness of living these conditions generated from an accident of birth, is made explicit by Jack:

> In fact anyone has to feed their children, what's so working-class about that? But there is a more major concern if it's made impossible to do.
>   (Jack, CoV 2006)

Jack points to the consequences of their accident of birth: just making ends meet, facing the possibility that all be lost, to keeping a floor on their circumstances involves a great deal of time and energy. This is a very different time/space orientation to that of the middle class 'subject of value' documented in CSC that constantly propels itself into the future through accruing cultural, social, economic and symbolic value.

All of my previous research on working class lives and the research of many others in the UK such as (Charlesworth, 2000; Gillies, 2007) reveals that working-class people harbour a ubiquitous sense of injustice. Expression of this injustice can be brought to the surface through specific encounters, especially those which involve judgement, resulting in comments like Ken's:

> What gets me is the people who are sent to judge you, in some many ways, have no idea of the type of life you've had to live. And for most they wouldn't even be able to keep alive. But they are in the position to judge. They've never *struggled* for anything in their lives and yet they are given the power to tell you how you should behave. It gets to me.
>
> (Ken, CoV, 2006)

Ken brings together the accident of birth as it structures economic and cultural possibilities to the moral judgement to which he feels subject. Judgement is the value practice that hinges the economic, cultural and moral. Being born into inequality then judged for not living up to the standards of others in very different circumstances generates affects of resentment and understandings of injustice.

Steve also points to the brutal differences in the ability to provide and care for families:

> We live in a society of haves and have nots and it's brutal. We're made to think that if we want the same things for our kids—education, nice life, things—that we're wrong. We shouldn't expect them. But that's what I've learnt. I've seen another world and I want it, I want if for my kids. A world where you can take for granted that you have the things that stop life being a struggle. Yes I am envious of their lives, why shouldn't I be? They have everything.
>
> (Steve, CoV, 2006)

Comments such as Ken's and Steve's are often read as envy, chips on shoulders, a sign of lack of aspiration. Ngai (2005) points to how envy is considered to be a 'bad feeling' read as a static subjective trait, a pathology of the person speaking the 'lack', a 'deficiency' of the person who envies:

> Hence, after a person's envy enters a public domain of signification, it will always seem unjustified and critically effete—regardless of whether the relation of inequality it points to (say, unequal ownership of a means of production) has a real and objective existence. Although envy begins

with a clearly defined object—and it is the only negative emotion defined specifically by the very fact that it addresses forms of inequality—it denies the very objectivity of this object.   (Ngai, 2005, p. 21.)

Envy, Ngai notes, has become stripped of its potential critical agency—as an ability to recognise and respond to institutionalised forms of inequality. Yet the comments above recognise inequality but also reveal the sheer frustration of being unable to counter injustice. Injustice becomes even more unpalatable when one has made huge investments in justice through labour and affect.

Investment in an unfair nation: Conned, used, abandoned

For the CoV elderly 'ladies' (their term), the scale switches: they felt they were 'all in it together' against the Fascists in WW2. Their value and values were generated from their commitment to producing a fair and just nation. Sheila, Gracie and Beryl identify their own bitterness at what they feel is unfair treatment:

> *Sheila*: It's not right no ... and the thing is some people now are getting stuff who haven't worked for what they're getting, and this is the thing, you think well what's she bloody getting that for, she wasn't ... you know, why is she getting a bus pass?
> *Gracie*: This is what makes you bitter.
> *Beryl*: Yeah and that's true it's what makes us bitter.
> *Bev*: Do you think you are bitter or just like 'this is wrong'?
> *Beryl*: No, bitter and it's wrong. When you think what you went through in those, that blitz (the aerial bombing of London) was terrible, terrible and living right near the docks as we live, and the gas works at the top of the road, ... at the top of the road.
> *Beryl*: A lot of them went when the blitz started and the children were evacuated. Whole families were split up.
> *Beryl*: I think we feel as though were being left on the side, you know what I mean?
> *Sheila*: yeah ...
> *Gracie*: We're left on the side yeah ...
> *Beryl*: Let's face it, we was conned, used and abandoned.   (CoV, 2006)

These are stories of a more intense and longer-term suffering attached to national recognition and value distribution. They express a concern that not just their labour (their working in an armaments factory) but also their suffering has no value; it did not produce a return. And this is not just an economic metaphor, it is based on life and death: their lives were put at risk and they all lost close family members. The use of the term bitter points to another 'ugly feeling' (Ngai, 2005), which like envy, is an affect that structures our lives but is read as if it is a personal disposition. These ugly feelings are generated through our relationship to much larger structural objects, in this case, the nation. Their bitterness and resentments are, I'd argue, legitimate responses to value (all that labour) and values (for the nation) not recognised over time: the nation does not care, their investments are wasted. Their understanding of national investments are contrasted and developed into a political critique of greed, of those who do not make investments in others, those who do not care.

Care and greed

Greed is something that research respondents identify as an oppositional value to which they orient themselves:

> We've not got values anymore ... because we live in a society of commodity, of materials: 'we've got to get that', a greedy society, a let's have society. I don't want to know the price of everything and the value of nothing (paraphrasing Oscar Wilde), I want to know what's what. What we want as human beings, human beings have run out of humanity.
> (Gerry, CoV, 2006)

> Everyone's now pitted against everyone else. (Pat, CoV, 2006)

> They just don't care, it seems to me that nobody cares about anybody anymore. (Florrie, CoV, 2006)

> We look out for each other, we've always looked out for each other. Nobody seems to do that anymore. (Esther, CoV, 2006)

The promoted values of the proper subjects of capital: individualism, self-interest, self-accrual, instrumentalism and competitiveness are considered with suspicion, operating as the constitutive limit to what matters, what counts and what has value. The significance of care has also been well documented in studies of many varieties of working-class life (Duneier, 1992; Lamont, 2000; Mac an Ghaill, 1994; Willis, 1977). Likewise, the majority of research on working lives (such as Beynon, 1975; Cavendish, 1982; Metzgar, 2000; Pollert, 1981; Westwood, 1984) identify a distinct moral code focusing on care and personal integrity in which the quality of inter-personal relationships and a very different form of sociability is generated from working conditions. These are values generated from value extraction. To care for (labour) and about (affect) is an investment made in others, not in one's self.

Different forms of care offer a heated ground for contestations over value. In FCG, middle-class mothers are frequently accused of 'not-caring', evidenced by not spending time with their children and by sending their children to child-minders and boarding schools. The extensive research of Reay (1998), Lawler (2000), Walkerdine and Lucey (1989), Lareau (2003) and Gillies (2007) point to very different class values about care. In the television project (MCS), motherhood was revealed as the major site for intense value struggles. Likewise, Val Gillies' (2007) research demonstrates how working class mothers are appalled by the imposition of values of achievement, competition, entitlement and instrumentalism (displayed in explicit grotesqueness on www.mumsnet. com) by middle class mothers, which are read as evidence of self-centredness, conceit, pretentiousness and exploitation. Caring, as demonstrated by full-time motherhood, is a value practice by which the excluded generate value for themselves.

In the Formations research, the women learnt to support each other in the best ways they could; the giving of time, energy and attention was crucial to a supportive sociality. They learnt to 'duck and dive' (surviving on little through various means, passing on useful knowledge and things) and tried to protect each other against the financial, physical and psychic depressions that regularly threatened their already precarious lives. They 'looked out' for each other and developed localised spaces of protection but also fun. They learnt how to have a good time in bleak conditions and cramped spaces in which increased state interference and middle-class spectral judgement repeatedly threatened to intervene. They made the best of their limited circumstances in the present where the future seemed bleak and their best chance of value was moral and affective not financial—love. Love was for children (not often men) and family and friends. Theirs was a revalorisation of relationships made from local, familial sociality where other people were supportive connectivities, not sources for self-accumulation.

Friendships were not without problems, and it is impossible to do justice to an eleven year ethnography here: who they sought out friendships with was crucial to their maintenance, but they did spend time and energy very differently to the 'subject of value', the self-accruing subject of capitalism. They generated what Simmel in his 1910 essay calls sociability: 'the pure essence of association' (p. 49), that which is left when the serious interactions are removed. Simmel calls this a 'play form of association', which may be generated from necessity or locality as the research suggests. And whilst the middle class is put under pressure to make every activity a form of serious (often educational) enterprise, and every association instrumental (what will I learn, how will it help, am I wasting my time?), the working class excluded from the forms of capital (social, symbolic) exchange can remain connected to 'the pure essence of association'.

This association offers protection against precarity and judgement. It enables one to live with wasted investments. The CoV ladies now dedicate their lives to 'having the laugh', coming to the community centre to meet friends:

> Beryl: Life! It's what you make it darling ... I mean we could sit in-doors, but now we've got a, you know, ... we've got a life. We deserve it.

They now sneer about their prior investments in respectability, 'we wore ourselves out scrubbing ... pointless', and were completely invested in 'living life to the full', doing as many things as their pension could support or they could find for free. They all looked after each other, spending more time with their friends than their families who they felt had 'abandoned us now'. The desire for attaching value via respectability to themselves as defence was gone; they didn't care what judgemental middle-class others thought anymore, only their friends mattered and they were evaluated through the gift of attention over time in the form of the pure essence of association.

This was not unlike our media research project on the moral economy of reality television, 'Making Class', where our working-class participants spent most of their time with friends and family in home and local spaces, not involved in improving activities but just 'being', 'with mates', 'chit chatting', and 'hanging out'. In contrast our middle-class participants were anxious to convert all their time into events and activities to generate cultural and social capital. They considered television viewing to be a 'waste of time', suggesting that time was a premium value to be used productively to develop a future. All friendship networks were connected to future enterprise, producing a perfect empirical example of Bourdieu's bourgeois *habitus* production. Sociality was of made from a very different order of things. They also disliked working-class uneducated reality TV participants for 'getting something for nothing' and tightly hinged the right sort of education and culture to social and economic rewards.[29] Simmel's (1910) idea of 'pure play' versus Bourdieu's account of the bourgeoisies' instrumental use of time epitomise the differences in class relationships. The different orientation to fun, pleasure and friendship may point to very different forms of sociality and relationality. Likewise, the history of pleasure, can for the working class Peiss (1986) argues, be read as both a challenge to authority and a statement of different desires. Zizek (2000) maintains that through their demands for decadence, fun and pleasure, the working class produces a necessary defence against the grim conditions endured.

Conclusion

If we link these contemporary snapshots to wider historical research, we can see how the working class has developed different circuits of value to those of the dominant symbolic, existing alongside the dominant economic and symbolic but different nonetheless. Stallybrass' (1998) account of the precarious lives of working class clothing and objects demonstrates entirely different values generated through attachments to commodities and memory. Likewise, Stedman-Jones's (1971) account of the strategies of survival of the urban poor, Rose's (2002) detailed account of the history of the autodidact, Ranciere (1989) and Vincent's (1981) descriptions of the working class desire and struggle for learning, or E.P. Thompson's (1966) vivid accounts of a different history in the making in which time and space have substantially different meanings, all vividly detail very different value practices. We can build a picture of working class relationships that produce different forms of attention, different desires and very different value/s.

In all my research projects (including issues of class, gender, race and sexuality) people experience the accident of birth as injustice, an injustice which establishes very different conditions for doing and being. Yet the working class know they are blamed and judged for doing and being differently. Inhabiting social relationships over which they have no control generates ugly feelings: resentment, bitterness,

---

29 Skeggs, B. and H. Wood (2011a), Turning it on is a Class Act: Immediated Object Relations with the Television, *Media, Culture and Society* 33(6): 941-953..

envy and a repulsion to judgement by those who have no understanding and inhabit radically different conditions. Yet they produce a different form of caring and association in response. The different possibilities they inhabit, such as precocity, enable them to connect to others differently.

When understandings of inequality and injustice were connected to understandings of class, judgements that located one as the site of pathology, individual responsibility and immorality could be deflected, relocated and defended against. But when they could not be, people were left perplexed. The women of the Formations research, who were young (sixteen to seventeen years-old) when the research began, were more often than not confused, irritated and disturbed by what they considered to be repeated misrecognition—what they felt when subject to the bourgeois gaze of judgement which they felt devalued and degraded them, but were not sure why. They formed themselves against the judgements that were made of them. As they grew older, they became more aware of the restrictions upon their opportunities, which led them to understand the inequality and injustice they experienced. If they connected these perceptions to the concept of class, their experiences were re-interpreted through a political analytic lens, just like the CoV respondents. If they were not able to do this, they were able to generate an agenda around fairness and care.

Kathleen Stewart (1996) describes how a whole community forms itself through 'just-talk': talk of fairness and kindness that glues people together and is based on values of care rather than exchange. Care was seen as a personal disposition to others but also a collective value, it was to labour and to connect to others. To care was not to be greedy, to pay taxes, to always help others if they needed help, to show consideration. The distribution of care, through its various practices, was something that mattered very much and was seen to be a specific classed practice. If we focus on how attachments are made to others through the gift of attention over time, through relational extension (Latimer and Munro, 2009), we can see other ways of living, precisely how sociality is formed through different material conditions. This is not an idealised account of working class values, but an attempt to show how very different material conditions produce different orientations to self/other, future/present, work and consumption. This is about different emplacements in time and space where time is used differently and movement through space is imagined differently. Attempts to produce value in these different circumstances do not take us beyond the value form, nor reduce analysis to only exchange. Instead, we need to think how bodies are inscribed with different value potentials and how these are reworked in local spaces of sociality, beyond the dominant symbolic and beyond capital exchange. We need to include relational value in our understandings of value production; in this way 'person-value', rather than an accruing subject of value, offers us an alternative to traditional bourgeois understandings.

References

Anagnost, A., (2004) The corporeal politics of quality (suzhi), *Public Culture*, 16(2): 189-208.

Beynon, H., (1975) *Working for Ford*, London: EP Publishing.

Bourdieu, P., (2000) *Pascalian meditations*, Cambridge: Polity.

Boyne, R., (2002) Bourdieu: From class to culture, *Theory, Culture and Society*, 19(3): 117-128.

Cavendish, R., (1982) *Women on the line*, London: Routledge.

Charlesworth, S., (2000) *A phenomenology of working class experience*, Cambridge: Cambridge University Press.

du Gay, P., (1986) *Consumption and identity at work*, London: Sage.

Duneier, M., (1992) *Slim's table: Race, respectability and masculinity*, Chicago: University of Chicago Press.

Foucault, M., (1988) *The ethic of care for the self as a practice of freedom. The final Foucault*. J. Berauer and D. Rasmussen, Cambridge, MA: MIT Press.

Gillies, V., (2007) *Marginalised mothers: Exploring working-class experiences of parenting*, London: Routledge.

Gilligan, C., (1982) *In a different voice: Psychological theory and women's development*, Boston, Mass: Harvard.

Hartigan, J. J., (1997) Unpopular culture: The case of white trash, *Cultural Studies*, 11(2): 316-343.

Heelas, P., (2002) Work ethics, soft capitalism and the 'turn to life', in P. du Gay and M. Pryke (eds.) *Cultural economy*, London: Sage, 78-97.

Lamont, M., (2000) *The dignity of working men: Morality and the boundaries of gender, race and class,* Cambridge, Mass: Harvard University Press.

Lareau, A., (2003) *Unequal childhoods: Class, race and family life,* Berkeley, CA: Univerisity of California Press.

Latimer, J. and Munro, R. (2009) Keeping and dwelling: Relational extension, the idea of home and otherness, *Space and Culture*, 12(3): 317-331.

Lovell, T., (2000) Thinking feminism with and against Bourdieu, *Feminist Theory*, 1(1): 11-32.

Mac an Ghaill, M., (1994) *The making of men: Masculinities, sexualities and schooling*, Buckingham: Open University Press.

McRobbie, A., (2002) A mixed bag of misfortunes? Bourdieu's weight of the world, *Theory, Culture and Society*, 19: 129-138.

Metzgar, J., (2000) *Striking steel: Solidarity remembered*, Temple University Press.

Ngai, S., (2005) *Ugly feelings*, Cambridge, Mass.: Harvard University Press.

Preiss, K., (1986) *Cheap amusements: Working women and leisure in turn of the century*, New York, Philadelphia: Temple University Press.

Pollert, A., (1981) *Girls, wives and factory lives*, London: Macmillan.

Ranciere, J., (1989) *The nights of labour: The worker's dream in the nineteenth century France*, Philadelphia: Temple University Press.

Rose, J., (2002) *The intellectual life of the British working-classes*, New Haven: Yale University Press.

Skeggs, B., (2004a) *Class, self, culture*, London: Routledge.

Skeggs, B., (2004b) Exchange value and affect: Bourdieu and the self, in L. Adkins and B. Skeggs (eds.) *Feminism after Bourdieu*, Oxford: Blackwell.

Skeggs, B., (2005) The making of class and gender through visualising moral subject formation, *Sociology*, 39(5): 965-982.

Skeggs, B., (2009) The moral economy of person production: The class relations of self-performance on 'reality' television, *Sociological Review*, 57(4): 626-644.

Skeggs, B., (2010) The value of relationships: Affective scenes and emotional performances. *Feminist Legal Studies*, 18(1): 29-51.

Skeggs, B., (2011) Imagining personhood differently: Person value and autonomist working class social relations, *Sociological Review*.

Skeggs, B. and Wood, H., (2011) Turning it on is a class act: Immediated object relations with the television, *Media, Culture and Society*, 33(6): 941-953.

Stedman Jones, G., (1971) *Outcast London: A study in the relationship between classes in Victorian society*, Oxford: Clarendon.

Stewart, K., (1996) *A space on the side of the road: Cultural poetics in an 'other' America*, Princeton: Princeton University Press.

Thompson, E. P., (1966) *The making of the English working class*, Harmondsworth: Penguin.

Tyler, I., (2008) Chav mum chav scum: Class disgust in contemporary Britain, *Feminist Media Studies*, 8(1): 17-34.

Vincent, D., (1981) *Bread, knowledge and freedom: A study of working-class nineteenth century autobiography*, London: Europa Publications.

Westwood, S., (1984) *All day and everyday: Factory and family in the making of women's lives*, London: Pluto.

Willis, P., (1977) *Learning to labour: How working class kids get working class jobs*, Farnborough, Hanst.: Saxon House.

Zizek, S., (2000) Class struggle or postmodernism: Yes, please!, in J. Butler, E. Laclau and S. Zizek (eds.) *Contingency, hegemony, universality: Contemporary dialogues on the Left*, New York: Verso, 90-136.

Part 4: Girlhood

Chapter 11

All sexed up? Reflections on researching girls, sexuality and active girlhood

Mary Jane Kehily

Meeting Tuula, Elina and colleagues has special significance for me as a critical event in my academic biography that opened up space for new friendships and fresh dialogue with fellow travellers. As school-based ethnographers with strong interests in gender and sexuality, we had much to talk about. And it's always been such good fun. Tuula and Elina's approach to research is an infectious fusion of the personal and professional. Demonstrating their commitment to feminist modes of care and collaboration in and out of the field, we have shared our experiences at conferences, seminars, restaurants and bars all over the world. Swapping tales and exchanging papers over the years has been a rare and special gift, hugely pleasurable and deeply moving. The research teams that Tuula and Elina build around them are, for me, a model of successful group-work and feminist praxis. Our first meeting was at the British Sociological Association conference in the early 1990s. Unaware of the irony at the time, Anoop Nayak and myself were conference virgins, presenting our first paper while trying to learn the codes and address the conference theme—sexuality. We were also mistaken for a prostitute and pimp at a local boarding house, but that's another story. Tuula introduced herself at the end of our session, setting in motion long-term forms of support, dialogue and mutual affirmation. My memories, distilled through free-flowing bottles of white wine, include many end-of-night scenes of linked arm singing at night clubs and bars and, on one occasion, while crossing a bridge in York city centre. I was delighted to be treated as one of the Finnish team, holding a temporary one-night pass. Sting provided the signature tune that celebrated their dedication to the ethnographic endeavour of observation in the song *Every breath you take* with the phrase 'I'll be watching you'. The Finnish ethnographers are at their most observant when watching girls paying attention to girls' talk and action and, somewhat uniquely, noticing the silences and periods of inaction that also contribute to an analysis of gender relations in school. Reading their work over the years has been a joy and inspiration. The highlights of this impressive body of work, for me, include the creative use of metaphor in an early paper, *School is like an ant's nest* (Gordon and Lahelma 1996), the insightful descriptions of girls and boys being ordinary in the in-between spaces of the school (Gordon et al., 2000) and the later work on femininity and citizenship (Gordon et al., 2008). Their approach had an influence on my ethnographic practice, encouraging me to attend to the basics of looking, listening and feeling, inflected with an account of the researcher as an individual girl and a girl within a group. As a tribute to Tuula and Elina, this paper traces some of the ideas we have discussed and developed in the course of researching girlhood over time. It's terrain we have shared from the 1990s to the present and forms part of a wider landscape of feminist education scholarship. The following sections draw upon extracts from my work that are most inspired by Tuula and Elina, and owe a great deal to our on-going dialogue. They are selected here to provide a space for commentary and reflection on our joint interests—the practice of researching girls and the changing experience of girlhood. Taking a loosely chronological approach, the first three sections are extracted from a paper prompted by feelings generated in a research encounter, originally published in *Feminism and psychology* (Kehily, 2004). Section 4 draws upon my work and parallel studies to consider girls experience in the 'bigger picture'; the social context and local practices that shape young women's coming-of-age. The final section of the chapter draws up recent work with Anoop Nayak (Nayak and Kehily, 2008) to offer a commentary on recent feminist scholarship, pointing to the widening social division between girls in late modernity, reflected in the positioning of young women as 'ideal' neo-liberal subjects and the abiding significance of class-specific productions of femininity.

Girls on girls

One day I found myself lying on the floor pinching my fat bits. This was followed by the serious business of comparing the wad of flab squeezed between thumb and forefinger with that of other girls in the room. There were moans, waves of disgust and shrieks of laughter. Her tummy, my upper arms and, oh my god, look at that blubber around the thighs. Was this a scene recalled from adolescence or a more recent memory—a Bridget Jones moment of weakness on a girlie night in with your mates? Well, actually it happened during a research encounter not so long ago, while I was doing an ethnographic study in a primary school.[30] The girls I was working with were age ten at the time and I was, er,

30 The project, Children's Relationship Cultures in Years 5 and 6, was funded by the Economic and Social Science Research Council, award reference no. R000 23 7438.
cont. over

about forty-two and three quarters.[31] After years of involvement in feminist politics and a few more years as a feminist researcher, I thought I had acquired something of 'the knowledge'—that unique blend of theoretical insights and feminist sensibilities that equip 'us women' for social situations. But knowing what I know about body image, fat and self-regulation, why was I engaging in such an activity? What's more, this isn't the only dubious practice I can recall from my time in the field. There were many other moments during the course of fieldwork when, as a participant observer, I was all too ready to participate. In this short chapter, I want to consider some of the tensions and conflicts involved in the process of carrying out feminist research with girls. I do not intend to discuss the methodological issues *per se*, rather I aim to engage with some of the feelings invoked by this style of research and reflect upon the emotional investments involved in sustaining such a project. I draw upon my research experience in two ethnographic studies; the primary school-based project[32] on children's relationships referred to above (Kehily et al., 2002) and my doctoral study of sexuality and gender carried out in two UK secondary schools (Kehily, 2002). This part of the paper considers, firstly, the collective practices of girls as observed in group settings, and secondly, the thoughts and feelings of girls as individuals, as expressed in one-to-one interviews.

'We girls': Collectively practised cultures of femininity

After several weeks of fieldwork in a Year 5 (age nine to ten year-olds) class in the West Midlands School, I stumbled across the existence of the diary group. This group, I learned, were a self-styled network of eight girls, four core members and four less regular participants, who regarded themselves as friends and confidants. With the exception of Sarah who was white British, the group was of south Asian heritage; however, they did not regard themselves as ethnically homogenous and in the conversations with me, indicated that their different religious affiliations to Sikh, Hindi and Islamic traditions existed as points of difference and diversity within the group. The diary group met in the school playground at lunchtime and playtime to discuss issues of mutual interest,

cont./ Other members of the project team were Debbie Epstein, Mairtin Mac an Ghaill and Peter Redman. Our aim was to explore the ways in which children in the nine to eleven age group made sense of emotional, caring and family relationships.
31 The fieldwork was carried out by Mary Jane Kehily between March-October 1998.
32 Discussions of material feminisms refer to a wide range of themes of embodiment, lived experience, emotion and affects as well socio-economic issues (see e.g. Alaimo and Hekman, 2008; Delphy, 1975/2005; Gordon, 2008; Hird, 2003; Irni, 2010; McNay, 2004).

such as friends, boyfriends and puberty. Over time, they devised a format for conducting their meetings, which consisted of deciding collectively on the topic of discussion and then allowing each member in turn to ask a question which the others must answer. Evading the question is not allowed and misleading responses are also not permitted. The structure of the meetings indicates that the group operated within clearly defined parameters through which discussion and silence are constantly regulated. The structure of diary group meetings can be seen as an appropriation of 'circle time' discussions in Personal and Social and Health Education, where social learning is encouraged through themed talk and turn-taking.

The name of the group appeared enigmatic to me at first as no member of the group kept a diary, nothing was ever written down, neither did members of the group bring along pieces of personal writing. However, in other ways the name 'diary group' can be seen metaphorically as a device, which allows for the interplay of public and private. In literary terms the diary is a conceit; individuals commit to writing their innermost thoughts knowing that they will be shared by a reading public. As such, the keeping of a diary is an act of self-disclosure, a private-made-public that centres upon the speaking into being of an interior landscape. In this way, diaries and the diary group can be seen to provide a space for the production of identities, a moment of intensity, which bespeaks versions of self. In the context of the school playground, the interplay of public and private is given a further twist. The playground is of course a highly public space that is open to all children to play, talk, and move freely. In practice, the space is shaped and regulated by children themselves. The diary group huddle together in a particular corner of the playground that they regard in territorial terms as 'theirs'. Repelling all intruders, the diary group turn a public space into a private one that is highly prized and zealously guarded.

A preoccupation with erotic attachments emerged as a feature of diary group discussions. The ways in which the girls talked about and related to boys and men involved imaginative projections of desire that we placed alongside romantic fiction as an induction into the practice of heterosexual relationships (Christian-Smith, 1993; McRobbie, 1981; Tinkler, 1995). While this appeared to be in keeping with the version of normative femininity invoked in other discussions, there was a facet of this activity that we were concerned to document and understand. These seemingly 'sensible' girls, invested in being good at every turn, were all attracted to boys in their class who were 'bad boys': good looking, high profile boys who had status among their peers and treated girls badly as a matter of routine. In one discussion, the girls' desire for two such boys is expressed as a form of masochistic pleasure in the pursuit of romantic love. We argued that the diary group provided the girls with a relatively safe performative space for the enactment of versions of femininity. We proposed that in the context of the individualising culture of school and courtship, the existence of the diary group offered girls an arena for trying out forms of desire and intimacy while simultaneously drawing strength and pleasure from the collective experience of female friendship. There was a clear sense of comfort to be derived from the diary group's collectively practiced femininity. I recognised that joining in marked you out as one of the girls—part of a supportive network that echoed your thoughts and feelings; enjoyed the same things as you and wanted to be good like you. It is the experience of belonging that our earlier work focused upon; however, this contrasted sharply with experiences that we did not write up—the levels of anxiety expressed by individual members of the group in one-to-one discussions. The following section explores some of these issues to suggest ways in which tension and conflict among girls may be articulated and managed.

'I-girl': Individuality and anxiety

During the time I spent as honorary member of the diary group, my presence as a researcher and 'grown up girl' was quickly integrated into the structure and ritual of diary group meetings. I could be called upon at different moments as group member, invited audience, moral arbiter and source of knowledge about the adult world. In one-to-one discussions with diary group girls, I was invariably related to as confidant. Individual girls shared their secrets and concerns with me amid entreaties not to tell the other girls. All eight girls expressed concerns about being liked, and privately feared that their presence in the group generated feelings of animosity and aversion:

'I know we all get on but, really, I know the others don't like me'

'They talk about me behind my back'

'No-one likes me, they say they do but they're just saying that. Selina is the worst. She's always saying things to the others about me'

'I don't know what to do. I can't make them like me'

Individual interviews were characterised by the expression of fears that were unspoken in group discussions. Feelings of being disliked, the duplicity of other girls and a sense of aloneness and impending rejection became the repeated refrain of one-to-one interviews. Yet why did our earlier work focus upon the activities of the collective at the expense of the uncertainties of the individual? The answer may lie in the subjective investments that researchers and respondents make in the research process. As a researcher, I was emotionally invested in feminist research and the project of feminism as a politics and a lived practice. I wanted to believe in the power of the female friendship group to hold girls together. Girls holding each other in this context would represent a symbolic chain of connection, each link providing a touch of security and a warm embrace in the less than cosy environment of the primary school classroom. Focusing upon the collective practices of the diary group at the expense of individual fears may be, simultaneously, a way of preserving the imagined ideal of sisterhood and a defence against the anxieties involved in feminist endeavour. Following psycho-social perspectives, Hollway and Jefferson (2000) and Walkerdine et al. (2001) point out that anxiety is inherent to the human condition and that subjects routinely mobilise defences against anxieties. It would be possible to see the encounter as one in which the anxieties of the girls collided with my own anxieties about doing feminist research. It may be that I did not know how to make sense of their individually experienced fears, or maybe acknowledging them was too painful, bringing to mind my own history of being a girl and a friend in the past and the present. In retrospect I recognise that there was a sense in which I was fending off the anxiety of acknowledging that the feminist ideal of female friendship is a fiction. I could speculate further, but the outcome remains the same—the girl's fears were written out of the earlier account of the diary group. But how does this help us to understand the girls' feelings of anxiety at the level of the individual?

The diary group girls found it difficult to express tension and conflict openly within the group. To do so would have challenged their highly prized status as *good* girls who are *nice* at all times. But tensions and conflict remained within the group and were dealt with in two ways. Firstly, as the earlier paper pointed out, the diary group produced themselves as good by collectively projecting negative qualities onto others. Secondly, further points of tension and conflict emerge as personal anxieties to be internalised by individual members of the group. It was the dynamic involved in the latter that was difficult to acknowledge the first time round. Volosinov (1973) suggests that all forms of communication and experience are socially oriented and dependent upon social context and socio-ideological structure. Volosinov identifies two poles of social experience: the 'I-experience', which tends towards 'extermination' as it does not receive feedback from the social milieu, and the 'we-experience' which grows with consciousness and positive social orientation. Volosinov would interpret an individual's self confidence as an ideological form of the 'we-experience' derived from confident social relations with the outside world. The diary group draws our attention to the gendered nature of communication and experience. The 'I-experience' of individual girls cannot be articulated and does not receive social recognition in the context of the friendship group. However, rather than tending towards extermination, in Volosinov's terms, the anxieties of individual girls may be internalised and given voice in moments outside the friendship group, thus preserving the stability and coherence of the group itself. Which brings me back to the memory of lying on the floor pinching fat bits. My participation in this diary group incident is indicative of the strength of my investment in female friendship as an agentic, self-determining and self-regulating experience. Wanting to be 'one of the girls' and wanting the group to work leads me participate in such activities, despite personal reservations. Like the other girls, I did not want to challenge the will of the collective or diffuse the empathetic glow of being, albeit temporarily, a diary group girl.

The bigger picture

Moving on from early work, the Finland–UK connection remains a generous and generative sounding board for new work on girlhood. In looking at contemporary gender relations, sexual coming of age in the UK has been framed by the post war period of intense social change. The loosening up of traditional structures and the emergence of 'permissiveness' and countercultural forms in the 1960s (Green, 1999) signalled a changing sexual climate. Philip Larkin (1974) famously summed up the changes in his poem *Annus Mirabilis* declaring that 'Sexual intercourse began in 1963'. The date may be speculative, but Larkin's poem imaginatively, if a little miserably, captures the zeitgeist of the 1960s and 70s as a period of sexual liberation that changed the lives of young people forever. The period was marked by significant social and scientific advance: the advent of the pill, gay liberation, second wave feminism, abortion rights and a proliferation of ways to talk about and practice sex—in Foucaultian terms an 'incitement to discourse'. By the end of the 1980s, sexual practices were changing further in the light of HIV/AIDS.

Influential parallel studies of young people's sexual relations also highlight the asymmetrical gender relations that characterise young people's sexual cultures and early sexual experiences. The Women, Risk and Aids Project (WRAP) (Holland et al., 1990; Thomson and Scott, 1990; 1991) and the Men, Risk and AIDS project (Holland et al. 1993) interviewed a large sample of young people in London and Manchester, aged between sixteen and twenty-one. Focusing on the disjuncture between young people's heterosexual relationships and practices to safeguard sexual health, the studies provide an up-close account of the conservatism inherent in young people's practices of intimacy. Young people's sexual encounters are strongly shaped by normative gender arrangements that define young men as active and young women as passive to the point where masculine dominance exists for young women as 'The male in the head' (Holland et al., 1998). At the younger end of the age range, respondents reported same sex friends and peer groups to be significant in mediating and regulating sexual relationships. The public character of intimate encounters placed young men in the impossible position of sexual hero and conqueror, while young women remained vulnerable to male advances and a damaged reputation. Importantly for sexual health, young people's sexual practice was shaped by peer group values and normative gender relations, rather than sexual safety. Young women, for example, did not like to ask their partners to use condoms as, in keeping with local mores, this indicated that they might be sexually loose and open to the charge of 'slag'. To avert the moral pincer movement of entrapment and censorship, young women tended to characterise all sexual encounters as a pursuit for love, trust and companionship. Some young people in the study did successfully negotiate more equal relationships, usually in contexts where they could establish some privacy and develop a sense of themselves as a couple.

Following some of the themes of the WRAP project, I explored the ways in which sexuality weaves into young people's lives and considered why the sexual arena is so highly charged, contradictory and combustible (Kehily, 2002). Ethnographic observations led me to conclude that in the context of the increased regulation of school life through testing, monitoring and processes of individualisation, school-based sexual cultures become important to young people as autonomous, peer generated sites of resistance, providing 'adult-free and education-free zones in which students can collectively negotiate what is acceptable, desirable and what is 'too much" (Kehily, 2002, p. 207). Drawing strength from each other, young people can use sexuality to challenge adults, generate humour, flout middle-class norms and define their own rules (Kehily and Nayak, 1997). Creative, multiply invoked expressions of an ever-present sexuality remain a recognisable part of young people's social worlds (Nayak and Kehily, 2008).

A further portrayal of young people's sexual initiation is provided by the modern artist Tracey Emin's (2004, 2005) autobiographical account of sexual initiation in her hometown of Margate, UK. As a working class girl growing up in a down-at-heel English seaside resort in the 1970s, Emin recalls a local practice in which teenage girls were 'broken in' for sex by local boys. First sex for young women in this context could involve the less than romantic experience of penetration, and possibly coercion, in the public pleasure zone of the sea front. Emin herself was 'broken in' at the age of thirteen. Characteristically, she turns personal experience into art in the feature film *Top Spot* (2004). Emin introduces the film with an establishing narrative:

> *Top Spot* was here. Here somewhere. Giant ballroom with chandeliers and red velvet curtains. We'd snog and kiss, be fingered, titted up. It was a place to experiment. You know what top spot is don't you? Top spot is when a man has sex with a woman or a girl, when the penis hits the neck of the womb. That's when it hits top spot. I mean who would ever call a teenage disco *Top Spot*?

Top Spot creatively reveals the messiness of adolescent girls' life-worlds as they seek pleasure, encounter pain and have fun. Teenage protagonists retell Emin's story and that of her friends as they come-of-age in the faded splendour of Margate's tourist attractions. Sexual experimentation became part of the girl's repertoire in the real-life seaside postcard of snatched moments and erotic opportunity redolent with comedic potential. Controversially, the film includes Laura's experience of teenage pregnancy and her subsequent suicide. Emin's collected volume, *Strangeland* (2005), further explores the pain of teenage sexual activity in its documentation of incidents of unplanned pregnancy, sexual coercion and sexually transmitted disease. Emin's work and the WRAP research projects serve as a powerful reminder that the sexual liberation heralded by the 1960s and 1970s remains patchy, haphazard and contextually specific. Working class young women, for example, remain subject to structures of constraint. Amidst all the trauma of showing and telling, however, Emin insists that the overarching message of *Top Spot* is an empowering one:

When you're growing up things can look really desperate and really totally bleak. And I'm here to tell you it doesn't have to be like that. You can turn every thing around. You can turn your experiences into something positive and that's what I hope the film gives to people, a positive outlook in the end.   (Emin, 2004).

Post-feminism and active girlhood

How do girls feature in the changing landscape of late-modernity? How has the experience of being a girl changed since Tuula and Elina first started researching and writing? Contemporary research on girlhood points to different ways of doing girl in which femininity is no longer so rigidly defined. Terms such as 'post-feminism', 'third wave feminism' and 'new femininities' have been deployed to characterise young women's embracing of pleasure and their increased visibility in the social world. The terms themselves are open to contestation in different contexts, signalling both an anti-feminist backlash and new ways of understanding feminism in contemporary times (Hollows and Moseley, 2006).

At its most generative, the 'post' of post-feminism signifies a way of thinking and acting beyond the rubric of feminism and may imply some critique of former orthodoxies. However, as with other terms such as post-colonialism or postmodernism, the new moment grows out of the past and cannot fully escape the shadow of the earlier period. As Sonnet (1999, p. 170) suggests, 'The current post-feminist 'return' to feminine pleasures (to dress, cosmetics, visual display, to Wonderbra 'sexiness') is 'different' because, it is suggested, it takes place within a social context fundamentally altered by the achievement of feminist goals'. In this respect, gender in late-modernity is characterised by a blurring of boundaries between the feminine and feminist. Young women's presence in the nighttime economy is equally as visible as young mens', as the girls' night out, birthday celebrations and hen parties become a high profile feature of the city centre pub and club scene. The contemporary moment appears to further enhance the emergence of new femininities in its appeal to individualised subjects as agentic controllers of their own destiny (Beck, 1992; Giddens, 1991). This poses complex issues for sexual politics when girls and young women come to regard a right to pole-dance, sport playboy bunny logos or have drunken one-night stands as an expression of autonomous girlhood. Like feminist forms, 'active girlhood' places an emphasis on the rights of the individual to be an active sexual subject without recourse to moral judgement.

Active girlhood extends beyond the sphere of leisure, sex and sociability. The processes of globalisation have increasingly relied upon the flexible labour of young women. Shaped by the contours of a girls-own success story narrative in the educational sphere, young women appear as well-groomed, well-governed subjects at the heart of neo-liberal reform. The education of girls and their increased visibility in the social domain coincides with the decline of radical sexual politics in the West and particularly young women's rejection of feminism as a political project. There are of course many ways of reading these changes. A well-rehearsed view, sometimes posited by young women themselves, suggests that feminism has 'eaten itself'. Young women have new-found freedoms as the inheritors of a feminist movement that has successfully made itself redundant. While not necessarily acknowledging the impact of second wave feminism, young women report feeling estranged from publicly available versions of feminist politics; the anti-male sentiment, the language of oppression and feelings of anger, marginality and missed opportunity rarely resonate with their lives or experiences. In a critical commentary, McRobbie (2009) suggests the fashion and beauty industry regulate young women through a self-imposed drive for complete perfection. McRobbie argues that the new social contract of late-modernity offers young women political subjectivity in exchange for the evolving capacity to work, consume and be sexually independent. Simultaneously, a 'new sexual contract' is taking shape in which women conform to the regulatory powers of the fashion and beauty industry, while renouncing any critique of patriarchy.

Walkerdine et al. (2001) offer a perspective on new femininities premised upon the salience of social class. Providing a counter narrative to the self-invention of late-modernity, they argue that the remaking of girls and women as modern neo-liberal subjects needs to acknowledge the ways in which social class shapes young women's experiences of education, academic attainment and their subsequent life trajectories. Class is commonly viewed as a feature of modernity associated with fixed employment, stable regional identities and meritocratic forms of social mobility based upon educational and economic success. Walkerdine et al.'s study of young women in the UK is a salutary reminder of the centrality of class in young women's lives. Their analysis points to the ways in which the regulation of femininity is related to sexuality and crucially works differently upon the bodies of working-class and middle-class girls. For middle-class girls, the emphasis is upon educational success and a professional career in which the possibility of early pregnancy is not allowed. By contrast, academic success for working-class girls involves identity rupture, the transformation of self and a move away from family and community. Working-class girls bear the emotional cost of becoming bourgeois subjects in forms of pain, loss and fragmentation. From the perspective of working-class young women, early pregnancy may be an attempt to resolve some of the contradictions involved in the transition to adult womanhood. Becoming a mother disrupts the educational process while affording young women a particular role and status in the local community. Walkerdine et al. suggest that working-class and middle-class girls become 'each other's Other' (2001, p. 209) existing as cautionary examples of what you could become by transgressing the regulatory framework.

Aapola et al. (2005) provide a fitting summary in an account that pays further attention to intersectional perspectives. They suggest that the lives and experiences of young women can be understood in relation to two competing discourses—'girlpower' and 'girls at risk'. Girlpower—the active girlhood discussed above—suggests to young women that they can get what they want and do what they want. In this respect girlpower exists as a seemingly new version of femininity for new times that can be seen in a range of assertive and individualised expressions of power, characterised by third wave feminism. Girls at risk, on the other hand, articulate a set of moral and social concerns in relation to young women such as: teenage pregnancy and sexually transmitted disease; drug taking; involvement in crime and particularly young women's participation in gangs and violent crime. What is apparent in these representations are class-specific productions of femininity, which are each tropes of excess. Furthermore, the excesses of 'girlpower' and 'girls at risk' discourse cannot be seen as literal expressions of where girls are in relation to each other; rather, they make subject positions available to young women across a range of social sites (Gonick, 2006). Given the life experiences, trajectories and resources available to working- and middle-class girls, this is not, of course, a relationship of equivalence.

References

Aapola, S., Gonick, M. and Harris, A., (2005) *Young femininity, girlhood, power and social change*, Basingstoke: Palgrave.
Beck, U., (1992) *Risk society: Towards a new modernity*, London: Sage.
Christian-Smith, L., (1993) Sweet dreams: Gender and desire in teen romance novels, in Christian-Smith, L (ed.) *Texts of desire: Essays in fiction, femininity and schooling*, London: Falmer Press, 45-68.

Emin, T., (2004) *Top Spot* (screenplay and direction), London, BBC3.

Emin, T., (2005) *Strangeland*, London: Spectre.

Giddens, A., (1991) *Modernity and self identity, self and society in the late modern age*, Cambridge: Polity.

Gonick, M., (2006) Between 'girl power' and 'reviving Ophelia': Constituting the neo-liberal girl subject, *National Association of Women's Studies Journal*, 18(2): 1-23.

Gordon, T. and Lahelma, E., (1996) 'School is like an ant's nest': Spatiality and embodiment in schools, *Gender and Education*, 8(3): 301-310.

Gordon, T., Holland, J. and Lahelma, E., (2000) *Making spaces: Citizenship and difference in schools*, London: Macmillan.

Gordon, T. et al., (2008) Young female citizens in education: Emotions, resources and agency, *Pedagogy, Culture and Society*, 16(2): 177-191.

Green, J., (1999) *All dressed up, the sixties and the countercultural*, London: Pimlico.

Holland, J., Ramazanoglu, C., Scott, S., Sharpe, S. and Thomson, R., *"'Don't die of ignorance'—I nearly died of embarrassment": Condoms in context*, London: Tufnell Press.

Holland, J., Ramazanoglu, C., and Sharpe, S. (1993) *Wimp or gladiator: Contradictions in acquiring masculine sexuality*, London: Tufnell Press.

Holland, J., Ramazanoglu, C., Sharpe, S. and Thomson, R., (1998) *The male in the head: Young people, heterosexuality and power*, London: Tufnell Press.

Hollway, W. and Jefferson, T., (2000) *Doing qualitative research differently: Free associations, narrative and interview method*, London: Sage.

Hollows, J. and Moseley, R., (2006) Popularity contests: The meaning of popular feminism, in Hollows, J. and Moseley, R. (eds.) *Feminism in popular culture*, Oxford: Berg.

Kehily, M.J., (2002) *Sexuality, gender and schooling: Shifting agendas in social learning*, London: Routledge.

Kehily, M.J., (2004) Girls on girls: Tensions and anxieties in research with girls, *Feminism and Psychology*, 14(3): 366-370.

Kehily, M.J., Mac an Ghaill, M., Epstein, D., and Redman, P., (2002) Private girls and public worlds: Producing femininities in the primary school, *Discourse: Studies in the cultural politics of education*, 23(2): 167-177.

Kehily, M.J. and Nayak, A., (1997) Lads and laughter: Humour and the production of heterosexual hierarchies, *Gender and Education*, 9(1): 69-87.

Larkin, P., (1974) *High windows*, London: Faber.

McRobbie, A., (1981) *Just like a Jackie story*, in McRobbie, A., and McCabe, T., (eds.) *Feminism for girls: An adventure story*, London: Routledge and Kegan Paul.

McRobbie, A., (2009) *The aftermath of feminism: Gender, culture and social change*, Basingstoke: Palgrave.

Nayak, A. and Kehily, M.J., (2008) *Gender, youth and culture: Young masculinities and femininities*, Basingstoke: Palgrave.

Sonnet, E., (1999) 'Erotic fiction by women for women': The pleasures of post-feminist heterosexuality', *Sexualities*, 2(2): 167-187.

Tinkler, P., (1995) *Constructing girlhood, popular magazines for girls growing up in England, 1920-1950*, London: Taylor and Francis.

Thomson, R. and Scott, S., (1990) *Researching sexuality in the light of AIDS: Historical and methodological issues*, London: Tufnell Press.

Thomson, R. and Scott, S., (1991) *Learning about sex: Young women and the social construction of sexual identity*, London: Tufnell Press.

Volosinov, V., (1973) *Marxism and the philosophy of language*, New York: Seminar Press.

Walkerdine, V., Lucey, H. and Melody, J., (2001) *Growing up girl: Psychosocial explorations of gender and class*, Basingstoke: Palgrave.

Chapter 12

Buttons, zippers and dresses:
Constructing agency in day care

Elina Paju

This chapter explores the concept of agency with reference to day care practices. The analysis draws on my ethnographic doctoral research, which I conducted in a Finnish day care centre during the school year 2003-2004. The centre offers day (and night) care for families working in shifts. The centre is open twenty-four hours a day, seven days a week throughout the year. The children spend time in day care according to their parents' working-hours. I followed the practices of two day care groups in which the children were aged from three to five, and five to seven years respectively (Paju, forthcoming).

I analyse how the coming together of certain practices, gender and materiality evoke different positions for children as actors, and whether the actors can be seen as agents. The focus of the analysis is on situations during the day care day where the children change from one activity to another, that is, situations of transition. The focus is on action containing both verbal and embodied features. The underlying assumption is that embodied ways of being in the world count at least as much for the human experience as does verbal utterances (cf. Merleau-Ponty, 1998).

The empirical research process was influenced by both feminist ethnography and ethnography conducted by childhood researchers (James, 2001, pp. 253-54; Skeggs, 2001, p. 437). I was also inspired by school ethnographies (Gordon et al., 2000; Tolonen, 2001). School resembles day care. In addition to the care provided by day care, the other function of Finnish day care is the education of children, which is also the main objective of schools. Day care with its practices can be seen as preparation for school and future citizenship, and that is indeed the explicit function of the pre-school system in Finland, which is mainly located in day care centres (Lappalainen, 2004, p. 646).

Conceptual framework—action, agency, materiality and gender

This chapter does not explore or even present the differing takes on agency in sociological and philosophical debates. Rather, I will make use of my empirical data to highlight agency in action. By action I understand, slightly in pragmatistic terms, that which we are and do. According to this conception, the way to exist as a human being is to act. This conception differs from a rationalist perspective on action, one that has for long influenced social sciences and often supports the view of an autonomous and individualised agent. (Joas, 1996.) According to the critique of sociologist Hans Joas, conceptions of agent should also take into account action that is passive and receptive. (ibid., p. 167-68.)

The assumption of a reflexive, conscious, goal-calculating agent can translate into different forms. An agent can be self-empowered or competent, depending on how one employs the concept. Here, I am trying to challenge *such* interpretations and interpret agency as being part of *all* action. This opens up the possibility that not only human beings are agents, but also nonhuman beings, such as material artifacts, can be agentive (cf. Hultman and Lenz Taguchi, 2010; Latour, 2007). Artifacts do not just form a background for action, but also actively shape it. By taking passive and receptive behavior into account, the compulsiveness of an overtly activistic view on agency disappears.

In the empirical part I discuss 'girls', but it is important to notice, that this category is not all embracing: there are differences amongst those who are labeled as girls as well as those who are labeled as boys. Pursuing a phenomenological standpoint, I understand gender to be about embodied situatedness in the world. We are being posited as either female or male, and different assumptions about the way we move and physically act as 'women' and 'men' shape our experience of the world (Young, 2005). The basis for this perspective is in the thinking that we as humans are situated in the physical and social world first and foremost as embodied beings (cf. Merleau-Ponty, 1998). I will add to this view with a stronger take on materiality. Humans are situated in the world surrounded by specific kinds of material objects, which guide the actions of humans into particular directions. In this chapter, the directing features of particular objects are analysed in relation to gender. Some artifacts are considered to be primary artifacts for women, and others for men. Thus, for example, women's artifacts, such as skirts and dresses, shape the way one moves and the action one is allowed to perform whilst wearing a dress. In western societies, the experience of wearing a dress is limited almost exclusively to girls and women. Similarly, in the yard of my research day care centre, boys could be seen operating the big plastic toy trucks.

Situations of transition

The focus in this chapter is on situations of transition, as the staff called them. The day care day was organised around a schedule that assigned different activities to different spaces in the day care centre. This practice is not, however, a peculiarity of this particular day care centre. Rather, this practice seems to penetrate educational institutions in Western societies in general. Tuula Gordon notes that for instance schools establish 'time-space paths in order to reduce the potential chaos in an institution with a large membership' (Gordon, 2000, p. 157). Transition situations occurred many times during the course of a regular day care day, and fell in between the 'proper' activities, such as eating and resting, or adult-led activities like crafts or educational classes. Children changed from one activity to another in these situations, for example, from a class led by the staff to playing outdoors. As the activities often took place in different rooms and spaces, these situations usually involved movement from one room to another.

The days followed a roughly similar path in the two groups. Transitions situations took place in the hallways—one for the group of older children, another one for the group of the younger. In the hallways each child had their own clothes hangers for their outdoor clothing and spare clothing. The transition situations quite often involved changing clothes. This happened after getting up in the morning before going to breakfast, when the children changed from their pyjamas to day clothes. After breakfast and one lesson, the children changed clothes in order to go out. When they came back in, they changed their clothes again and went to lunch. After lunch, it was time for a nap, and the children undressed, leaving on only their t-shirt and underwear or stockings. They again dressed up after their nap, and after the snack and the second lesson of the day they went out again, before which they changed their clothes. After this, they changed from their outdoor clothing into their indoor clothing, and finally, they put on their pyjamas before going to bed. So, the changing of clothes took up a vast amount of time, and it was repeated many times during the day care day.

Agency in the situations of transition—an empirical analysis

The activistic view on agency interprets an agent to be someone (human) who, in one way or another, takes part in shaping a course of action, for example by starting it. Moreover, an agent is seen as being competent and goal-oriented, and because of this, reflexive and conscious. In this view, material surroundings become either limitations or resources for employing or practicing agency. Agency is something a person does, and material surroundings either enhance or restrict it.

This view is well suited to analysing the overall possibilities for children's agency in situations of transition during the day care day. When physical surroundings and material conditions are seen as either enhancing or restricting agency, the functionality of the physical space in relation to the action performed becomes vital. In the hallways, the racks were packed tight with the children's clothes. The children had quite a lot of clothes in day care, especially during winter, when their thick overalls took up a lot of space in the racks. Besides outdoor clothing, which also included raincoats, the children had an extra layer of clothes in case of very cold weather; extra clothes in case the ones they had on would get dirty; and pyjamas for the night. The hallway of the younger children was not designed for the number of children in the group. This meant that not everybody had their own rack; some only had a hook on which to hang their clothes. An extra shelf had also been installed above the racks to provide more storage space for the children's clothes. This was by no means an ideal situation from the staff's point of view, and they saw the results of the material conditions they were working in to their own and the children's activities.

Below, Soile,[33] a member of the staff in the younger children's group, describes the hallway and its effects to me:

> I sit on the bench in the hallway. Soile stays and talks to me and says that the space is rather poor, and that one harms the children when one has to do so many things for them—things the children would be capable of doing themselves. Soile points at the rack that is divided between two, sometimes three children, due to the lack of space. The shelves hang too high on the wall to be reached by the children. They can't be reached even by school children, says Soile. Adults need to help the children more often than they otherwise would. If the space was better, the children could be let in three at a time to take their [outdoor] clothes off and put on their indoor clothes, Soile says, but now adults need to help to take down the baskets etc. A couple of children only have a hook for their clothes. Staff tries to give these to children who seldom attend day care, Soile says.   (Fieldnotes, translation from Finnish by EP)

33 The names of the children and the staff are pseudonyms.

Soile's remarks highlight the importance of everyday functionality in day care spaces. When the space is too crowded, its functionality suffers, and this has consequences for the practices of the day care groups. The staff might have more useful things to do than taking down baskets. Soile's remarks point out how this especially affects the children: they cannot manage on their own due to the poor material conditions of the hallway.

There is a notion of agency to be detected in Soile's remarks. Children have the capability to manage on their own. Due to material conditions, the children cannot behave in as agentic a way as they might do otherwise. This is one way of looking at the interplay between materiality and agency, to see materiality as either enhancing or limiting agency. I now move on to analyse agency further, in order to make sense of action that at first glance seems passive.

In the group of older children, the children could dress by themselves, so they did not need any practical help in that respect. Instead, the staff instructed them what to wear, or negotiated with the children about their choice of proper clothing for each occasion. The children were able to dress and undress; they could use a zipper and knew how to do up their buttons. In other words, the children were capable of managing one basic aspect of their everyday life in day care. There was just one exception to the rule: the girls who had buttons or zippers at the back of their dresses.

Because the zippers and buttons were usually located at the back of the dresses, the girls wearing dresses could not reach these themselves. The adults had to help the girls both when putting the dresses on and when taking them off. Occasionally the girls helped each other, but they more frequently asked an adult for help—either the staff or me. I was not in a teaching or caring position in the day care centre and did not interfere with instructing or caring for the children. My aim was to differ from the other adults—i.e. the staff—and so I aided the children in situations where I figured that another child could help them. In the following extract, Tinja, who is a child, gets help from Marika, who is a teacher in the older children's group.

> Tinja comes back to Marika and turns her back on Marika, says: 'Open these buttons'. Marika opens them. (Fieldnotes, translation from Finnish by EP)

Being able to do things was highly appreciated amongst the children. They compared their knowledge and skills with each other, and skillfulness raised a child's status among her/his peers. Since the practice of changing clothes was repeated several times a day, girls who wore dresses experienced the inability to dress and undress by themselves multiple times a day.

Iris Marion Young (2005) has analysed the movements of girls and women and contrasted them with those of boys and men in her essay *Throwing like a girl*. From a phenomenological perspective, Young asks why girls and women throw a ball in a way that will not make it go as far as when boys and men throw a ball. Young argues that the technique of throwing a ball is quite different, and she goes on to ask what does to girls' the relationship with the world. Young sees fear and fright of the world in girls' timid postures as well as in the short curve of the ball. The world is not as open—full of positive possibilities—for the girls as it is for boys.

Young's analysis is, of course, not as straightforward as presented here. She also states that girls, in general, are taught from an early age to avoid physical harm being done to their bodies and so to also avoid physical activity that might lead to cuts and bruises. (Young, 2005.) If one follows Young's reasoning, one may wonder what it does to a girls' relationship with the world when she repeatedly experiences the incapability to perform the most everyday task of changing her clothes. One may indeed wonder what it does to the girls' sense of agency.

The picture may not be as bad as it seems, however, since a slightly different interpretation is possible. The first interpretation renders the buttons a 'silent' role as an obstacle in the way of true agency. The other possibility is to see the buttons as being part of an action that can lead to extra attention from the adults, and so, the button or zipper and the girl work together to shape the action. For example, the girls in the older children's group asked for help with the buttons and zippers on the backs of their dresses, but they did not stop there; they asked for help from the adults also when they were perfectly able to dress or undress by themselves. This happens in the next extract below where Milla, Emma and Pilvi are children and Marika and myself are adults:

> The children are taking their sweatshirts off. Milla goes up to Marika, and says: 'Can you take this off?' Marika: 'Surely you can take the sweatshirt off on your own.'   (Fieldnotes, translation from Finnish EP)

On another occasion Emma and Pilvi approach me:

Emma comes up to me and says that she wants me to put her scarf on her head … Emma positions herself with her back towards me, her hair is in two small bunches. She tells me how the scarf should be put on in regard to the bunches. I tell her to tell me if I put the scarf on too tight. Emma tells me when it's tight enough. Pilvi, too, wants me to put a scarf on her head. I put it on and Pilvi tightens the scarf herself.

(Fieldnotes, translation from Finnish EP)

On several occasions I noticed how the children tried to avoid being labeled a baby, and how they wanted to show their skills and their knowledge in every way. In this respect, I was quite surprised that the girls asked for help in situations when they could have managed the tasks perfectly well on their own.

In order to understand the girls' behavior, the practical organisation of the day care centre needs to be taken into account. The staff described the day care centre as being like a railroad station. There are days, one of them said with regret, when she realises she has not been able to talk with all of the children in her group. One conclusion from this is that the attention and company of staff is not always there; it needs to be sought.

Girls asking for help did so in both verbal and bodily ways. A girl could just come and stand before an adult with her back towards the adult without uttering a word when she wished for her dress buttons or zipper to be opened. In a crowded group, then, one way to get the attention of the adults was to ask for help, either by stating it out loud or through bodily interaction, for example pointing to the buttons on the back of one's dress to an adult.

Non-agentic action as agentic

Tuula Gordon, Janet Holland and Elina Lahelma (2000) have analysed silence in the classroom context and particularly silent girls. The generally accepted idea concerning silent girls is based on the assumption that girls adapt naturally to the school system. The idea also contains an assumption concerning girls' physicality: they are seen to require less physical activity than boys. Gordon, Holland and Lahelma have made the opposite conclusion: rather than seeing girls as naturally quiet and tranquil, so depriving them of any agency whatsoever, they state that girls have to focus as hard as boys to keep themselves still and quiet. Girls are *determined* to do so; they focus on their studies or daydream, creating their own mental spaces. In this sense, silence is an expression of competence (Gordon et al., 2000; Gordon, 2006, p. 7).

Gordon, Holland and Lahelma's analysis is important to the question at hand. In addition to giving the silent girls the credit of agency the analysis expands the concept of agency and raises questions concerning its limits. In similar ways to how silent girls can be seen to perform agency, action, which is normally regarded as non-agentic, can be seen as agentic.

The compulsion for competence has also been placed under scrutiny (cf. Brembeck et al., 2004). Especially the Nordic conception of childhood has been seen as reflecting a compulsory quest for competence. In this conception, children are interpreted as autonomous and competent. This conception is well suited to the ideology of lifelong learning, which understands learning as a continuous activity from the cradle to the grave. The competent Nordic child manages her/himself without being fussed over too much by adults. (Kryger, 2004.)

If one deserts the idea of competence as a manifestation of agency and takes a closer look at the material objects involved in situations of transition, the picture changes somewhat. Whilst the poor functionality and crowdedness of the hallways deprived the children of the capacity to manage by themselves, the crowdedness and poor functionality nevertheless shaped the direction of action so that the children benefitted from increased interaction with staff. In situations of transition, the poor functionality—seen from the competence-emphasising angle—of the hallways and of the buttons on the back of the girls' dresses, work in the same direction: they enhance the interaction between the children and the adults.

The competence connected to clothes, to seeking help or managing on one's own, was connected to the part that material objects played in educating and instructing the children. The relatively wide gap observable between adults and children became narrower when an adult was teaching or instructing a child on how to use or manage an object, for example a knife or a pair of scissors. The object, and the instruction around it, brought the child and the adult together. Once the child had acquired the necessary competence for properly manipulating an object, the adult moved away from her/his side. In this sense, because the children had already acquired many skills in manipulating different objects, the gap between adults and children was wider in the older children's group. The older the child, the more capable s/he was in managing different chores and the less time s/he spent in the proximity of adults. The help requested by the older girls can be seen as having been a way to bridge the gap between the girls and their care providers.

School has been analysed by dissociating formal and informal school from one another. The formal school refers, among other things, to school rules and regulations as well as the hierarchical relationship between teachers and pupils. The informal school points to informal interaction during lessons or in between them. (Gordon et al., 2000; Tolonen, 2001, pp. 77-78.) Pursuing this conceptualisation, transition situations in day care could be interpreted as moments where informal day care takes place within the aims of formal day care. The situations offered a place for informal discussion, and when the staff helped the children, they could engage in a brief private conversation. Compared to other situations during the day where children and adults' positions were fixed, here they could come closer to one another. As the adults leaned over toward the child, the difference between their heights diminished as their heads were positioned at roughly the same level. As I observed children and the adults in these situations, I sometimes noted that they seemed for a brief moment like an island in the middle of the ongoing movement and buzz of the day care centre. The physical proximity, the embodied sensing of being close to one another, was a big part of the interaction between the girls and adults, in addition to their verbal interaction.

Eeva Jokinen describes in her research on the everyday lives of Finnish adults a situation told by one of her informants. The morning ritual of combing her daughter's hair before rushing to day care and work, even if ordinary and every day, was described in tender words as a beautiful moment and experience, and Jokinen concludes that the narrator of the story reaches out and opens up to the world in the moment of brushing her daughter's hair. (Jokinen, 2004, p. 297-98.) One may wonder if the short moments when the girls sought out adults' help during the course of the day care days contained similar emotional experiences.

Material artifacts have different consequences for action. The shelves that were out of reach for all the younger children affected the ways both boys and girls were able to dress by themselves and the ways they needed—and were entitled to—the assistance of adults. Dresses and the consequences of wearing a dress affected only the girls. The material design of the girls' dresses helped them gain more attention than the boys from the adults. Dress buttons and zippers were free tickets to the proximity and attention of the adults. The functionality of the outdoor overalls and indoor clothing was designed, for the most part, to support the children's autonomous management of dressing and undressing.

In this sense, the dresses formed a sharp contrast to the otherwise functional clothing for children.

Conclusion

In this chapter, I have presented an empirical analysis of the interplay between materiality and agency. I have defined an agent as something practiced in action, as an actor. I have analysed the overall functioning and practices of a normal day in the day care centre for the children of shift-working parents. I have focused my gaze situations when the children changed from one activity to another. These transition situations usually involved moving from one room or space to another, and often also the changing of clothes. In these situations, the positioning of both the children and the staff was more flexible and their interaction more informal than in many other situations during the day care day.

I have introduced different takes on agency in relation to my empirical data. In the first case, that of the clothes' rack, I presented an interpretation of the material conditions as depriving the children of their agency. There lies a hidden interpretation concerning agency in this reasoning, namely, the idea that agency equals individual capability to manage by oneself, reflecting the competence of the actor.

When defining agency this way, the limitations to and possibilities for managing on one's own, are important. Material limitations posed by the structure of the spaces—hallways that are too small for the number of children, and shelves that are too high for the children to reach them—affect and limit agency. This affected all the children, girls and boys, equally. From this point of view, however, the buttons and zippers on the backs of the girls' dresses limited the girls'—and only the girls'—agentic action and their sense of agency. In this way, gendered clothing constructed the girls as less agentic than boys.

However, pursuing the interpretation of agency as linked to competence and capability, the girls could surely be seen as lacking something in these situations. In line with Young's (2005) theory, they were also lacking in their relation to the world. The picture can, however, be turned upside down. The calls for aid and the unpractical clothes offered the girls a means to access the presence and proximity of adults. In this view, the material objects function as actors; precisely because of the buttons, the girls could ask for help. The buttons in the back of the dresses push a certain kind of action forward.

Agency, then, can be defined from slightly different angles. In analysing the silence of girls in high school, Tuula Gordon, Janet Holland and Elina Lahelma

(2000) put forward a definition where agency is not just about loud and active action; stillness and silence can also be interpreted as constituting agentic action, once an action is contextualised and analysed from a larger framework. They have further analysed activity and passivity in ethnographic fieldwork. They note how easily the researcher's gaze turns toward visibly active and loud action. However, silent action may be equally active, such as when a student is focusing in her/his studies, for example. Gordon and her colleagues (2005) argue that in school studies, activity has been related to visible and audible signs, and the possibility of a student's active mind is ignored.

Gordon, Holland, Lahelma and Tolonen's (2005) analysis provides an important insight for methodological improvement. However, one does not have to stop there. The underlying assumption that directs the gaze towards active action is based on a particular definition of action, and in order to re-orient the gaze, a revision of the assumptions related to action might prove useful. The definition of active action, which also often conceptualises action as rational, lies at the root of sociology and many other social sciences. Hans Joas suggests many revisions to this concept of action, and one of them is to widen up the scope of action: Joas maintains that action theory as a whole should take into account action that is not just 'activist', but also passive, sensitive and receptive (1996, pp. 167-68). In line with Joas' arguments, anthropologist Marja-Liisa Honkasalo notes, that the receptive part of action is so minimalistic that it has been categorised as constituting experience rather than action (Honkasalo, 2008, p. 249).

The insistence on a competent, autonomous, active agent is an idea both in academic thinking and in societal discourse. To see it differently in research, to pay attention to passive, silent and almost invisible agency, is by no means an easy task. I found myself perplexed by the girls repeated cries for help and quite frankly, also annoyed. I interpreted the girls as disempowering themselves. Even though I wanted to challenge the overtly activistic take on agency, I valued the competence of the children and could not see the seemingly passive way the girls acted as demonstrating competence. This competence in procuring extra attention from adults differs from competencies that are openly valued in day care, such tying up shoelaces, writing one's name, using scissors.

This is an important point to keep in mind when reflecting on the ways material artifacts are part of everyday action in day care. They do not merely provide a backdrop for action to occur; they take part in shaping the action, side by side with human beings (cf. Hultman and Lenz Taguchi, 2010). The zippers and buttons were not just a hindrance for the girls' competence; they also nudged the girls towards other people, mostly the adults. Dresses, scarves and ponytail-ribbons became a habitual means to procure the attention of adults. In line with Young's (2005) theory, I asked earlier what kind of relation with the world the girls experience when they are unable to dress by themselves. To conclude, I answer by noting that the girls experience the closeness of other people. They experience ease in reaching out to others.

References

Brembeck, H., Johansson, B. and Kampmann, J., (2004) Introduction, in Brembeck, H., Johansson, B. and Kampmann, J., (eds.) *Beyond the competent child. Exploring contemporary childhoods in the Nordic welfare societies*, Roskilde: Roskilde University Press, 7-29.

Gordon, T., (2006) Girls in education: Citizenship, agency and emotions, *Gender and Education*, 18(1): 1-15.

Gordon, T., (2000) Tears and laughter in the margins, *NORA*, 3(8): 149-159.

Gordon, T., Holland J. and Lahelma E., (2000) *Making spaces: Citizenship and difference at school*, London: MacMillan Press.

Gordon, T., Holland J., Lahelma E. and Tolonen T., (2005) Gazing with intent: Ethnographic practice in class-rooms, *Qualitative Research*, 5(1): 113-131.

Honkasalo, M.-L., (2008) *Reikä sydämessä. Sairaus pohjoiskarjalalaisessa maisemassa. [Hole in the heart. Sickness in North-Karelian landscape.]*, Tampere: Vastapaino.

Hultman, K. and Lenz Taguchi, H., (2010) Challenging anthropocentric analysis of visual data: A relational materialist methodological approach to educational research, *International Journal of Qualitative Studies in Education (QSE)*, 23(5): 525-542.

James, A., (2001) Ethnography in the study of children and childhood, in Atkinson, P., Coffey, A., Delamont, S., Lofland, J., and Lofland, L., (eds.) *Handbook of ethnography*, London: Sage Publications, 246-256.

Joas, H., (1996) *The creativity of action,* Cambridge: Polity Press.

Jokinen, E., (2004) Kodin työt, tavat, tasa-arvo ja rento refleksiivisyys. [The labours, habits, equality and laid-back reflexivity], in Jokinen, E., Kaskisaari, M. and Husso, M., (eds.) *Ruumis töihin! Käsite ja käytäntö. [Put the body to work! Concept and praxis]*, Tampere: Vastapaino, 285-304.

Kryger, N., (2004) Childhood and "new learning" in a Nordic context, in Brembeck, H., Johansson, B. and Kampmann, J. (eds.) *Beyond the competent child. Exploring contemporary childhoods in the Nordic welfare societies*, Roskilde: Roskilde University Press, 153-175.

Lappalainen, S., (2004) They say it's a cultural matter: Gender and ethnicity et preschool, *European Educational research Journal*, 3(3): 642-657.

Latour, B., (2007) *Reassembling the social. An introduction to actor-network theory,* Oxford: Oxford University Press.

Merleau-Ponty, M. (1998) *Phenomenology of perception,* London: Routledge.

Paju, E., (forthcoming) *Sidoksellinen toiminta. Etnografinen tutkimus toimijuudesta päiväkodissa. [Relational action. An ethnographic research of agency in day care].*

Skeggs, B., (2001) Feminist ethnography, in Atkinson, P., Coffey, A., Delamont, S., Lofland, J., and Lofland, L., (eds.) *Handbook of ethnography*, London: Sage Publications, 426-437.

Tolonen, T., (2001) *Nuorten kulttuurit koulussa: ääni, tila ja sukupuolten arkiset järjestykset. [The cultures of the young in the school: Voice, space and the everyday organisation of genders]*, Helsinki: Gaudeamus.

Young, I. M., (2005) *On female body experience: "Throwing like a girl" and other essays*, New York: Oxford University Press.

Chapter 13

Strawberry ice cream and other episodes: Tracing spaces for feminist agency during life transitions

Seija Keskitalo-Foley

Prologue

In this chapter, I examine transitions and spaces of feminist agency using my own experiences and memories as data. My aim is to reflect on and analyse possibilities for cultural and social change, which feminist scholars and actors have been—and are—calling for, and thus inspire those who call themselves feminists to ponder and reflect on options for feminist agency. I define myself as a feminist but cannot situate myself strictly within one particular branch of feminism or feminist tradition. In using different approaches, I follow Christina Hughes' (2002, p. 421) advice to 'more self-consciously read, speak and write ourselves into possibilities of different discourses'. My approach here draws on both poststructural and materialist feminist traditions. Poststructuralism, which emphasises language and text, also 'directs us to understand ourselves reflexively as persons writing from particular positions at specific times' (Richardson, 2009, p. 309). By 'feminist materialism' I refer to experiences of embodied, lived social relations (Ramazanoglu and Holland, 1999) based on understanding knowledge as localised in a certain time, place, situation and actor. Autoethnography offers one way to utilise both approaches adopted in this chapter.

Drawing on the autoethnographic tradition means using opportunities to connect personal experiences to the cultural context (see, e.g. Coffey, 1999). My interest in autoethnography emerged during research processes in qualitative and feminist studies that encourage the researcher's visibility in the text. Moreover, after becoming familiar with (auto)biographical research (see Stanley, 1992), I find autoethnography—where the self can be treated as a unit of analysis (Coffey, 2003, p. 59)—to be a promising and productive approach that shares many features with research drawing on memory work (see, Haug, 1987). Both draw on personal subjective experiences and memories, but memory work emphasises a collective method in interpreting and analysing. The research process is also different: where memory work draws on the memories of the group that gathers together to share, analyse and interpret their lived experiences (see, e.g. Autti,

1996), in the autobiographical process, the writer can work alone, choosing the best way to shape her- or himself as data into text.

Amanda Coffey (2003, p. 64) defines autoethnography as a genre, which includes personal and autobiographical narratives. Encouraged by Coffey's idea (1999, p. 117) that '[t]he autobiographical mode of ethnographic writing reflects wider cultural emphasis on self-revelation and confession, and an appeal to subjectivity and lived experience', I will dissect several episodes and periods in my life in which gender has figured prominently. The episodes are part of my memories and span several decades.

Being aware of power and the ways in which we accept and shape cultural assumptions (see, e.g. Davies, 1993), I am not going to construct a heroic feminist narrative of 'right' consciousness. My aim is to discuss culturally shared meanings by exploring some everyday episodes in detail. I am aware that my data is lacking many of those instances where spaces for feminist agency were available but I did not seize these opportunities. By focusing on and analysing everyday practices and cultural meanings, I examine how spaces of agency have appeared in different positions in my lifetime. I will analyse the theme from the positions of kindergarten teacher, mother, university teacher and researcher. These positions provide me a great amount of material on everyday encounters, episodes and memories that include gender issues. They also illustrate transitions and continuities over two generations in my life history. While my analysis is mostly episode oriented, I also examine spaces for agency in general, aiming to illustrate transitions in, opportunities for and limits to my feminist agency.

Feminist consciousness, experience, memory and feminist agency

What does it mean to have feminist consciousness? The theme of consciousness has not been popular lately in feminist discussions. It was crucial in the women's liberation movement in the 1970s, when raising one's consciousness meant helping oneself and others to become politically aware (see, e.g. Peltonen, 1988). Briefly, consciousness-raising can be interpreted as efforts aimed at better understanding of women's oppression. The concept has not figured recently in feminist discussions for several reasons, one being that it implies an essentialist perception of women and men as two monolithic, opposite groups. In other words, consciousness-raising seems to belong to the history of feminism, that is, the era of first- and second-wave feminism. However, some researchers (see, e.g. Sowards and Renegar, 2004) have argued that in third-wave feminism consciousness-raising instils a critical perspective on personal and social injustices. References to consciousness-raising have also been rare in Finland; the term 'gender awareness' has often been used instead when referring to the need to change the prevailing gender system.

Even though I find the concept of gender awareness useful, I prefer 'feminist consciousness' precisely because of its political history, as this is a part of my own history. I associate feminist consciousness with feminist agency, because I find the connection inevitable: when one has developed a certain consciousness, it will somehow show in one's life, in choices, practices and actions.

My data include experiences and memories, both of which are problematic concepts and cannot be taken as given. Experience has been a focal and widely discussed concept in feminist research (see, e.g. Ramazanoglu and Holland, 1999). In interpreting my data I am aware that my writing comes from a particular position at a specific time. Even though I have not assumed that my experiences somehow represent those of potential feminist readers of my text, there may be something to be shared. Moreover, although my subjective experiences are embodied, that is, they relate to me as a material body, they are linked to culture and society; and they can be told in terms of language and meanings that are available to the reader (see Ramazanoglu and Holland, 1999, p. 385). Writing about my experiences now as a middle-aged feminist researcher, I have a different language at my disposal than I did several decades ago.

Memory has also been extensively discussed, especially in biographical and narrative research (see, e.g. Hänninen, 1999). Many researchers problematise the notion of human memory as a transparent window to reality (see, e.g. Hänninen, 1999, p. 108; Määttänen, 1996) even though human memory and consciousness have shaped people's subjective memories; nevertheless, as experiences and memories can be valued as an important source for analysis and interpretation. Also of importance for the analysis of my memories is Kirsti Määttänen's idea that the remembering process cannot reach or repeat the 'real' situation, but rather in remembering one creates something akin to what happened (Määttänen, 1996, p. 20). Although I will try to provide a detailed description of the episodes chosen, I am aware that it is not possible to reproduce an episode perfectly.

Agency was a popular theme among feminist scholars in both Britain (see, e.g. McNay, 2004) and Finland (see Honkasalo, 2006; Ojala et al., 2009) in the early 2000s. Here, we can perhaps see this interest as a tendency similar to the perceived need to 'turn back to the material world', as turning from discourses to materialism is interpreted. Agency has been analysed as having many different variations; in particular, feminist theory has problematised the narrow understandings of the concept as rational and target-oriented action (Honkasalo, 2006). According to Hanna Ojala, Tarja Palmu and Jaana Saarinen (2009, pp. 14-15), agency in feminist studies has been perceived in many ways, one form being 'small agency' (Honkasalo, 2006). Ojala, Palmu and Saarinen have pointed out that agency has been divided into three levels: the macro, meso and individual. The first is where the spaces for agency produced by discursive structures can be analysed. The second embraces institutional practices and dynamics that define societal, cultural and material resources for agency. The third—the individual—is the focal one for the present autoethnographic analysis, for it prompts the questions: 'What may—or what must—a person do in different contexts and situations?' and 'How can a person negotiate his or her own agency?' (op. cit., pp. 15-16).

In this chapter, I interpret feminist agencies as being based on what has been called feminist consciousness and issues of power. In keeping with Finnish feminist research (see, e.g. Honkasalo, 2006), I do not interpret feminist agencies solely in terms of acts but also as awareness of alternative courses of action.

Strawberry ice cream

At the end of the 1970s, I was a young kindergarten teacher working in a day care centre. There were about twenty children between the ages of three and six years in my group. Once, when we were having lunch, the children talked about the colour of their clothes. They were enthusiastically dividing the colours according to gender: 'Blue is for boys, red is for girls'. There seemed to be a mutual understanding of what colour 'belonged' to whom, and none of the girls or boys objected to this idea. I joined in the discussions, saying: 'What if we happened to get strawberry ice cream for dessert; because it is pink, should it only be served to girls?' The children, mostly the boys, protested loudly. I continued: 'And what should we do about the playroom: the floor is blue, so should the girls walk on the walls because the floor is a boy's colour?' This suggestion made the children laugh out loud. Satisfied, I finished the episode by saying something about how colours belonged to everyone, and that it was not necessary to make distinctions according to gender.

In this episode, one can easily read the cultural conventions of gender that children learn at a very early age in a world that has been gendered by adults (see, e.g. Grabrucker, 1985). Not only colours, but toys, games and behaviours become culturally gendered. This process takes place everywhere in children's lives—at home, in day care and in the media. Their understanding of gender emerges when watching the people around them (Grabrucker, 1985). Kindergarten teachers—as focal persons in children's lives—have possibilities to strengthen these cultural stereotypes but also the power to problematise and deconstruct such conventions. Colours have different meanings depending on the culture; not all cultures share the same ideas that are 'natural' in Finland.

In this episode, I was using the power that a teacher has over children. I took the position of knowing better (see, e.g. Hakala, 2007) by telling the children 'the truth'. My purpose was to prompt the children to think about how funny the idea of gendered colours is. In as much as I made the children protest and laugh, I felt that I had succeeded in this aim. Asking children 'What if?' can evoke alternative and imaginary visions of the matter being discussed. In this episode, my aim as a feminist teacher was to deconstruct cultural, unchallenged assumptions of the relations between gender and colours. When a familiar thing is made strange, we can be challenged to see familiar practices from a new perspective (Naskali, 2010). The gendered colour issue is one among many distinctions that structure cultural thinking regarding what is feminine and what is masculine.

In the 1970s, 'gender roles' was the most frequently used term when talking about girls and boys or women and men. This concept was used in research as well as in guides for kindergarten teachers (Heikkinen and Rautakivi, 1972) and public discussions. Gender roles were rarely discussed in the training for kindergarten teachers, and gender was a marginal issue in the early childhood education literature, one hardly mentioned. When it was visible in the guides, it referred to cultural change and presented early childhood education as including the principles of equality between girls and boys. Gender in early childhood education has since been studied using constructionist theories and, most recently, from power perspectives as well (see, e.g. Ylitapio-Mäntylä, 2009).

Possibilities and limits of a feminist mother

Once, when my daughters were under ten years old, one of them said: 'Mom, please, let's make pancakes; we haven't had them in a woman's memory!' In Finnish 'in living memory' is *miesmuistiin* (literally, 'in a man's memory'). Here by changing the word 'man' to 'woman', my daughter showed that she understood that language can be shaped. I happily made the pancakes with my daughters to reward them for such creativity.

Mindful of the fact that language is something that one can shape and still be understood, I wanted to encourage my daughters to problematise language and not take it as given. Language has been an area of interest in feminist research. Some scholars (see e.g. Penelope, 1990) see language in general as the language of a patriarchal universal discourse. The Finnish language also has gendered vocabulary and several proverbs, in which the word *mies* (man) is often used when referring to people in general, one example is given above, *miesmuistiin* (see, e.g. Jaatinen, 1988). Becoming aware that language is constructed and can be refigured and deconstructed is crucial for understanding the relationship between language and power. Paying attention to language is important for parents, teachers and educators because through language we can produce, reproduce or shape and deconstruct cultural meanings.

When my older daughter started school in the late 1980s, I started studies at university. With feminist studies offered early in the degree programme, this academic experience was a pivotal turn for me in conceptualising my experiences. Even though I already had some kind of feminist awareness, I was now exposed to concepts and theories which could help in analysing my ideas related to gender. I could now call my ideas about upbringing at least 'anti-sexist' (see Gordon, 1990, p. 87) or 'feminist'. Of course, earlier I did not have or use these concepts. By trying to deconstruct gendered cultural conventions and the binary opposition of difference between girls and boys, my aim was to offer my daughters more possibilities than the traditional stereotype for girls. I could define my aim in almost the same way as Tuula Gordon (1990, pp. 129-30) has described the goals of feminist mothers: ' ... most women did not consider it desirable to approach the task of upbringing with clearly defined goals; their daughters were growing up in a society where women were subordinated, but they could fight against that'.

Still, reflecting on my daughters' childhood, I understand well Marianne Grabrucker's (1985, p. 11) thoughts when she wrote: ' ... I realised how I and the surrounding world were constructing stone by stone a woman governed by patriarchy, not a human person with feminine and masculine features. And this happened mostly unconsciously, without purpose and without really thinking or understanding the situation'. Feminist poststructuralist theory argues that people go through subjectification as part of a process whereby 'each person actively takes up discourses through which they and others speak/write the world into existence *as if they were their own*' (Davies, 1993, p. 13). In the school context, this process can be interpreted as 'professionalisation', learning the routines (Gordon et al., 1999) and learning to be a 'professional pupil' whose 'professionalism is to have some agency, but in appropriate ways' (Lahelma and Gordon, 1997, p. 134).

Later, when my daughters were teenagers, they often criticised me for being prejudiced in favour of women. For example, if I commented on the risky driving of a male driver, they would say: 'Of course you said that because he is a man!' This criticism also related to my feminist identity, which was problematised:

> Once, I collected their storybooks and toys, telling them I was going to save them for my grandchildren, and one of them said: 'You say you are a feminist and yet you think conventionally that everybody will have children. What if you don't get any grandchildren? What if I bring home a bride?' I answered that she was right. I was thinking conventionally in this case and added that she was welcome to have a partner she loves and all that mattered to me was that she would be happy. After I had said this, my daughter smiled and gave an amused sigh and said: 'Oh, Mother, I knew you would say that!'

The conventional thinking my daughter justly accused me of reflected notions of heteronormativity. For example, Lauren Berlant and Michael Warner (1998, pp. 555-56) point out that heterosexual privilege is 'a tacit but central organising index of social membership'. Even as a feminist who has knowledge of gender and sexual diversities, intersectional and queer studies, I made this comment from my own position as a member of a heterosexual culture that cannot recognise or remember much of what people know and experience of the cruelty of 'normal culture'. The hegemony of normality is also cruel to people who can otherwise include themselves in heterosexual culture, for example, single and divorced people. Heteronormativity is maintained by both public and social norms. Social norms favour and present heterosexuality as self-evident. The assumption that everybody will have children is exclusive of single people, people who cannot have children, and people who have chosen not to, and puts them in a marginal position in culture and society. This cruelty of 'normal culture' surrounds us in many ways: for example, most theories of upbringing assume heteronormativity. Erica Burman (2008, p. 8) crystallises this tradition, arguing that the discipline of psychology treats gender in a 'finished' form, as it were, as a stable, fixed, singular identity within the dominant discourses of heteronormativity. She adds that developmental approaches to gender have functioned as the key route for legitimating such conceptions.

Even though my feminism and feminist identity were challenged and problematised by my daughters, they still often demonstrated that they could 'read' the world and were able to recognise gender and sex diversity as well as challenge the gendered culture. For example, when they were in high school, they sometimes told me school anecdotes that were related to gender and could analyse these anecdotes from feminist perspectives. One of these episodes was a teacher's comment on boys' expertise in technology, which my daughter interpreted as reflecting an old-fashioned attitude.

Spaces for agency as a feminist teacher and researcher

Feminisms and feminists have organised themselves according to several traditions, waves and groups, yet I find it hard to locate myself in any particular feminist wave or position. When thinking about feminist agency in my present life as a university teacher and a researcher, I have even chosen not to analyse any particular episodes but to discuss space for and limits on agency in the academic context more generally.

I have been working in a university since 1993 and from the very beginning have studied, done feminist research and participated in developing Women's Studies. For me, feminist research offered an academic and intellectual challenge, an opening to see the political, social and societal corollaries of knowledge. In our faculty, gender issues have been part of the curriculum for almost twenty years. Despite this tradition, persons with hostile attitudes to gender and equality issues can still affect the programmes. This means that we have to go on defending and justifying gender studies and equality issues in our work.

As part of this effort, we have to confront the challenge of neo-liberal managerialism in Finnish universities. The phenomenon is not exclusive to Finland and has been discussed widely elsewhere (see, e.g. Davies 2005). According to Bronwyn Davies (2005, p. 4), we 'need to understand how this major shift in the culture has occurred, what it does to us, and how to crack it apart'. She asserts that we should give our students a double gaze for seeing both the pleasure and the danger of being drawn into the neo-liberal discourse (op. cit., p. 13).

Even though we do not want to, we have to work on the terms of the present academic culture with its structures, practices and discourses. When I consider the history of Finnish women and gender studies, I draw an analogy between the discipline and work towards equality. Even though both of these areas have developed for several decades in Finland, they have not been fully integrated into the country's institutions and society, but need to be defended and justified repeatedly. This can be done in many ways. When defending women's studies and gender studies in an administrative context, one can appeal to both theoretical arguments and equality legislation.

Discursive, political and ethical agency?

In what follows, I reflect on feminist agency, analysing the dimensions that I have identified in the positions of kindergarten teacher, mother and university teacher and researcher. They are all powerful positions in the sense of Michel Foucault's idea of productive power. A kindergarten teacher, for example, has considerable power. She or he often has a close relationship to the children: they form strong emotional ties with the teacher, who is a focal part of their everyday life and whom they depend on in many ways. Of course, the same applies to a mother's power. Adults have a great deal of power in their interaction with children. In everyday practices, kindergarten teachers and mothers have chances to break or problematise the gender stereotypes that children are exposed to at an early age. University teachers and researchers also have at least intellectual power: choosing one's approaches, topics and what to teach or research has been the basis of academic freedom. However, this freedom has had its limits and constraints, which of late are increasingly defined by economic efficiency.

Before studying feminist theories, as a mother and as a kindergarten teacher, I did not have the concepts and language that I now have for articulating feminist issues such as sex and gender diversity. My aim was simply to open up space for thinking otherwise, asking 'What if?' The cultural resources for bringing up children in a spirit of gender equality were poor. At the time, equality issues were marginal, even though they were mentioned in texts on early education. Today, thanks to the feminist activism of past decades, we have equality legislation, government programmes and other resources that promote gender equality and provide a justification for feminist work. In terms of the macro level of agency (see Ojala et al., 2009, p. 16), feminist agency has much more space and many more opportunities than in the 1970s.

Looking back on the episodes that I have analysed, I find that rewarding my daughters for alternative ideas is a case where I could define my agency as having been discursive: it enabled me to see the world in alternative ways. Discursive agency is related to changing language. When meanings are constructed by discursive repetition, one sees the vulnerability of the dominating structures: they leave space for refiguring and even for resistance. I interpret discursive agency as an opportunity to create or reinterpret cultural conceptions. Even though I could also define my acts as emancipatory—given that their ultimate goal was to change the world—I share the idea that Tuula Gordon (1990) has identified in the goals of feminist mothers. There are multiple processes that aim to achieve equality, and we can ask whether feminists throughout the world share precisely the same vision of equality. Also asking 'What if?' may open up new perspectives and alternatives and thus create new ways of referring to politics of differences and postmodern and poststructuralist feminisms.

Feminist researchers (Burman, 2008) have problematised theories of mainstream upbringing and education, which, it is argued, are universalist, male-centred and gender blind. It is surprising that these theories are taken as given and still dominate the studies for teachers and other educators-to-be. Individual- and psychology-centred theories can be problematised from a feminist perspective, yet many times students are surprised to hear that traditional theories have even been challenged. For feminist teachers, including critical discussions of traditional theories in their teaching is one aspect of agency. I find that in my life feminist agency could be largely interpreted as habitualised, or routine (see Jokinen, 2005), because it has been part of my work for such a long time. What I want to point out is that spaces for feminist agency are everywhere—not only in day care centres, homes, schools and academic forums.

Feminist and other critical scholars have argued that science is political: it cannot step outside of power, nor can the scholars who practice it. On this basis alone, feminist agency can be considered political, and the demand for cultural and social change makes the political dimension even more visible. I would point out that feminist agency includes ethical agency, for gender, power and equality also deal with questions of rights, justice and values. When defining feminist agency as ethical, it is important to reflect on and analyse one's position as 'knowing better' (see, e.g. Hakala, 2007) and also see the danger of creating a heroic feminist narrative. I am aware of the fact that most of the episodes analysed in this chapter are ones in which I can portray myself as 'a good feminist', and my analysis does not extend to situations where I have either chosen to stay quiet or pulled back from confrontation because of fear or feeling vulnerable. The theme of vulnerable feminist agency would merit another article. Many scholars (see, e.g. Peltonen, 1988; Lahelma and Öhrn, 2003) have problematised the construction of 'a strong Finnish woman', which rhetorically may transfer all responsibility to individual women instead of leaving space for discussions of cultural, social, political or other constraints on activism.

My aim in this chapter has been to examine transitions and spaces for feminist agencies using my own experiences and memories as data. As a facet of the general criticism against qualitative research, autoethnography has been warned of the potential of romanticising the self (see, e.g. Coffey, 2003, p. 66); in my case this could be fashioning myself as 'a proper strong feminist'. This danger may be real, even though I mostly consider my feminism to be ordinary, everyday work, perhaps sometimes reflected on in a relaxed way (Jokinen, 2004).

Although I have, for the most part, examined episodes where my agency seems to have a specific target, I can also recognise experiences of enduring and tolerating inequalities in the hope of a better future. This kind of patience could be defined as 'small agency' (see Honkasalo, 2006). I would associate small agency with relaxed reflectivity (Jokinen, 2004), where one is aware of gendered housework, for example, but does not keep on fighting and arguing against the role that this inequality entails. According to Eeva Jokinen's idea of reflecting on equality, this can lead in two different directions: the desired and real change, or cynicism (ibid., p. 301). I wish to avoid cynicism by reflecting on what can be done. Among the many concrete things that I can do, perhaps the most important aim is to inspire people to ask 'What if?' This question is important because it may open spaces for imagination, for seeking new knowledge and possibilities, and for offering analytical tools that might lead to social and cultural change.

References

Autti, M., (1996) Muistelutyön kautta mielen omakuvaan. [In Memoria Veritas. Memory work as a path to a self-portrait of the mind], in Naskali, P., (ed.) *Pulpetti ja karttakeppi. Feministisen pedagogiikan kysymyksenasetteluja. [The desk and the pointer. Questions in feminist pedagogy]*, Lapin yliopiston kasvatustieteellisiä julkaisuja C 14, 79-86.

Berlant, L., and Warner, M., (1998) Sex in public, *Critical Inquiry,* 24 (2): 547-566.

Burman, E., (2008) *Deconstructing developmental psychology,* 2nd ed., London: Routledge.

Coffey, A., (1999) *The ethnographic self. Fieldwork and the representation of identity,* London: Sage.

Coffey, A., (2003) From over-rapport to intimacy and autoethnography, in Atkinson, P., Coffey, A., and Delamont, S. (eds.) *Key themes in qualitative research. Continuities and Changes,* Walnut Creek: AltaMiraPress.

Davies, B., (1993) *Shards of glass: Children reading and writing beyond gendered identities,* Sydney: Allen and Unwin.

Davies, B., (2005) The (im)possibility of intellectual work in neo-liberal regimes, *Discourse: studies in the cultural politics of education*, 26(1): 1-14.

Gordon, T., (1990) *Feminist mothers*, New York: New York University Press.

Gordon, T., Lahelma, E., Hynninen, P., Metso, T. Palmu, T., and Tolonen, T., (1999) Learning the routines: "professionalisation" of newcomers in secondary school, *Qualitative Studies in Education*, 12(6): 689-705.

Grabrucker, M., (1985) *Siinäpä vasta kiltti tyttö. [Now that's a good girl!]*, "Typisch Mädchen ... " Prägung in den ersten drei Lebensjahren, translated (abridged) into Finnish by Bützow, H., Helsinki: Kääntöpiiri.

Hakala, K., (2007) *Paremmin tietäjän paikka ja toisin tietämisen tila. Opettajuus (ja tutkijuus) pedagogisena suhteena. [The position of knowing better and the space for knowing differently. Teacherhood (and researcherness) as a pedagogical relationship]*, Kasvatustieteen laitoksen tutkimuksia 212, Helsinki: Helsingin yliopisto, Thesis (PhD), University of Helsinki.

Haug, F., (1987) *Female sexualisation. The collective work of memory*, London: Verso.

Heikkinen, A. and Rautakivi, S., (1972) *Esikouluikäisten ohjaus. [Guidance of pre-school-aged children]*, Jyväskylä: Gummerus.

Honkasalo, M-L., (2006) "Aika aikaa kutakin". Naisnäkökulmia toistoon ja toimijuuteen ["There is a time for everything". Feminist perspectives on daily routines and agency], in Kupiainen, T. and Vakimo, S., (eds.) *Välimatkoilla. Kirjoituksia etnisyydestä, kulttuurista ja sukupuolesta. [Journeys between. Essays on ethnicity,culture and gender]*, Joensuu: Suomen Kansantietouden Tutkijain Seura.

Hughes, C., (2002) Beyond the poststructuralist-modern impasse: The woman returner as 'exile' and 'nomad', *Gender and Education*, 14(4): 411-424.

Hänninen, V., (1999) *Sisäinen tarina, elämä ja muutos. [Internal narrative, life and change]*, Acta Universitatis Tamperensis 696, Thesis (PhD), University of Tampere.

Jaatinen, J., (1987) Miehen puhetta ja akkojen löpinöitä. Eräiden sävyjen ilmaisemisesta kielessä. [Men's talk and gals' chatter. The expression of certain shades of meaning in language], in Laitinen, L., (ed.) *Isosuinen nainen. Tutkielmia naisesta ja kielestä. [The big-mouthed woman. Studies of women and language]*, Helsinki: Yliopistopaino, 103-121.

Jokinen, E., (2004) Kodin työt, tavat, tasa-arvo ja rento refleksiivisyys. [Housework, customs, equality and relaxed reflexivity], in Jokinen, E., Kaskisaari, M. and Husso, M., (eds.) *Ruumis töihin. Käsite ja käytäntö. [Putting the body to work. Concept and practice]*, Tampere: Vastapaino, 285-304.

Jokinen, E., (2005) Aikuisten arki. [Everyday life of adults], Helsinki: Gaudeamus.

Lahelma, E. and Gordon, T., (1997) First day in secondary school: Learning to be a 'professional pupil', *Educational Research and Evaluation*, 3(2): 119-139.

Lahelma, E. and Öhrn, E. (2003) "Strong Nordic women" in the making? Educational politics and classroom practices, in Beach, D., Gordon, T., and Lahelma, E., (eds.) *Democratic education. Ethnographic challenges*. London: Tufnell Press, 39-51.

McNay, L., (2004) Agency and experience: Gender as lived relations, in Adkins, L. and Skeggs, B., (eds.) *Feminism after Bourdieu*, Oxford: Blackwell, 175-190.

Määttänen, K., (1996) Muisti ja muistamisen tunnot. [Memory and feelings of remembering], in Määttänen, K. and Nevanlinna, T., (eds.) *Muistikirja. Jälkien jäljillä. [A daily reminder. Tracking traces]*, Helsinki: Tutkijaliiton julkaisusarja 80, 10-25.

Naskali, P., (2010) Kasvatus, koulutus ja sukupuoli. [Upbringing, education and gender], in Saresma, T., Rossi, L-M. and Juvonen, T., (eds.) *Käsikirja sukupuoleen*. [*A handbook on gender*], Tampere: Vastapaino, 277-288.

Ojala, H., Palmu, T. and Saarinen, J., (2009) Paikalla pysyvää ja liikkeessä olevaa — Feministisiä avauksia toimijuuteen ja sukupuoleen. [Stationary and mobile—feminist positions on agency and gender], in Ojala, H., Palmu, T. and Saarinen, J., (eds.) *Sukupuoli ja toimijuus koulutuksessa*. [*Gender and agency in education*], Tampere: Vastapaino, 13-38.

Peltonen, E., (1988) *Tiedostaminen naisliikkeen ja naistutkimuksen strategiana*. *[Developing awareness as a strategy of the women's movement and gender studies]*, Naistutkimusraportteja Sosiaali- ja terveysministeriö, Tasa-arvojulkaisuja D, Naistutkimusraportteja.

Penelope, J., (1990) *Speaking freely. Unlearning the lies of the fathers' tongues*, New York: Pergamon Press, the Athene Series.

Ramazanoglu, C., and Holland, J., (1999) Tripping over experience: Some problems in feminist epistemology, *Discourse: studies in the cultural politics of education*, 20(3): 381-392.

Richardson, L., (2009) Writing theory in(to) last writes, in Puddlephatt, A. J., Shaffir, W. and Kleinknecht, S,W., (eds.) *Ethnographies revisited. Constructing theory in the field*, London and New York: Routledge.

Sowards, S. K. and Renegar, V.R., (2004) The rhetorical functions of consciousness-raising in third wave feminism, *Communication Studies*, 55(84): 532-552.

Stanley, L., (1992) *Auto/biographical I: The theory and practice of feminist auto/biography*, Manchester: Manchester University Press.

Ylitapio-Mäntylä, O., (2009) *Lastentarhanopettajien jaettuja muisteluja sukupuolesta ja vallasta arjen käytännöissä. [Daycare center teachers' shared memories of gender and power in everyday practices]*, Acta Universitatis Lapponiensis 171. Rovaniemi: Lapin yliopisto, Thesis (PhD), University of Lapland.

Part 5: Equality

Chapter 14

The interconnections between class, gender and agency in higher education

Kirsti Lempiäinen

This chapter[35] discusses the interconnections between agency, academic class and gender in higher education. The purpose of the analysis arises from the change, or even turmoil, that universities are facing in many places in Western Europe. At the national level, one example of current changes in higher education is the British government's decision to cut public funding to the social sciences and humanities. The system of governance in the universities is heading towards a strictly managerial model in which departmental managers hold decision-making power that was previously distributed more widely, if not necessarily more democratically. However, despite the obvious turbulence in higher-education institutions, it would be too simplistic to assume that the space for agency in the academia is automatically being diminished.

As a feminist researcher, I take it as axiomatic that action is not just bound to university structures, for example, but that these structures also enable action and thus restructure and re-institutionalise that action (Giddens, 1984; McNay, 2003). In this chapter, academic space will be analysed in the light of data generated through interviews and auto-ethnography. An understanding of social action as permeated by social divisions and categories such as gender, age and class, informs how I approach agency. The research question this chapter seeks answers to are how academics and students negotiate their agency, and how this negotiation can be explained along the axes of class, gender and other intersecting differences.

In the next section, I will present the data and methodologies used in the analysis. The intertwining character of gender, class and other differences will be illuminated by feminist theoretical discussion (Skeggs, 1997; Lawler, 2005). In the concluding remarks, I will suggest that a social division between an academic underclass and upper class is being inscribed into institutional and physical

---

35 I want to thank the Apaja academic writing collective at the University of Tampere, the gender studies scholars at the University of Lapland, and the referees and editors and Merl Storr for their valuable comments.

spaces—and sometimes also the mental spaces of universities—in ways, which sometimes require that the agent pay special attention to gender.

Data and methodologies

The data collection methods included both auto-ethnography and interviews.[36] In the auto-ethnography, I used my own memos, discussions, email messages, literary material and experiences at the University of Liverpool, the University of Milan-Bicocca and the University of Tampere. I visited university departments or schools (mainly the social sciences and humanities), administrative offices and student unions, and wandered around campus. I took part in seminars, staff meetings and official festivities. All this space I call the academia (see Husu, 2001).

The division between the ethnographer and the field is always somewhat blurred—the field is in the ethnographer as much as the ethnographer is in the field. In auto-ethnography the emphasis on the researcher's subjective interpretation is even greater. Her feelings and emotions, a sort of sense of 'social flesh'—a notion that Chris Beasley and Carol Bacchi (2007) have introduced to capture 'human embodied interdependence'—is crucial. The form of auto-ethnography applied here is based on the principles of materialist feminism that Tuula Gordon, Janet Holland and Elina Lahelma (2000a) advanced in their study. In their approach, experience, spatiality and embodiment are essential. Gordon, Holland and Lahelma looked at 'processes and practices in everyday life at school' to contextualise their ethnography in a societal and historical frame (ibid., p. 4). Elizabeth Ettorre (2010) points out that for (feminist) sociologists, it is relevant to reflect upon the analyst's own knowledge and feelings in sociological accounts of relationships. Moreover, arguments for strong objectivity in the style of Sandra Harding (1993) favour a form of auto-ethnography in which one encounters witnesses rather than observers.

Drawing on Pierre Bourdieu's (1986) cultural theory of class, feminist class theorists point out that class is lived and acted upon in meaning-giving processes. Embodied, gendered and layered experiences carry classificatory systems, which men and women invest in. Class position goes hand-in-hand with social capital. Gender is an important division and category directing action, and is often hierarchically detectable and reflexively approached (Jokinen, 2004; Lawler, 2005; Skeggs, 2004; Tolonen, 2008). In my own analysis, I will not use social

---

36 The interview themes were the quality of teaching and research, mobility, employment, and university structures of governance.

class as a theoretical tool in this way, although I acknowledge its importance in feminist social research. Rather, class will gain its meanings through the analysis. I proceed with the recognition that 'gender is often hidden in the structuring of categories,' and that this is also true of class (Skeggs, 2004, p. 23).

The points where I agree with previous analyses are that the upper academic class (the well-off) has a legitimised social position from which to drive their subjectivity without having to justify their choices or actions to those in subordinated positions, and gender affects these choices and actions (Bourdieu, 1986; Skeggs, 1997). The academic underclass (the not-so-well-off) does not have the same legitimation, and is obliged to discuss and justify its choices and actions.[37] These features of class are as vivid in academia as they are in society. Upper-class agency has implications for many aspects of academic life, such as having a permanent job, having one's own office, scholarship (for researchers and students alike), the opportunity to teach, invitations to parties organised by the well-off (professors), whether one's parents have enough money to pay for one's studies, and so on. Underclass agency refers to the lack of these things. These class properties are not merely human qualities, and could also be applied to subject fields, disciplines, departments or other institutional agents. But what is seen as valuable varies somewhat according to the agent her/himself. One Finnish study on non-permanent university workers has shown that some academic workers voluntarily choose fixed-term jobs, although insecurity in this group is generally rising (Kinnunen, 2010). A permanent job is thus not a universal value. What is more, the underclass actors' status is valid only inside academia, because all agents in academia have at least some power to define and value different sorts of phenomena, and this is not comparable to the situation of not-so-well-off people in general.

My compilation and use of interviews in this analysis requires a caveat. The different pieces of data are not comparable in the strict sense of the word. I stayed in Liverpool for more than three months, whereas I visited Milan-Bicocca only for two weeks, and I have studied and worked most of my life in the University of Tampere. Hence I have most experience of the Finnish case. I will analyse the data as three case studies. In Milan I received help with the interviews from Carmen Leccardi, and in Liverpool from Elizabeth Ettorre. One final note on the data is that in all places it was difficult to get undergraduate students to join the study; in Liverpool and Tampere I therefore interviewed a student activist.

---

37 For a critique of the notions of the upper class and underclass, see Skeggs (1997, p. 6).

Material realities: Space and time for agency

The three universities are different in many respects. The University of Liverpool (the acronym L in the interview extracts) is one of the UK's top 20 research-led universities (the Russell Group universities). The university has an active partnership in China, which is also one of the University of Tampere's (T) areas of collaboration. The University of Milan-Bicocca's (M) main international partnerships are in Latin America. Both Liverpool and Milan-Bicocca charge student fees according to the socioeconomic situation of the student, while there are no student fees at the University of Tampere (as is the case generally in Finland)[38].

When it came to cuts in jobs and funding, no one was harbouring any wishy-washy ideas about academic freedom or the glory of having one's own space. A cause for concern was the way disciplines were approached in an instrumental rather than intellectual manner in the 'new' university:

> What the universities are for, now, is socialising people, keeping people out
> of the labour market. Students are asking about how to pass assessments,
> but university teaching is not instrumental. We used to be reading
> sociology—now it's studying sociology. (L3)

The restructuring process in universities was said to disturb academic work, and in the interviews, time resources in particular were discussed a lot. What is more, the current academic work climate emphasises the futurity of the labour rather than the present. Lisa Adkins (2008) has analysed the ways in which current workers must be oriented to an open future in many fields that require expert knowledge and skills. Now-time in the universities is increasingly limited, and thus it may seem that the space for action as such is also limited. Furthermore, in the new university, writing reports and articles is valued more than research itself, and we could ask whether doing research has been reduced to writing and publishing. Heavy criticism was directed at politicians and governments in many comments, such as, 'The Ministry in Rome is not interested in our results, it just wants products' (M8).

38 The University of Liverpool is the oldest of the three universities, founded in 1881, with
    27,000 students and 2,200 staff (5,000 including all the research staff). The University
    of Tampere (founded in 1960—it started as Civic College in Helsinki in 1925) has the
    same number of staff (2,200) and 15,200 enrolled students. The University of Milan-
    Bicocca, founded in 1998, has 30,000 students and 1,700 staff.

The so-called node individuals were quite visible in all three places, either by their busy schedules, the queues outside their doors, or in Milan the constant ringing of their hands-free mobile phones. Their embodied agency appeared to be moving, handling many things seemingly at same time, always being busy and a little tired. They performed a nomadic subjectivity, which tied them to various moving and changing networks. The fixed points creating stability were their capabilities and relationships with others (Braidotti, 2011; Haraway, 2004). The higher one stood in the university hierarchy, the less free time one had, and working hours from seven a.m. until eleven p.m. were not unusual. These material realities no longer even cause surprise, but are merely stated as facts. If one evaluates the space for agency solely in terms of time and how much one can control one's working hours, for example, an academic is not very independent. Even a professor's workload did not look enviable in any of the universities I studied.

I would like to emphasise that in a stable faculty with no immediate threats of cuts, the restructuring did not affect agency to great extent: rather, it was pressures to produce results such as books, publications, getting research grants and so on. One scholar in the data (L7) emphasised that no one was actually counting successful research applications yet, and it was enough if one was applying and being as busy as everyone else. In other words, being a successful academic can mean *performing* a successful academic. Many of the interviewees in all three universities concentrated on their core tasks of research, teaching and studying as business as usual. In Tampere one interviewee (T9) spoke especially warmly about the essence of work as 'being in the right mental environment with other people interested in societal issues', despite the rapid restructuring of the university. Although in Milan many postdoctoral researchers were working on small research grants and were not part of the permanent staff, they still appreciated academic work.

> A student who starts a PhD doesn't consider a career different from an academic one … I decided to do a PhD because I like academic career. If I would have to think of another career than academic today, I couldn't … I'm one of the youngest … I started at twenty-four … we have the PhD but we don't have experience [to go outside university]. I think that we have a different passion, different desire for our career.   (M4)

Emotions were attached to one's academic career, and in this interviewee's case at least this had started early, as he was doing his postdoctoral research at thirty-one years of age. The interviewees with more established positions denied any diminution of their space of agency at all:

> [The new liberal university] encourages academics to self-censor or self-discipline ... academics discipline themselves even before they are told to do something, and I look around and some of my colleagues, I think that at some times they can be quite pathetic, responding immediately to the university's demands because there is still a lot of academic freedom, there is a lot still and people don't think about ...   (L4)

A proud academic position denies that there is any outside controlling mechanisms, or even the slightest suggestion that any kind of control might form part of one's own agency in a Foucauldian fashion. This, I would argue, is a well-off, upper-class position.

Sensing class and gender

Although I did not address gender directly in my questions, the issue came up in many interviews, perhaps because the interviewees noted that I was a feminist researcher. I also paid reflexive attention to gender and equality issues during the auto-ethnography.

> *Example 1.* This morning I went to the administration building, which was modern and quite new. It looked efficient and fresh after the somewhat older and shabbier building I had been in earlier. The man who I'm meeting, quite high in the university hierarchy, smiles pleasantly, we say hi and he immediately asks whether I would like to have a cup of coffee. As I agree, he brings the coffee himself in a taking-care kind of manner. I thank him and silently wonder whether this happens with every visitor regardless of the visitor's gender. Instead of a calculated game the whole situation seems to me natural, as if two of a kind have met. The space is delightful, with huge windows, which let in a lot of daylight. The room gives the impression that an important manager works in it. (L8)

> *Example 2.* The room is small but there is a window, a narrow one, in the background. Although there are a lot of books and papers, everything

seems to be somehow in the right place, and the room looks familiar because it reminds me of an academic's room. We start our discussion, and after awhile someone knocks on the door and a young man enters the room. I try not to listen to the discussion, although the tone appears to be rather heated from the start. When I move away as if to leave the room, the person I'm meeting asks me to stay and continues to speak in an authoritarian manner to the man. The up-front, frank manner seems to me to be a performance of power in which I cannot recognise gender, no matter how hard I look, or any of the hegemonic masculine conventions of solidarity between men. The possible conflict of interest is also not being hidden as one would expect it to be if the incident had occurred in the realm of patriarchy. Somehow, I feel appreciated. (L3)

Example 3. I'm interviewing a young scholar who represents the so-called hard sciences. As my women's studies background is known to the interviewee, I wonder how we will get along, but soon I throw myself into the interview routine, forgetting our backgrounds. After a while I find myself hearing that 'women are better than men in all possible ways'. Would the interviewee have said that if my position had been hidden? Should I ask if women are so good, how come I hardly ever see any in the faculty we are in? (M3)

The gendered class divisions in university are more complex than the 'male domination, female subordination' model would suggest. Nevertheless, when discussing gender, this kind of model—conceived as historical rather than current—was a point of separation and differentiation for these male interviewees. They reflexively constructed their own gendered agency in the situation (cf. Jokinen, 2004). Chivalrous gestures and ways of action also confirmed and underlined their separation from that model. It could be argued that some of the meanings I read as reflections of gender were simple signs of friendliness. Either way, the negotiation of difference and patriarchal power structures was apparent. Nonetheless, I do not want to draw the conclusion that there would have been only one masculine frame of acting in these situations, but rather that a certain negotiation was offered for me to detect ('I know that you know, so this is the way I act as a man'). The *doxa*, a common understanding, was also created by bending or breaking gender divisions, as in the second example (Connell, 1995; Lawler, 2005). From another angle, the second example strengthens the masculine hierarchy while calling for a female eyewitness to the situation.

One of Beverley Skeggs's strongest arguments is about the (dis)identification of class that she demonstrates in her study *Formations of class and gender* (1997). Skeggs argues that her interviewees did not want to be included in the working class, which was conceived as an underclass and as a category of failure, unemployment, poverty and other negative features with which obviously no one would wish to identify (ibid.)[39]. So class is not necessarily positively made by one's identifying with and becoming part of it, but rather by one's negating and dissolving it. A similar mechanism can be traced in relation to gender in the extracts above: there are expectations about gender hierarchies, which are acted upon and worked out. A man in a high position serves coffee to a woman in a low position. Supposedly the interviewee wanted to step out of the cultural position that his well-off space and male gender were offering him.

Spaces were hierarchically divided so that there was more space, light and convenience for those in the higher positions. Agents would step down from this privileged position in those moments when they were providing services and acting 'like everybody else' in academia. Students had their own spaces in separate buildings, but with big common rooms or indoor arenas with a lot of noise and little natural light. An exception to this was Tampere, where many of the postgraduate students had their own rooms:

> *Example 4.* We sit in a small room, which is quite gloomy. The interviewee has an errand still to take care of, and I prepare my papers and things in the meanwhile. The room is not full of stuff, as if its tenant is there only temporarily. It's Friday afternoon and the long office-like corridor outside seems to be empty. The interviewee looks eager to start. However, she wants to keep the door open during the interview. As far as I recall, we have not met before. Although we are from different generations, I have a strong feeling that we understand each other perfectly.   (T3)[40]

The sense of being two of a kind, as in an earlier example, is linked in this case to gender and the underclass position. It feels as if the interviewee were half my age, although she is actually older than the impression she gives. Usually

---

39 Skeggs (1997, p. 95) asks 'who would want to be seen as working class?' and then gives an answer in parentheses: 'possibly only academics are left.'

40 I've translated all the T-marked extracts from Finnish to English.

interviews are private situations, but the interviewee here keeps the door almost ceremonially open. It might be because her boss has an office nearby and the interviewed woman wants her employer to be included in the circle of trust, which I sensed from the beginning. The interviewee seems cautious not to jeopardise her position in the eyes of the boss, and thus underlines her own underclass position.[41]

Gendered intersections of age and academic class

While I was visiting the faculties, my own ideas about equal treatment as a doctor among doctors were perhaps a bit naïve, but I was shaken out of my fantasy world by the next interviewee. She had a small, brownish and gloomy office with a window onto an inner courtyard. I had already begun to wonder whether the academic underclass experience was more directly linked to gender and women.

> Until comparatively recently and certainly within our school, things are now much more transparent. You knew absolutely, and it was a male environment, and it was a white male environment … in truth you didn't know what they were [doing] … it really amazes me that in 2000, you know the new millennium this can happen. The first staff meeting in which one of these white male heads of departments, that involved all of the staff, you can imagine how expensive it was for everybody to be there, and he starts by reading off a paper and I ask him, 'Do you take questions as you go along or at the end?' And he said, 'There will be no questions, I'm head of the department, I'm reading a paper, it will take an hour and then it's over.' And if I've read in a Dickens novel I would have … and this was not an old man talking here, most of these men that I have experienced this way are actually, quite a lot of them are quite young.. (LX)

Gender is not the only important division brought up in the extract above, but age and skin colour (ethnicity) are important as well. Authoritarian leadership and governance is considered to be something from the previous millennium, and old ways of acting are contrasted with intelligible ways of acting. I am suggesting here that although 'these men' have had power over the interviewee in the university hierarchy and thus she could conceive herself as part of the

41 I thank Virve Peteri for this observation.

underclass, she in fact turns the power position upside down by means of her slight contempt. What this story underlines is that the interviewee's agency is not dependent on how 'these men' act, even though her request in the meeting was not answered. The affect alludes simultaneously to horror, disappointment, disrespect and pride.

Another interesting response concerning gender and age came from a young female PhD student whom I asked to reflect on whether the university was a bureaucratic organisation:

> It's difficult to say because I don't have much experience or evidence to base it on, but my impression is that it is old fashioned, very male, very white, the university here is appalling, it seems a very science- or medicine-orientated. I just have this image of some very old white men who are doctors or scientists doing things ... in an old-fashioned way and not really up to social science or other subjects.   (L2)

Again, the combination of whiteness, age and male gender comes to the fore as hideous. However, her own field, social sciences, is exempt from the science-oriented picture. The 'old men's science over there somewhere' is an impression which arises from her own imagination. Valerie Hey and Carole Leathwood (2009) have argued that the power of white men is written into the bureaucratic, frightening university. The power is emotionally strong, as was also shown in the interviewee's expression.

When it comes to Milan-Bicocca, many people seemed to be proud of their young, research-oriented and highly ranked university (sixth in the national ranking of seventy-seven universities in 2010), and one interviewee highlighted this by saying that 'we are working in a good way' (M1). A generally expressed wish in the Milan interviews was 'to open up the university more to the world'. The most critical stances were those taken against the new right-wing attitudes of the higher-education reformists who did not see the value of subjects such as the humanities and the so-called soft sciences:

> Everyday we are realising how little our students know their own language ... It is a moment when humanities, the study of humanities should be supported, but this is just the opposite.   (M3)

And this is happening ... exactly the same what is taking place in Great
Britain and universities are cutting, cutting, cutting jobs there.   (M2)

Although these two interviewees do not directly address gender here, later
in their interviews they create a very clear division between humanities and the
technologically oriented sciences, and between the soft and the other-than-soft.
The traditionally signified set-up is adopted rather rigidly. These women actually
reinforce the idea of a strong sexual difference in academic fields.

> The [Italian] university system is ... very peculiar ... we are a little bit, I
> would say culturally, because of the language, a periphery ... particularly
> me working on gender issues and not having women's studies fully
> institutionalised, it's very difficult because I always have to do sociology of
> culture *and* gender, and for these people here, it does not mean anything,
> gender, so it's just M/F in statistics, so this is something that is really
> difficult and we will have to continue to work on.   (M4)

The overall critique of a peripheral academia without books or connections
is described as a lack here. In this context the interviewee is locating herself
as a marginalised young feminist researcher. Later she discusses her good
international contacts, research projects and politically engaged networks. Being
marginal and underclass in one area of academia does not imply that the agent's
whole academic position can be characterised in that way—quite the contrary.
  All the interviewees were concerned at the restructuring of academia, if not
for their own sake, then for that of their students. The next interviewee in
Tampere does not divide agents according to their age (or gender), but instead
he discusses the promises made by staff (or academia) and those who believe
such promises:

> The only thing that one [a student] can do is to read extensively and then
> decide what one wants to become, that this is not a polytechnic. But the
> way of thinking [is] like in a polytechnic. I feel we somehow enhance it,
> or the system in some peculiar ways enhances it. And then we cannot
> answer to the enhancement. So the result is a lot of very disappointed
> people. Kind of people who want to read and roam about and finally get
> tired of not becoming anything ... It feels like this world is no longer the
> right place. One would think that university would be the last bastion of

thinking, but perhaps it is not. At least I think that myself, and ponder how I have been naïve. Yes.   (T1)

An emphasis on 'people', as if dissolving age and gender differences, was not rare in the data. In the Milan-Bicocca departments, the same kind of acknowledgement by upper-class agents was made without any young-versus-old dichotomy, although the age structure was quite obvious: elderly scholars had permanent positions and young scholars had no positions. The fault was seen as lying with the system:

> In the Italian system ... all the rules have been in favour for the internal career of the professors, favouring the growing old of the professor and not the qualities ... like European research cooperation etc. ... we are not able ... to mobilise the system, to make our young people going around in the world, in other Italian universities, and so on, so we are stuck with a lot of young people who have done PhD here, that have a postdoc fellowship here and then they are stuck here and they have no job here but cannot win a job elsewhere.   (MY1)

Here the interviewee is thinking not just of his own position, but of all those that he represents, and of those who are not so well-off and whose existence his good share of academia hinders. The same kind of solidarity among actors from different levels of the hierarchy could be found in the other two universities. It appears when a common enemy or problem is identified or imagined by the actors.

Conclusion

My focus has been on the particular ways in which gender, age and academic class weave possible understandings for academics to pursue agency and comprehend their space in the academia. As hierarchical organisations, universities have embedded power divisions. The obvious halt in one's career after a PhD for younger generations is the deepening gap between the upper class and the underclass in all the researched universities. This has also been my own motivation for this study.

Gendered orders are actively created and recreated in everyday practices in the university. The space for gendered agency becomes more nuanced when it is analysed with and through the concept of class. Gender is also intertwined with other differences, such as age or ethnicity (skin colour). The interconnections of class, gender, age, ethnicity and agency are not permanent and fixed, but they are nonetheless central to narratives about one's work and study in current academia. What is more, 'questions about centres and margins are complex' when discussing the space for agency in the university (Gordon et al., 2000b, p. 201). What the materialist feminist standpoint here suggests is that the conceptualisation of material realities and agents has to be reassessed as the study proceeds. Thus conceptions of margins and centre, for instance, move and change together with the analysis. In this chapter, the division between the academic upper class and underclass was both produced and simultaneously deconstructed in the interviewees' speech and acts. In other words, an underclass agent could temporarily be an upper-class agent in another context in academia, and vice versa. What is more, time to research and write, and for some also to study and teach, has become scarce in a way, which also affects class positions.

My own position as a feminist scholar contributed to the research setting in many ways. For instance, a male interviewee might step down from his upper-class position by performing emotional labour (taking care and serving coffee), which is often culturally expected from female agents (Hochshild, 2003). I suggest that the social division between an underclass actor and an upper class actor is inscribed into the academic institutional, physical and mental space in a way, which occasionally awakens reflexive attitudes towards gender. From time to time, gender-reflexive action contradicts cultural gender expectations and deconstructs the gendered orders of academia. To conclude, Tuula Gordon's (2005) concept of *felt agency* materialises in the analysis. Class and gender are felt very concretely in relation to other actors.

References

Adkins, L., (2008) From retroactivation to futurity: The end of the sexual contract?, *Nora: Nordic Journal of Feminist and Gender Research*, 16(3): 182-201.

Beasley, C. and Bacchi, C., (2007) Envisaging a new politics: Beyond trust, care and generosity—towards an ethic of 'social flesh', *Feminist Theory*, 8(3): 279-296.

Bourdieu, P., (1986) *Distinction: A social critique of the judgement of taste*, London: Routledge.

Braidotti, R., (2011) *Nomadic subjects: Embodiment and sexual difference in contemporary feminist theory*, 2nd ed., New York: Columbia University Press.

Connell, R. W., (1995) *Masculinities*, Berkeley: University of California Press.

Ettorre, E., (2010) Autoethnography: Making sense of personal illness journeys, in Bourgeault, I., DeVries, R., and Dingwall, R., (eds.) *Handbook on qualitative methods in health research*, London: Sage.

Giddens, A., (1984) *The constitution of society: Outline of the theory of structuration*, Cambridge: Polity.

Gordon, T., (2005) Toimijuuden käsitteen dilemmoja. [Dilemmas of agency as a concept], in Meurman-Solin, A., and Pyysiäinen, I., (eds.) *Ihmistieteet tänään. [Humanities today]*, Helsinki: Gaudeamus.

Gordon, T., Holland, J., and Lahelma, E., (2000a) *Making spaces: Citizenship and difference in schools*, Basingstoke: Macmillan.

Gordon, T., Holland, J. and Lahelma, E., (2000b) Moving bodies/still bodies: Embodiment and agency in schools, in McKie, L., and Watson, N., (eds.) *Organising bodies: Policy, institutions and work*, London: Macmillan.

Haraway, D., (2004) *The Haraway reader*, New York: Routledge.

Harding, S., (1993) Rethinking standpoint epistemology. 'What is strong objectivity', in Alcoff, L., and Potter, E., (eds.) *Feminist epistemologies*, New York: Routledge.

Hey, V., and Leathwood, C., (2009) Passionate attachments: Higher education, policy, knowledge, emotion and social justice, *Higher Education Policy*, 22: 101-118.

Hohchschild, A., (2003) *The managed heart: Commercialization of human feeling*, Berkeley: University of California Press.

Husu, L., (2001) *Sexism, support and survival in academia. Academic women and hidden discrimination in Finland*, Helsinki: Department of Social Psychology, University of Helsinki.

Jokinen, E., (2004) Kodin työt, tavat, tasa-arvo ja rento refleksiivisyys. [Work at home, habits, equality and casual reflexivity], in Jokinen, E., Kaskisaari, M. and Husso, M., (eds.) *Ruumis töihin. Käsite ja käytäntö. [Body to work: Concept and praxis]*, Tampere: Vastapaino.

Kinnunen, U., (2010) Määräaikaisten epävarmuus kasvussa. [Insecurity of fixed-term workers rising]. *Aikalainen*, http://aikalainen.uta.fi/2010/06/14/maaraaikaisten-epavarmuus-kasvussa-2/ [Accessed 9 December 2011].

Lawler, S., (2005) Introduction: Class, culture and identity, *Sociology*, 39(5): 797-806.

McNay, L., (2003) Agency, anticipation and indeterminacy in feminist theory, *Feminist Theory*, 4(2): 139-148.

Skeggs, B., (1997) *Formations of class and gender*, London: Sage.

Skeggs, B., (2004) Context and background: Pierre Bourdieu's analysis of class, gender and sexuality, in Adkins L., and Skeggs, B., (eds.) *Feminism after Bourdieu*, Oxford: Blackwell.

Tolonen, T., (2008) Menneisyyden dinosauruksen luiden kolinaa? [Clattering the past bones of dinosaurs?], in Tolonen, T., (ed.) *Yhteiskuntaluokka ja sukupuoli. [Social class and gender]*, Tampere: Vastapaino.

Chapter 15

Gender in Finnish school textbooks for basic education

Liisa Tainio

Gender equality is one of the most widely accepted goals in education (e.g. UNESCO, 2007). In addition to struggling with such urgent and important goals as to eliminate gender disparity and ensure equal access to basic education all around the world, the documents also encourage paying attention to issues that affect the learning process itself, such as classroom interaction and teachers' treatment of students and the representation of gender in textbooks and other kinds of learning materials used in schools (Blumberg, 2007; Gordon et al., 2000). Interestingly, one of the most geographically widespread phenomena is the gender bias of school textbooks. Blumberg (2007) demonstrates that research on textbooks is numerous and available in all continents, and according to these studies, gender bias in learning materials follow the same pattern, namely that females are underrepresented and that both females and males are depicted in gender-stereotyped ways.

In this chapter, I analyse school textbooks for basic education in Finland, focusing on thirty books for Finnish language and literature education[42]. My aim is to study whether there is a gender bias in these books and in what ways gender is represented in the illustrations and texts of these books. My analysis is based on an earlier study involving quantitative and qualitative analysis of books that are in current use (Tainio and Teräs, 2010). All school textbooks in Finland are designed in the spirit of the National Core Curriculum for Basic Education (2004). This document explicitly mentions that 'gender equality is promoted by giving girls and boys the ability to act on the basis of equal rights and responsibilities in society, working life, and family life' (National Curriculum, 2004, p. 12).

I take it for granted that all texts involve and communicate ideologies, and that those ideologies matter for the reader (Fairclough, 1989; Oteiza, 2003). Critical discourse analysts use the concept of naturalisation to refer to those

---

42 In the National Curriculum (2004) this subject is called Mother tongue and literature (L1). For the sake of clarity, I use the term Finnish language and literature.

recurrent explicit and covert ideological meanings, represented through linguistic or semiotic features that become common to the extent that they are seen to represent the natural and legitimate state of affairs (Fairclough, 1989, p. 91-93). The systematic and dominant character of these features make them influential, and strangely enough, also hard to notice. Fairclough (1989, p. 92) sees naturalisation as 'the royal road to common sense', meaning that when an ideology becomes dominant, it also becomes invisible to a certain point, and will be seen as core to the discourse or the institution it represents. This is why it is especially important to pay attention to and analyse the ideologies present in official textbooks used in schools. School textbooks have 'the power to impose cultural meanings and to structure student's perceptions of reality' (Oteiza, 2003, p. 640).

In classrooms, teachers often rely heavily on textbooks, spending sometimes eighty to ninety-five per cent of the teaching time by using them (see Blumberg, 2007, p. 6). According to earlier studies on Finnish basic education, also in Finland teachers seem to spend a lot of their time in classrooms using textbooks, and the contents of textbooks have been shown to influence both teaching practices and subject didactics (e.g. Heinonen, 2005). Although teachers are certainly able to make use of textbooks in their teaching in several ways—also in critical ways (Sunderland, 2000)—the importance of textbooks for teaching and learning should be taken seriously. While students learn subject matter through texts and through teachers' use of textbooks, students are not able to avoid the impact of the ideologies embedded in the texts, even if they read the texts in different or critical ways. Therefore it is important to find out how teachers perceive the ideologies of textbooks. This is why I explore teachers' ways of observing the gender ideology of textbooks in this chapter, analysing a discussion between two teachers as they study a set of textbooks.

Earlier studies on textbooks and gender

School textbooks are institutionalised and authoritative texts produced for the purpose of teaching and learning. In these texts, the authors' thinking is visible but it is constructed through several actors and instances, such as the national curriculum, the discourses connected to the scientific fields of different subjects, dominant educational ideas about learning and teaching, and of course, through the editor's and publisher's instructions (Oteiza, 2003). Finnish school textbooks usually consist of different kinds of material, for example, informational texts, extracts from other literary sources, exercises, examples, lists and abstracts, and illustration (pictures and photos). The style of the informational texts has been described as factual, authoritative, objective, and general; it is also usual that facts and interpretations are provided as if they were the only ones. There are usually several series of volumes available in the market for teachers and schools to select.

Gender bias and the representation of gender in school textbooks has been one of the interests, although not a very popular one, for Finnish researchers on education and linguistics. One of the pioneering works was Elina Lahelma's (1992) analysis on textbooks for subjects connected to social studies. According to her analysis, women were seen as more responsible for care work and men as more powerful and active participants in society. Women remained more or less invisible, especially in history textbooks. Also more recent studies of Finnish school textbooks have recurrently reported gender bias and stereotyped images of gender (see Tainio and Teräs, 2010). Analyses of heteronormativity and heterosexism show that the diversity of sexes and sexualities are not represented or receive only minimal attention in school textbooks.

Earlier analyses of Finnish language and literature textbooks show that also in this field, women are underrepresented in texts and illustrations, and that gender images are traditional. This is displayed both in informational texts and in the numerous citations of fictional texts, which are typical elements in first language textbooks (Palmu, 2003). The textbooks for first grades contain a lot of fictional texts and illustrations, but the characters in the fictional texts as well as in the pictures are mostly masculine (Palmu, 1992). Also references to persons, for example to writers of fiction and other authors, contain more references to men (Palmu, 2003).

A closer look at textbooks

In this chapter, I analyse Finnish language and literature textbooks that are currently in use in grades 3, 6, and 9 (students aged nine, twelve, and fifteen), available on the market by the biggest publishers in Finland in 2011. I wanted to focus on this subject because, first, Finnish language and literature is seen to be one of the most important subjects for developing students' academic and literacy skills, such as reading and writing. Consequently, there are more Finnish language and literature lessons than there are of any other subject in basic education. Secondly, the image of this subject is said to be gendered: it is seen as a 'feminine' subject (Lappalainen, 2009). This might even be one reason behind the fact that, in average, female students achieve better results in language and literature education throughout basic education, and they are more motivated to learn this subject than boys (Lappalainen, 2009). The gendered image of the subject appears also in the gender division of the textbook writers: the vast majority of the writers of these textbooks are women (eighty-six women to twenty-three men, see Tainio and Teräs 2010, p. 21).

I will analyse the texts and illustrations of the textbooks with the help of content analysis (e.g. Krippendorff, 2003). Content analysis is used as a method in studies that aim for an overall picture of very large data. In this analysis, I use both quantitative and qualitative content analysis to reveal a possible gender bias in the books. I also draw on critical discourse analysis to interpret the kind of cultural meanings of gender embedded in the books more qualitatively (Fairclough, 1989).

In this chapter, I also study the ways in which teachers observe gender in textbooks. Applying the method of conversation analysis, I explore a conversation between two teachers who talk about five text books for ninth grade and who I asked to pay attention to the representations of gender in the books. Conversation analysis is a method that analyses everyday interaction as a fundamentally organised social activity (e.g. Hutcby and Wooffit, 2001). According to conversation analysis, participants collaborate and negotiate during the course of an interaction with the help of shared practices on a turn by turn basis. The teachers were asked to 'think aloud' about what they saw in the books and on what grounds they would choose a textbook for themselves if they were able to select one of the books they looked at for use in their classroom (see Sasaki, 2008).

Objects for analysis: Illustrations, gender specific words and passages about gender

As in the earlier analysis (Tainio and Teräs, 2010), my first aim was to find out if there was a gender bias in the illustrations: every person and gendered fantasy character in the illustration (pictures and photos) was counted. Some characters and persons were impossible to categorise as male or female; they were categorised as 'other'. My second aim was to analyse the texts, or more precisely, the words used in the texts, to find out if there was a gender bias in references to persons (and fantasy characters); all those words that carry markings of gender were counted. Finnish language is considered to be genderless since there is no grammatical gender and, for example, even in the third person singular (cf. *he/she* categorisation in English) the personal pronouns do not carry reference to gender (Tainio, 2006). This means that in Finnish there are gender markings only in certain nouns, such as first names, which in Finnish reveal the sex of the person, and certain nouns such as *tyttö* 'girl', *kuningas* 'king', and *lentoemäntä* 'air hostess'. My third aim was to explore if the textbooks contained information on gender equality or on sex and gender divisions in culture and society. In the following, I will present some of the findings of the quantitative analysis of textbooks together with more qualitative analysis of extracts from textbooks and of the teachers' conversation.

Illustrations

All the textbooks contained lots of pictures and photos; the majority of the pictures depicted persons and fantasy characters. Gender bias favoring pictures of males was clearly prominent (see Tainio and Teräs, 2010). From 7,762 pictures of persons or fictional characters, 61.5 per cent were of males and 33.9 per cent of females. Only 6.7 per cent of the persons were not clearly marked as male or female. The proportion of pictures of males was lowest in the textbooks for third grade (males 58.5%, females 24.8%) and grew steadily up to ninth grade (males 65.3%, females 33.2%). Interestingly, the gender/sex of fantasy characters in particular was overwhelmingly masculine (1,089 male fantasy characters, 271 female fantasy characters). The majority of pictures of persons were of adults (3,475 altogether), and most of the adults were men (2,267). There were slightly more pictures of boys in the pictures depicting children.

When a reader picks up a new book, the first thing she explores is the illustration and overall typography of the textbook together with the contents. This happened also in my data. Most of the teachers' comments about gender bias in the textbooks focused on illustrations. In the selection of books they explored[43], they paid attention to the illustration of especially one textbook, *Sisu*. In this textbook, the number of pictures of male persons and characters was exceptionally vast (304 males to 73 females) which was noticed by teachers. The illustration of *Sisu* includes pictures of two cartoon characters that are displayed on almost every page. These characters are called Sisu and Pussi (fictional names with no reference to gender). The teachers Mari and Sini are seated next to each other and the textbooks are in front of them on a table. At the beginning of the example, Mari is holding *Sisu* and Sini looks at it while Mari shows her a picture[44].

43 The textbooks teachers were studying are *Loitsu 9*, *Sisu 9*, *Aleksis 9*, *Taju*, and *Aktiivi 9*.
44 See over

Example 1. [45]

01 *Sini*:	Siel on vähemmän ihmisten kuvii.=siel on luontokuvii enemmän (.) jos aattelee
	There are less pictures of people.=there are more pictures of nature (.) if you think
02	miten (.) niinku esimerkiks sitä (1.0) sitä sukupuolta tuodaan siel nyt (.) esiin.
	how (.)for example the (1.0) the gender is presented (.) in it.
03	(0.5)
04 *Mari*:	Tässähän on (.) tässä (.) on just nää Sisu (.) nää tällaset sarjakuvahahmot jotka
	Here there are (.) here (.) are those special Sisu (.) these cartoon characters who
05	on niinku Sisu ja Pussi?
	who are called like Sisu and Pussi?
06 *Sini*:	Joo.=
	Yeah.=
07 *Mari*:	=Nimeltään?
	=by name?
08 *Sini*:	Onks ne sit jotenkin niinku (.) £neutreja£? he he=
	Are they then like (.) £neuters£ ('without reference to gender') he he=
09 *Mari*:	=No niitten on tarkotus olla, mä tiedän ku mä ((lines omitted))
	=Well they are supposed to be, I know because I ((lines omitted)) [46]
10 *Sini*:	Joo.
	Yeah.
11 *Mari*:	Et niitten oli tarkotus olla mutta (.) onks £ne sun mielestä£.

44 The conversation was video recorded in September 2010. The recording lasted sixty-three minutes. The teachers Mari and Sini (pseudonyms) are experienced, acting teachers in mother tongue and literature. They did not know each other before the recording. They are about forty-years-old, and both teach on the upper grades of comprehensive school, including ninth grade.

45 Transcription conventions follow those of conversation analytic framework. Here are the key conventions: Brackets ([ ]) mean overlapping talk; pauses are marked as minimal (.) or longer (1.5), meaning length in seconds; £ means smiling or laughing voice; he he means laughter; = means latching of turns; intonation is marked as . /, /? marking falling/level/rising intonation; nonverbal behavior is described in double brackets (( )). The translations are under rows of the original talk in italics; the translations of all examples are mine.

46 A line in Mari's turn is omitted since through the information in it her identity could have been revealed.

So that they are supposed to be but (.) what £do you think£.

12   (0.5) ((*Mari* smiles, shows a page to *Sini*))

13 *Sini*:   No mun mielestä ne nyt on kyl (.) mielummin niinku (.)
          maskuliinisia hah[moja.
          Well I think that they are (.) much more likely like (,) masculine
          cha[racters.

14 *Mari*:   [Niin.
          [*Yes.*

15 *Mari*:   Niin munkin mielestä ne on (.) oli niinku alust saakka ihan
          selkeesti
          That is what I think too (.) I thought like that right from the beginning
          that

16   kuitenki poikia.=
          they clearly are boys.=

17 *Sini*:   =Mm.

18 *Mari*:   Eikä (.) niinku m- ei minkäänlaista niinku sellasta
          And not (.) like no- not a bit of any sort of

19   androgyn[iaa kuitenkaan myöskään.
          androgyny [either.

20 *Sini*:   [Ei:.
                [*No:.*

21 *Sini*:   Mm.

Mari appears to have more information about *Sisu*; she has been thinking about the gender of these cartoon characters already before this discussion (line 15). She also initiates the sequence about the two characters (lines 4-5). However, Mari points out only the existence of the cartoon characters but reveals nothing more about her reason for mentioning these figures. Sini acknowledges with a neutral uptake ('yeah'). While Mari continues, Sini takes it as an encouragement to continue on the topic and to talk about the gender of the characters (line 8). Sini's suggestion about the genderless character of Sisu and Pussi is formed as a question addressed to a knowing participant (e.g. Macbeth, 2004). Furthermore, the end of the turn is accompanied with laughter, a conversational cue of a humorous mode (Jefferson et al., 1987). However, the question is designed to predict a certain kind of preferred response, namely a yes-answer which, in this case, would have been something like 'yes, they are designed as genderless 'neuters''. However, in her answer Mari expresses some reservations and continues displaying the position of an expert (lines 9, 11). She asks Sini for an opinion with a turn accompanied by a smiling voice and pointing gesture (lines 11-12). Both teachers end up sharing the same opinion (lines 14-16). They agree that the two characters are boys, not neuters or even androgynies (lines 18-19), no matter how they were meant to be interpreted by the illustrator. In the course of their negotiation, this opinion and agreement is carefully built up step-by-step, and when it is said aloud, the teachers continue in full agreement with talking about the characters as males.

The two cartoon characters Sisu and Pussi are shown in Picture 1. This picture is presented in the context of learning about language history and analysing the style of old texts.

Picture 1. Sisu and Pussi.

The characters are depicted as looking at another character from a distance; this character is immediately identifiable as female (she has, e. g., big breasts and long eyelashes, both typical features for extremely feminine cartoon characters). Sisu utters a humorous remark, the lines containing several wordplays (the translation into English being something along the lines of: 'In/inside the past/ passing person there is a semen/seed for the future'). It is difficult to interpret these lines in any other way than as sexualising both the female character and Sisu and Pussi, and as reflecting a (heterosexual) gender ideology.

As illustrations are the first things readers pay attention to, it is probable that these kinds of humorous cartoons have a big influence on understanding of gender in the context of textbooks. Also, teachers choose to talk about these characters, and they make visible the importance of these figures to each other from the point of view of their task, to reflect on the representations of gender.

Gender specific words

School textbooks contain several types of texts, and in this analysis, all gender specific words were counted regardless of text type and context. By paying attention to gender specific words, it is possible to gain a picture of the representation of gender in textbook texts. This kind of a quantitative analysis leaves many questions unanswered and may not reveal a fair picture about the ways in which genders are represented. However, with the help of this kind of a content analysis it is possible to get an overall picture of who the authorities and other persons referred to in the texts are. It also provides us with an overall view on how much males and females are discussed in textbooks.

Textbooks for Finnish language and literature education have a prominent majority of references to males. 33,430 gender specific words were identified through the analysis, and of them 58.9 per cent referred to males. All in all, references to persons and fantasy characters were common since language and literature textbooks contain many narrative and fictional texts. In the ninth grade textbooks, there were far more male than female specific words, with 60.5 per cent of the gender specific words referring to male persons or characters. The variation between different textbooks was remarkable, shifting from a male representation of 56 per cent (*Loitsu*) to a male representation of 65 per cent (*Sisu*). In addition, about 70 per cent of the names of actual persons referred to males (4,532 men to 2,519 women). Fictional characters also contain overwhelmingly more references to males (10 413 male to 6 504 female characters).

It is much more difficult to evaluate the gender bias of texts than of illustrations when leafing through a book. The teachers in my data discussed the texts mostly through observing the titles and searching for those aspects or persons, for example writers, that they seemed to consider important in advance from the point of view of gender. In this negotiation, the teachers used their own professional expertise to evaluate the textbooks. However, they made fewer comments on gender in texts than they did on gender in illustrations. The most common discussion theme was the gender division of writers of fiction, as it is traditional for the textbooks for ninth grade to contain a section that introduces the history of literature in Finland. The next example illustrates Mari and Sini's attention to this fact.

Example 2.

01   (8.0)

02 *Mari*:   Ihan niinku tavallaan ne (.) kirjailijat joita tääl nostetaan nin, (.) niin kyl se on
            Just like those (.) the writers that are presented here so, (.) well it is more or less

03   lähinnä toi (.) Minna Canth joka=
            this (.) Minna Canth who=

04 *Sini*:   =Niin. [Se nousee sieltä.
            =Yes. [She gets attention.

05 *Mari*:   [naiskirjailijoista niinku (.) parhaiten, (.) on esillä mutta (.)
            [among the women writers well she (.) gets most, (.) of the attention but (.)

06   muuten se on aika (0.5) äijäin kirjallisuut[ta tää.
            otherwise there is more like (0.5) male litera[ture here.

07 *Sini*:   [Niin.
                                                      [Yes.

08 *Sini*:   Mitäs (.) tekstei onks siin mitään novelleja mites (.) kenen novelleja siin on tai muita
            What kind of (.) texts are there any short stories how (.) whose short stories there

09   tekstejä sitte tossa.
            are printed or other texts then.

10 *Mari*:   Tääl on täs (.) Siel on (.) Minna Canthin, (.) Canthilta on yks novelli, (.) ja sitte
            Here you find (.) There is (.) Minna Canth's (.) Canth's short story, (.) and then

11   muuten täs ei kauheesti,
            otherwise there are not many,

Mari and Sini are searching for references and texts about female writers. The most celebrated woman writer in the history of Finnish literature is Minna

Canth (1844-1897) who fought for equal rights and welfare for women and poor people and whose personal life was colorful. These facts make her a self-evident candidate for the introduction of Finnish literature. This seems to be shared knowledge for Mari and Sini (lines 2-5). As in the earlier extract, also in this extract Mari seems to be positioned as an expert. This is understandable because at the beginning of the conversation she told Sini that she uses this book, *Taju*, with her students. Mari is also the first to evaluate the balance between male and female writers in this textbook (lines 5-6). According to her, the book favours men writers; Sini agrees (line 7). This observation is also in line with my quantitative analysis of gender specific words used in this book: there are 712 references to men/boys compared to 320 references to women/girls. This bias is common and even more prominent in some other textbooks (Tainio and Teräs, 2010, p. 46).

All in all, the teachers saw it as being important to pay attention to the fictional texts and references to male and female writers, at least when they were asked to reflect on the ideology of gender. They found the lack of the references to women writers as a problem. The expertise of Mari on this specific book (*Taju*) made it easier for them to uncover the gender bias in the textbook. Teachers made several remarks on the titles in the text and, with the help of it, they also made observations about other matters concerning gender. Nevertheless, underlying values and ideologies related to gender cannot be revealed in a short time and without a deeper look at the texts.

Questions about sex and gender

Although gender equality is mentioned in the national curriculum in Finland, the writers of textbooks have not taken advantage of the different possibilities to share information about gender issues and gender equality and to analyse the category of gender in language, culture and society. From the point of view of quantitative analysis, the textbooks have a gender bias with the vast majority of pictures and references representing males. However, after a closer look, several sections were found where students could get information about gender issues, or were guided to analyse gender in different contexts (Tainio and Teräs, 2010, pp. 47-55). For example, in sections devoted to the analysis of fiction, it was not uncommon for students to be instructed to explore texts or characters with specific attention to gender. Gender issues were taken up also in the passages on sociolinguistics and media education.

For the casual reader of a textbook, it is often difficult to notice the covert ideologies embedded in the texts; this requires a careful analysis (Oteiza, 2003). The teachers who explored the five textbooks did not address detailed features of the texts, even though they are trained for linguistic analysis. However, some passages provided information about gender, and they did not always promote equality. I will analyse one such example here. The extract is about humour and joking as an important field of language use and as practices connected to social bonding; the title of the text is *Mikä suomalaisia naurattaa?* 'What do Finns laugh at?'

Example 3. (*Aleksis 9. Harjoituksia.* p. 67)[47]

Obscene jokes are usually told by men, and they do not tell them in the company of women. If women, for example in the workplace, have to listen to obscene jokes, this could be considered sexual harassment.

Obscene jokes are part of the culture of men and boys. In obscene jokes a woman is usually depicted as a stupid object, as in popular jokes about blonds. Joking together strengthens male social bonding and helps men survive in the world of mothers, sisters, women teachers, girlfriends and wives.

In the text, the woman writer introduces several fields of humor to readers, and one of them being obscene joking. Right at the beginning of the extract, the writer presents a stereotypical view on the gendered nature of (men) telling obscene jokes. However, the writer addresses an important sexual harassment issue, informing the readers quite correctly about the nature of this activity. Nevertheless, in the next paragraph the writer states that obscene jokes belong to male culture. This sentence is presented in indicative modus in present tense, which makes it a general statement (Hakulinen et al., 2004, p. 1510). Again, this claim is based on a stereotypical picture of men as a homogenous group with a particular culture. The description of typical women in obscene jokes is mentioned but with no reference to the range of different kinds of sexual or obscene jokes.

---

47 In Finnish: "Rivoja vitsejä kertovat enimmäkseen miehet, eikä niitä yleensä kerrota naisseurassa. Jos esimerkiksi työpaikalla naiset joutuvat kuuntelemaan heitä halventavia rivoja vitsejä, sitä voidaan pitää seksuaalisena häirintänä.
    Rivot vitsit kuuluvat miesten ja poikaporukoiden kulttuuriin. Rivoissa vitseissä nainen on yleensä hölmön objektin asemassa, kuten suosituissa blondivitseissä. Yhteinen vitsinkerronta lujittaa miesten ryhmätunnetta ja helpottaa elämistä äitien, sisarten, naisopettajien, tyttöystävien ja vaimojen maailmassa."

The last sentence in the example is written straightforwardly from the male point of view. This sentence suggests that the habit of obscene joking is a positive practice in the process of social bonding among groups of men. Furthermore, the world outside these groups is described as if women were in power in all contexts and recurrently restrict the life of men. The list of different groups of women who are in charge include not only family members (mothers, sisters, girlfriends, wives), but also women teachers are mentioned as making it difficult for men and boys to survive. According to this sentence, women are also the reason for obscene joking among men. The passage provides contradictory information about the organisation of gender in society and culture. It depicts women both as potential victims (of sexual harassment) and as the powerful group that restricts the life of boys and men. Without a very careful discussion, students can get very odd information about gender in language use and culture.

Concluding remarks

In this chapter, I have analysed Finnish language and literature textbooks, and I have also presented an analysis of a conversation between two teachers looking at five textbooks, and analysed a picture and a section of one of the textbooks in order to reveal the gender ideology embedded in them. The analysis of the conversation between two teachers shows that when teachers observe textbooks in order to discuss their suitability for different learning purposes, such as learning and discussing issues on the organisation of gender in culture and society, they analyse textbooks from particular perspectives. The teachers were asked to pay attention to representations of gender in the textbooks, and at least when asked to, they were able to identify the gender bias and comment critically on it.

Although the textbooks for Finnish basic education can be considered informative, rich, and attractive, they naturalise gender bias. Improving learning materials could start from the writers of textbooks and the publishing companies. They should pay more attention to illustrations, person references and the overall construction of texts. All texts are media for ideologies, including those of gender and sexuality. However, it is possible to diminish the gender bias of school textbooks (Blumberg, 2007; Stromquist, 2007). This appeared to be important also for the teachers in my data.

Finally, teachers are key actors in the process of promoting gender equality in schools. This leads us to take a critical look also at the teacher training programs in Finland. Teachers are the ones who use books in schools, and because courses on gender issues and gender equality still are rare in teacher training programs, they do not necessarily receive guidance on these issues. According to preliminary studies on textbooks used by teacher training programs, gender issues are not prominent or even considered an important focus area (cf. Zittleman and Sadker, 2002). This means that it is possible to graduate from teacher training programs without giving a second thought to gender issues in school, in the work of a teacher, and in Finnish culture and society. Without professional guidance on gender issues, future teachers may not be able to see ideologies of gender in school textbooks and to promote gender equality in their work.

References

Blumberg, R. L., (2007) Gender bias in textbooks: A hidden obstacle on the road to gender equality in education. Paper commissioned for the EFA Global Monitoring Report 2008, Education for all by 2015: will we make it?.

Fairclough, N., (1989) *Language and power,* London: Longman.

Gordon, T., Holland, J., and Lahelma, E., (2000) *Making spaces: Citizenship and difference in schools,* Houndsmills: MacMillan Press.

Hakulinen, A., Vilkuna, M., Korhonen, R., Koivisto, V., Heinonen, T.R., and Alho, I., (2004) *Iso suomen kielioppi. [Big grammar of Finnish],* Helsinki: Suomalaisen Kirjallisuuden Seura [Finnish Literature Association].

Heinonen, J.-P., (2005) *Opetussuunnitelmat vai oppimateriaalit? [Curricula or educational materials?],* Helsingin yliopisto: Sokla [University of Helsinki: Department of Teacher Education].

Hutcby, I., and Wooffit, R., (2001) *Conversation analysis: Principles, practises and applications,* Cambridge: Polity Press.

Jefferson, G., Sacks, H., and Schegloff, E.A., (1987) Notes on laughter in the pursuit of intimacy, in Button, G., and Lee, J.E.R., (eds.) *Talk and social organisation.* Clevedon: Multilingual Matters.

Krippendorff, K., (2003) *Content analysis. An introduction to its methodology,* 2nd ed., Thousands Oaks, CA: Sage.

Lahelma, E., (1992) *Sukupuolten eriytyminen peruskoulun opetussuunnitelmassa. [Gender differentiation in the curriculum of the comprehensive school.],* Helsinki: Yliopistopaino [University Press].

Lappalainen, H-P., (2009) Äidinkielenopetuksen kysymysmerkkejä. *[Question marks in mother tongue education], Virittäjä,* 4(113): 585-589.

Macbeth, D., (2004) The relevance of repair for classroom correction, *Language in Society,* 33: 703-736.

National Curruculum (2004) *National core curriculum for basic education 2004,* Helsinki: National Board of Education.

Oteiza, T., (2003) How contemporary history is presented in Chilean middle school textbooks, *Discourse and Society,* 14(5): 639-660.

Palmu, T., (1992) Nimetön Hiiri ja Simo Siili. Aapisten sukupuoli-ideologia. [Gender ideology in ABC-books], in Näre, S. and Lähteenmaa, J., (eds.) *Letit liehumaan. Tyttökulttuuri murroksessa. [Girls' culture in change],* Helsinki: Suomalaisen Kirjallisuuden Seura [Finnish Literature Association].

Palmu, T., (2003) *Sukupuolen rakentuminen koulun kulttuurisissa teksteissä. Etnografia yläasteen äidinkielen oppitunneilla. [Construction of gender in cultural texts in school An ethnographic research on mother tongue lessons in secondary school]*, Helsingin yliopiston kasvatustieteen laitoksen tutkimuksia 189 [Department of Education, University of Helsinki, Publications 189], Helsinki: University Press.

Sasaki, T., (2008) Concurrent think-aloud protocol as a socially situated construct, *IRAL,* 46: 349-374.

Stromquist, N., (2007) Gender equity education globally, in Klein, S., (ed.) *Handbook for achieving gender equity through education,* 2nd ed. Mahwah, New Jersey: Lawrence Erlbaum.

Sunderland, J., (2000) New understandings of gender and language classroom research: Texts, teacher talk and student talk, *Language Teaching Research,* 4(2): 149-173.

Tainio, L., (2006) Gender in Finnish language use: Equal, inequal and/or queer? *WEB-FU* 10/2006 (Wiener elektronische Beiträge des Instituts Finno-Ugristik). Universität Wien, http://webfu.univie.ac.at/inhalt.php [Accessed 2 December 2011].

Tainio, L. and Teräs, T., (2010) *Sukupuolijäsennys perusopetuksen oppikirjoissa. [Organization of gender in textbooks for basic education]*, Raportit ja selvitykset 2010: 8, Opetushallitus, www.oph.fi/julkaisut/2010/sukupuolijasennys_perusopetuksen_ oppikirjoissa [Accessed 2 December 2011].

UNESCO (2007) *Education and empowerment of girls and women* (August 8), www.unesco. org [Accessed 2 December 2011].

Zittleman, K. and Sadker, D., (2002) Gender bias in teacher education texts. New (and old) lessons, *Journal of Teacher Education,* 53(2): 168-180.

Chapter 16

Gender awareness in research on teacher education in Finland

Jukka Lehtonen

The Finnish education system is understood to be one of the most successful in the world. One reason underlying the success of the education system lies in its research-based Master's-level teacher education, which is highly regarded. Finland is often seen as a Nordic model country for gender equality. Gender equality and awareness are not adequately addressed by most of the universities giving teacher education, however. One of the reasons for this is the lack of relevant research literature on gender in teacher education. Much high-quality gender-related research on school and education in Finland has been conducted, and Tuula Gordon and Elina Lahelma are two key figures in this research field. At the same time, it has been asserted by many researchers that there is insufficient gender-aware research in Finland, particularly on teacher education and pedagogical practices (see Lahelma, 1992, p. 16; Naskali, 1993; Sunnari, 1997, p. 3; Vuorikoski, 2003, p. 41).

This chapter will examine research conducted in Finland between 1990-2010 on teacher education and teacherhood. I am interested in how gender has been addressed in research policy documents and what position gender has in research related to teacher education. I will thus be analysing the position of gender in this field of research. My data include official documents, databases and research literature. I ask how gender-aware research on teacher education has been handled in studies and texts on conducting research. The main reasons for the lack of relevant gender aware research on teacher education will be summarised in the conclusions.

This analysis became relevant in the *Gender Awareness in Teacher Education* (TASUKO) project. This nationwide project funded by the Finnish Ministry of Education and Culture (2008-2011) worked towards increasing gender awareness in teacher education and pedagogical practices. The project was led by professor Elina Lahelma and involved a wide network of experts, teacher educators and researchers of education at all universities offering teacher training in Finland. Gender aware research that can be applied and utilised at the practical level should form the basis of training in the field of teacher education, but for various reasons it has not been conducted very abundantly. One of the aims of the TASUKO project was to support the construction of a research programme that would create opportunities for further research on gender in teacher education and on pedagogical practices.[48] An analysis of Finnish research on teacher education and gender was conducted and published as part a book with a title that translates from Finnish as *Gender Perspectives on Research-based Teacher Education* (Lehtonen, 2011). In this chapter, I will concentrate on some of the key findings of this analysis.

This chapter is divided into four parts: a section that discusses the legislation mandating research on equality in education and analyses government documents related to research on teacher education; a section assessing research on teacher education, examining the appearance of the theme of gender in this body of research utilising various databases; a section dealing with gender-aware education research and committee reports from the perspective of the specific research needs of teacher education; and the conclusions section.

Equality requirements, Finnish law and teacher education

Gender equality has been established as a goal in education and related research in Section 5 of the Act on Equality: 'The authorities and educational institutions as well as other bodies offering education and instruction must ensure that women and men have the same opportunities for education and professional development and that instruction, *research* and teaching material support the realisation of the intent of this law' [italics my own]. The current law also includes an obligation to create equality plans for staff. Legislation thus unambiguously requires universities and institutions offering teacher education to participate in broader actions, including research, that facilitate the promotion of gender equality in the arenas of education and instruction. To uphold the Act on Equality, gender should be sufficiently analysed in research meaningful for teacher education. Teacher education could be grounded in this research in such a way that it would be possible to achieve the aims of the legislation at the practical level in schools and educational institutions.

---

48 As part of the TASUKO project, several small-scale research projects were conducted at various universities and specialist seminars were held. A survey regarding the needs and aims of research on gender and teacher education was distributed to the ninety members of the project's network of specialists. In addition, forty-nine specialists on gender awareness in teacher education were interviewed on their views regarding the current position of research in teacher training and future research needs.

The goal of equality was included in legislation affecting schools for the first time in 1978 for lower secondary education, and then in the early 1980s for compulsory education and general upper secondary education. For vocational education legislation, it occurred slightly later. At the end of the 1990s, the legislation for compulsory, general upper secondary and vocational upper secondary education was unified, and at this time the specific mention of gender equality was removed. In current legislation, then, either mention is made of equality in general (compulsory education) or equality is not mentioned at all (general and vocational upper secondary education). Furthermore, the legislation mandates that in basic education in instruction, particular attention is paid to the differing needs of girls and boys as well as differences in growth and development between girls and boys. This approach, which naturalises a binary gender division and emphasises differences between genders, does not necessarily open the path to gender-awareness or question conceptions that sustain gender inequality; instead, it may have precisely the opposite effect. In contrast, the legislation on general upper secondary education establishes the goal for students to learn to promote human rights, democracy, equality and sustainable development. Corresponding goals have not been established for vocational upper secondary education, even at the decree level, nor has gender equality been noted in legislation on universities and polytechnic universities. In terms of gender perspectives, then, 1999 resulted in a dilution of education legislation, which has perhaps undermined perceiving gender equality as a significant theme in educational and research policies.

Aside from legislative work, the Government has, at the level of the Government Programme and also through strengthening educational and research plans, taken a stance on gender issues related to education and research (see Brunila, 2010, pp. 16-27; Kuusi et al., 2010, pp. 13-16, 18-20). In the government programmes for the years 1995-2007, there is no mention of gender equality in terms of higher education and academia, but in the Government Programme for the years 2003-2007, the section Education, Academics, and Culture states that gender equality is one of the values of the civilised Finnish society, and the status of the coordination of investigative women's studies is presented in the Programme. In the last analysed Government Programme, it is mentioned that teacher education and kindergarten teacher education should include gender-aware instruction. Training teachers to become more aware of gender has been included in government equality programmes, but few concrete measures have been taken to achieve this goal, with the exception of funding to the TASUKO project. From the perspective of research, very marginal goals have been presented in equality programmes.

In the education and research development plans approved by the Government as well as in the deliberations of the national committee for developing teacher education, issues of gender have received little attention and these documents do not support the advancement of research that would be of use in gender-aware teacher education. This was noted in the report *Education and Gender Equality*, which proposes that 'in the future, development plans for education and research as well as the resource allocation of the Ministry of Education and Culture should take into account the goals for and measures aiming at gender equality included in the Government's equality programmes' (Kuusi et al., 2010, p. 67). According to this report, the mainstreaming of equality policies does not currently function sufficiently well in teaching activities.

A key problem in the government's development plans for education and research is the fact that they rarely deal with the goals noted in the government programs and equality programmes. Gender-aware research in teacher education is referred to only in the development plans for 2003-2008. These note the need to explain learning differences between girls and boys. In these development plans prepared by the Ministry of Education and Culture, then, gender themes and goals appear inadequate in comparison to the broader aspirations of the Government. In spirit, they steer less in the direction of equality awareness and research that supports this aim and more towards an emphasis on the existence and significance of differences between girls and boys. In its report on equality, the Government proposes to ensure the mainstreaming of gender perspectives as part of education-related decision-making and to utilise existing research data as well as good experiences in equality work achieved through development projects (Finnish Government, 2010, p. 35).

In terms of research that would be of use in teacher education, it is also meaningful to analyse documents and reports covering the national core curricula for basic education, as these determine development needs in teacher education and related research. The report *Education and Gender Equality* (Kuusi et al., 2010, p. 28) states that 'the national core curricula for basic education and research include extremely scant measures aiming at gender equality'. According to the report, the subject-specific core curricula do not support the development of gender-aware instruction either, although the subjects of history and social studies, for instance, would offer an opportunity to do so. The report advocates that goals and actions steering towards gender equality should be more extensively and clearly taken into consideration in the core curricula themselves, and that local curricula should be monitored and evaluated from the perspective of gender equality (Kuusi et al., 2010, p. 68).

The national core curricula for basic education states that equality between genders should be promoted during instruction 'by giving girls and boys the capacity to act with equal rights and responsibilities in society, in both working and family life' (Kuusi et al., 2010, p. 21). In specifying working methods, it states that during instruction, 'individual developmental differences and backgrounds, as well as those between girls and boys' should be taken into consideration. This attitude, which frequently appears in documents dealing with school, lends itself to constructing a dichotomic, mutually exclusive view of gender that emphasises and naturalises differences. This leads to a rather one-dimensional understanding of gender. In this instance, the central research question with regard to gender and equality appears to be: 'In what ways are girls and boys different from each other?' and not, for instance, 'How can gender-related inequality be dismantled?' The current curricular documents and their gender-related contents and perspectives do not encourage conducting gender-aware research.

To summarise the analysis of legislation, Government programmes, development plans for education and research, other official reports and the core curricula, it can be stated that the research aiming at promoting and supporting equality mandated in equality legislation since 1995 has not formed into a goal or tool in educational administration and in the development of teacher education. Excluding individual exceptions, research to support gender-aware teacher education has not been encouraged. In the 1990s and the 2000s, demands for achieving gender awareness in teacher education have remained overshadowed by educational-policy and media-nurtured discussions of equality and education, which have primarily stressed essential differences between girls and boys, as well as individual reports on the need for increasing the number of male teachers. This culture of discussion, which is also reflected to some extent in the educational policy documents that have been analysed here, has not sparked the possibility for arranging gender-aware research. Along with the repetition of conceptions that sustain traditional models of gender, the typical gender policy in the examined texts is silence on the issue of gender and its side-lining to a marginal note. Institutions offering teacher education have not, during the period of investigation, shouldered their responsibility for realising the Act on Equality (see e.g. Hynninen and Lahelma, 2008), nor have they actively encouraged gender-aware research. The report on equality and the investigations of degree programmes it relies on, focus on the insufficiency of research on teacher education and gender awareness (Brunila, 2010; Finnish Government, 2010, p. 128; Kuusi et al., 2010; Ministry of Education and Culture, 2010, p. 52).

The perspective offered by databases

In order to investigate the position of gender-aware research related to teacher education, I examined how gender and teacher education as topics intersect the kinds in various databases. I focused on the number of the research publications with a gender perspective in various education-specific categories and on the analysis of gender and sexuality specific keywords.

I conducted a Helsinki University Library (Helka) database search on the teacher education literature available in the Minerva Library of the Faculty of Behavioural Sciences. In this Helka database search, I used the term *teacher education* to search for publications available at the Minerva Library that were published in Finland during the period 1990-2010. There were 667 such publications; five of them were marked with the keyword *gender*. Of the five publications I found through the database search, gender was a central factor in three. In the other two, gender was one of several themes. I reviewed all the keywords of the 667 works on teacher education and noted that instead of the keyword *gender*, other keywords related to gender had often been used. Examples of this included *gender roles, gender structure, gender differences, women's studies, female predominance, women, men, women's status, women's history, women's organisations, Finnish Women's Association, feminists* and *soldier boys*. Some of the publications demonstrated a clear gender perspective and some only a partial one. Despite this broader examination of keywords, I only found twenty-three publications that included gender- or sexuality- themed keywords. This represents 3.4 per cent of all the publications analysed. If we remove the ten publications, which only touched on the theme of gender or sexuality briefly or in only part of the publication, we are left with thirteen publications that demonstrate a gender or sexuality perspective (1.9% of all publications). On the basis of this database search as well, then, the themes of gender and sexuality would seem to appear marginal in the research literature on teacher education.

With the help of TASUKO project intern Johanna Snellman, we conducted a survey of the National Library of Finland's publication reference database, LINDA, using the database's search engines. In this process, cross-searches were conducted between Finnish-language keywords linked to education research and those related to gender/sexuality. The keywords used related to education were *teacher education, teacher, pedagog*, didact*, teaching, school* and *education*. Truncated forms were used in some cases so that various forms of the words would be more likely to be included in the analysis. The gender-related keywords were: *gender, girl, boy, women, woman, man, men, feminine* and *masculine*.

The keyword *teacher education* identified a total of 4,495 publications in the LINDA database in August 2010, of which 2,501, over half, were in Finnish. In total, eighty-six of all the publications contained gender-themed keywords (1.9%); this figure was fifty-nine for the publications in Finnish (2.4%). When I conducted a comparable search in November 2010, focusing only on works published and recorded in the database during the years 1990-2010, the keyword *teacher education* was found in 2,845 publications, of which 1,499 were in Finnish. In all, eighty-eight publications contained gender-themed keywords (3.1%), and fifty-eight of the publications in Finnish contained these keywords (3.9%). Of these, the most common keywords were *gender, women, boy* and *men*. To conclude, the greater part of teacher education research with a gender perspective and all of the teacher education research with a sexuality perspective included in the database has been conducted after the 1980s. In addition, the percentage of such research has clearly grown in connection to research containing keywords such as *teacher education*, although it continues to occupy a rather marginal position. No publications at all were found before the 1990s for many of the gender-related keywords (*man, men, feminine, masculine*) or for any of the keywords referring to sexuality (*sexuality, homo*, hetero*, lesbian, queer*). Studies conducted earlier were classified using the keywords *gender, girl, boy, woman* and *equality*. This shift seems to suggest, in addition to changes in the classification system, that perspectives on gender and sexuality in research in the area of teacher education have diversified.

Education-related keywords located a significant number of publications, of which approximately half were in Finnish. Of all of these publications, only a very small amount dealt with gender and even fewer dealt with sexuality. In the period 1990-2010, only a small portion continued to be marked by keywords as being gender-themed, but this number was somewhat bigger than in the overall survey, indicating that research in the field has grown. The keywords *school, education, teacher,* and *pedagog** were more certain ways of locating information on gender than the keywords *teacher education, didact** or *teaching*. In terms of the number of publications, school-related Finnish-language research was found most frequently using the search terms *education, school, teaching* and *teacher*. Works with the keywords *pedagog*, didact** and *teacher education* appeared least frequently. This is explained by the fact that libraries have more school-related gender-aware literature than analyses of teacher education, pedagogy, or didactics.

A survey of articles contained in the ARTO database was also conducted with a comparable keyword search. I expanded my search to two other databases: 1) The KOTU (Education Research) database maintained by the Finnish National Board of Education and through it, the Register of Research on Education and Training that has been compiled there, and 2) The Dissertation Database of the Centre for Gender Equality Information in Finland contains approximately 280 dissertations stored there since 2000. They all demonstrated similar results in many respects as the LINDA database search.

In summary, the database searches revealed that relatively few gender-sensitive studies have been published, and that paucity characterises research related to *teacher education, didactics*, and *pedagogy*, in particular. More research is being conducted than before, that is, before the 1990s, but the number of research studies is still small. It is not likely that the registers of the National Board of Education and the Centre for Gender Equality Information in Finland are entirely up to date, but the impression they provide is much the same as that provided by the LINDA and ARTO database searches.

Research with a gender perspective

In this section, I provide a historical analysis of the kinds of gender-aware committee and research data that has been produced during the years 1980-2010, and the stance the publications from different decades have taken on gender-aware research on teacher education. The objects of my investigation included committee deliberations, reports and compilation publications as well as, first and foremost, dissertations in which questions of gender perspectives on education-related issues are a central theme. Only a few extensive reports and studies involving gender- and equality- oriented analysis of teacher education and related research exist (Brunila, 2010; Committee report, 1988; Jakku-Sihvonen et al., 1996; Kuusi et al., 2010; Ministry of Education and Culture, 2010).

It was not until the latter half of the 1980s that the thematics of gender and equality made a more forceful *entrée* into discussions on education policy. This was made particularly visible by the publication of a research report on gender equality (Lahelma, 1987), a report on equality pilots (Salonen, 1988) and the deliberations of the equality pilot committee (Committee report, 1988). Elina Lahelma played a major role in this development as the responsible official within the Ministry of Education and Culture and the secretary of the equality pilot committee. This committee offered stances on the development of research activities; for instance, the establishment of extensive pilot, research, and development projects focused on issues of equality was encouraged in the domain of teacher education for all forms of school (Committee report, 1988, p. 114). The deliberations also mentioned the 'Education and Gender' researcher network, which was directed by Tuula Gordon. It was established in 1987 (later the Eddi network, derived from the beginnings of the words for Education and Difference) as well as a pan-Nordic research and development project that was realised in the early 1990s (Nord-Lilia, see Arnesen, 1995).

In her dissertation *The Differentiation of Genders in Comprehensive School Curricula*, Lahelma analyses education research conducted in Finland in the 1980s that pursued a clear gender perspective (Lahelma, 1992, p. 19). She conducted a survey of these studies, conducting reference searches of literature and theses. According to Lahelma, one could characterise this type of Finnish research by saying that too little of it was conducted and it was conducted unsystematically. Lahelma highlights the need for continuing research on conceptions of knowledge related to degree programmes and their development work; analysis of textbooks; educational policy; special-needs instruction; careers in education; and the genderedness of everyday practices at schools. According to Lahelma, in the late 1980s and early 1990s gender research on educational themes and related discussion, as well as the number of publications on the thematic, increased in Finland (Lahelma, 1992).

Vappu Sunnari studied the gendered structures and processes of primary school class teacher education (Sunnari, 1997). The study examined, from a historical perspective, both the first teacher training seminar in Finland (in Jyväskylä in 1863) and the gendered structures of the class teacher training that took place in Oulu in the years 1988-1996, as well as pedagogical development challenges involved in the Nord-Lilia project, which was the most central development and research project in teacher education in relation to gender issues in Finland prior to TASUKO (see Arnesen, 1995). In the Nord-Lilia project (1992-1994) funded by the Nordic Council of Ministers, building on pan-Nordic cooperation methods, the aim was to develop teacher education into a more gender-sensitive direction. Twenty-six projects from Finland participated in the umbrella project, many of which involved research and investigative activities. Sunnari's study of the history of primary teacher education revealed the gendered history and nature of the field (Sunnari, 1997). According to Sunnari, there has been little research on teacher education, which she suggests reflects an ideology of neutrality: teachers and teacher educators assume they treat students equally, without gender-related differentiations and discrimination (Sunnari, 1997, p. 4; see Lahelma, 1992, 2006). If gender is not seen as a problematic issue in the everyday practices of schools or from the perspective of school goals, research on gender in education appears unnecessary.

In the late 1990s and early 2000s, several dissertations were published on gender in education. Many of these studies were directly linked to—or were influenced by—a large gender-aware school-ethnographic study led by Gordon, *Citizenship, marginality and difference in schools— with special reference to gender,* and the activities of the Eddi network, which to a large extent revolved around Gordon and Lahelma's studies on gender (see, e.g. Gordon et al., 2000). In the project, six researchers gathered data from two Helsinki-area lower secondary schools in the years 1994-1995 using ethnographic methodologies. The entire umbrella project, and many of the dissertation studies supervised by Gordon and Lahelma in and around it, analysed the everyday practices and cultures of schools. Consulting these dissertation studies has also been useful for teacher educators and the development of research in the field in a more gender-aware direction.

Most of the gender-specific school-related dissertation research did not though focus or even comment on teacher education or research on it. In the over fifty dissertations and other publications I have examined, some views on the need for, and lack of gender-aware research on teacher education were presented in few of them. Even though they dealt with various themes related to school and education, many of them did not consider there to be a need to examine teacher education, or to support research in conjunction with this. Only a small portion of the publications I examined had been prepared at institutions offering teacher education. Many of the school studies had been conducted in the areas of sociology, educational sciences and youth research. Of these, most utilised the feminist approach of research, but also other methods of examining gender were used. In publications that analysed teacher education and related research needs, note was made of the related deficiencies, needs, and future expectations. Many of the research needs were observed decades ago and have been reiterated in various forms since, but there has been scarce and infrequent analysis of a multifaceted nature that could be used to develop teacher education and the pedagogical solutions necessary to support it (see also Lahelma et al., 2007, p. 108).

Conclusions

This analysis investigated the position of gender-aware research in research on teacher education in Finland. As I have indicated in my analysis, insufficient gender-themed research on teacher education and pedagogical solutions has been conducted in Finland during the past twenty years. Despite the fact that legislation requires research related to the advancement of gender equality, such research has not received sufficient attention in documents and plans concerning teacher education and the development of the related research, in teacher education literature or teacher education programmes. Database searches reinforce the impression of the paucity of research on the topic, as does the analysis of gender-themed education research.

Several causes for this problematic situation have been suggested. Some of them are connected to conceptions related to gender and equality, some to traditions of teacher education. One explanation is that there is a perception that schools and teachers already operate on a basis of equality in Finland, and thus there is no need to conduct gender- and equality- aware research. Another explanation is that the inequality in question is not seen as constituting a major problem, and so research on it is not encouraged. A third is that gender-related (especially feminist) research is considered suspect and (overly) political. A fourth explanation—even though generally there is no desire to admit this—is the fact that research in the field is not desired because gender equality and change related to gender are not desired. These views have propped up regularly in publications on the field. (Hynninen and Lahelma, 2008; Vidén and Naskali, 2010.)

Reasons connected to teacher education traditions that emerged during the survey include the asocietal and uncritical nature of teacher education, as well as the relatively low emphasis on and competence in research in it. It has been stated that Finnish research on teaching has included little critical examination from a sociological viewpoint, which could also explain the lack of the gender perspective within it (Simola, 1997; Vuorikoski, 2003). This sustains the conception of school and the teacher's work as neutral and unbiased. According to Simola, didactic and psychological approaches have been emphasised in teacher research, and the sociological links of teaching have received little attention (Simola, 1997). This is also reflected in the scarcity of sociological and cultural analysis of gender in research in the field. The rarity research of dealing with sociological factors has been noted in assessments concerning the development of teacher education (Jussila and Saari, 1999).

On a concrete level, there is an absence of supporting factors for gender-aware research in teacher education units if gender awareness is not a significant theme in terms of pedagogy or content at even a general level in their education and research programmes. Often competent guidance, research literature, or research groups and networks on the topic are not available. (see Lehtonen, 2011; Pellikka, 2010; Vidén and Naskali, 2010.) Furthermore, the authorities at the Ministry of Education and Culture, with the exception of one-off position statements and actions, have not actively taking a stance on behalf of gender-aware research in planning and development work and in proposing and funding concrete methods of achieving this goal.

What could, then, be done differently? Gender awareness should be reinforced throughout society, within the Ministry of Education and Culture and the educational administration, universities, faculties and in particular institutions offering teacher education as well the teaching profession and municipal management. To advance gender-awareness, we need education and communication as well as thorough gender analysis and more-concrete objective-setting in education and research development plans and curricular work, in which gender themes are taken into account in both education and research. Educational administration should train itself to become an expert on the theme and actively promote gender equality. Funding should be organised for research with significantly more vigor, and special research programmes and projects should be funded. Teacher education, in its various forms and degree programmes, should include themes to increase gender-awareness in an integrated, compulsory fashion, as well as specifically organise mandatory and optional training in order to ensure a basic level of competence in gender issues. In addition to dealing with the theme in terms of content, current teaching and guidance practices should be examined critically and modified to be more gender-sensitive and to take diversity into greater consideration. Students and teacher educators should be encouraged more to conduct gender-themed research, and better opportunities to conduct this work should be created.

The TASUKO project lead by Lahelma has striven to link research to gender-aware teacher education through: networking, cooperation and the organisation of various events; building up a material bank on the topic; supporting research activities taking place at various universities; and the publication of studies on the thematic. The TASUKO project has succeeded in supporting teacher educators and researchers in the field towards more gender-aware research and co-operation, as well as in taking the long-simmering discussion on the goal of promoting equality to the national level. It has legitimised the often tenacious and long-term, but also just-begun work on behalf of gender equality in teacher education units that is frequently conducted by individuals or small groups within them.

References

Arnesen, A-L., (ed.) (1995) *Gender and equality as quality in school and teacher education*, Nordic Council of Ministers, Oslo: Oslo University College of Education.

Brunila, K., (2010) *Sukupuolten tasa-arvo korkeakoulutuksessa ja tutkimuksessa. [Gender Equality in Higher Education and Research]*, Helsinki: Ministry of Social Affairs and Health.

Committee Report, (1988) *Tasa-arvokokeilutoimikunnan mietintö. [Report of the committee on equal opportunities in education]*, Helsinki: Valtion Painatuskeskus.

Finnish Government, (2010) *Selonteko naisten ja miesten välisestä tasa-arvosta. [Government Report on Gender Equality]*, Helsinki: Ministry of Social Affairs and Health.

Gordon, T., Holland, J. and Lahelma, E., (2000) *Making spaces: Citizenship and difference in schools*, London: Macmillan.

Hynninen, P. and Lahelma, E., (2008) Tasa-arvoisuutta ja sukupuolitietoisuutta opettajankoulutukseen. [Equality and gender-awareness for teacher education], *Finnish Journal of Education*, 39(3): 283-288.

Jakku-Sihvonen, R., Lindström, A. and Lipsanen, S., (eds.) (1996) *Toteuttaako peruskoulu tasa-arvoa? [Is equality realised in primary education?]*, Opetushallitus [National Board of Education] 1/96, Helsinki.

Jussila, J. and Saari, S., (1999) *Opettajankoulutus tulevaisuuden tekijänä. Yliopistoissa annettavan opettajankoulutuksen arviointia. [Teacher education as the shaper of the future: Evaluation of the teacher training universities provide]*, Helsinki: Edita.

Kuusi, H., Jakku-Sihvonen, R. and Koramo, M., (2010) *Koulutus ja sukupuolten tasa-arvo. [Education and Gender Equality]*, Helsinki: Ministry of Social Affairs and Health.

Lahelma, E., (1992) *Sukupuolten eriytyminen peruskoulun opetussuunnitelmassa. [Gender segregation in the primary school curriculum]*, Helsinki: University of Helsinki.

Lahelma, E., (2006) Gender perspective: A challenge for schools and Teacher Education, in Jakku-Sihvonen, R. and Niemi, H., (eds.) *Research-based teacher education in Finland—Reflections by Finnish teacher education*, Turku: Finnish Educational Research Association, 203-213.

Lahelma, E., Saarinen, J., Guttorm, H. and Ojala, H., (2007) Kasvatuksen ja sukupuolen tutkimuksen matkassa. [Moving ahead with research on education and gender], *Finnish Journal of Education*, 38(2): 107-109.

Lehtonen, J. ed., (2011) *Sukupuolinäkökulmia tutkimusperustaiseen opettajankoulutukseen. [Gender perspectives on research-based teacher education]*, Helsinki: University of Helsinki.

Ministry of Education and Culture (2010) *Segregaation lieventämistyöryhmän loppuraportti. [Final report of the committee on alleviation of segregation]*, Opetus-ja kulttuuriministeriön työryhmämuistioita ja selvityksiä 2010:18, Helsinki: Ministry of Education and Culture.

Naskali, P. ed., (1993) *Moninaista—kasvatustiedettä naisnäkökulmasta. [(Wo)manifold—The educational sciences from a women's perspective]*, Lapin yliopiston kasvatustieteellisiä julkaisuja, C. Rovaniemi: University of Lapland.

Pellikka, L., (2010) *Katsaus kasvatustieteen koulutuksen sukupuolitietoiseen oppikirjallisuuteen. [An overview of gender-aware literature used in educational sciences programmes]*, Helsinki: Tasuko, University of Helsinki.

Salonen, A. ed. (1988) *Koulu matkalla sukupuolten tasa-arvoon. Kokeiluselvitys tasa-arvo kokeilutoimikunnalle. [Schools en route to gender equality: A report on pilots for the committee on equal opportunities in education]*, Helsinki: Valtion Painatuskeskus.

Simola, H., (1997) Pedagoginen dekontekstualisointi ja opettajankoulutuksen opetussuunnitelmat. [Pedagogical decontextualisation and teacher education curricula], *Finnish Journal of Education*, 28(1): 24–37.

Sunnari, V., (1997) *Gendered structures and processes in primary teacher education—challenge for gender-sensitive pedagogy*, Oulu: Universities of Oulu and Lapland.

Vidén, S. and Naskali, P., (2010) *Sukupuolitietoisuus Lapin yliopiston opettajankoulutuksessa. [Gender awareness in teacher education at the University of Lapland]*, Rovaniemi: University of Lapland.

Vuorikoski, M., (2003) Opettajien yhteiskunnallinen valta ja vastuu. [The societal power and responsibility of teachers], in Vuorikoski, M., Törmä, S. and Viskari, S., (eds.) *Opettajien vaiettu valta. [The silent power of teachers]*, Tampere: Vastapaino, 17-53.

Chapter 17

Words that matter: Revisiting equality work in education

Kristiina Brunila

In 2003 when I began my doctoral research on gender equality work in Finland (Brunila, 2009), I found myself in a troubling situation. Finland was presenting itself with pride as a model of gender equality. At the same time, equality was being presented as an export product, and equality policies appeared closely connected to the interests of the labour market. There was also a growing questioning within feminist research addressed to the various types of persistent inequalities in Finnish society. When looked at more closely, the promotion of equality seemed to be a rather women-based, project-based and marginalised political activity. Regardless of this, however, equality work seemed to be very active, carried out in kindergartens, schools and universities as well as in adult education and work settings.

For me as a researcher, these tensions anticipated questions and challenges concerning theorising and analysing equality work. What theories, methodologies and methods should be used and what questions should be asked? After finding myself embracing theoretical resources from the work of Michel Foucault, Jacques Derrida, Judith Butler and educationalists Patti Lather, Bronwyn Davies and Elizabeth Adams St. Pierre, I began to take the notion of power seriously. Feminist researchers in particular helped me to realise that, for the researcher, no outside positions are available. Hunting for a more liberating or emansipatory approach to determining 'right' or 'wrong' with respect to equality work was only going to reproduce the problems that equality work already faced.

In 2011 as I am writing this article, it seems that understanding equality work is even more important because of the rather extreme degree of marketisation and projectisation in the Finnish public sector. Regardless of these processes, equality work has still been widely conducted. I aim to revisit equality work once again and determine the societal and discursive power relations that have shaped it and with what consequences. My most important question is related to continuance. How is it possible that regardless of challenges including marginalisation, marketisation and projectisation, equality work has succeeded in maintaining momentum?

Gender equality work in Finland

In Finland the welfare state has traditionally been a major institutional supporter of gender equality work (Holli, 2003; Raevaara, 2005). Gender equality has been promoted largely through political struggles leading to changes in legislation as well as through positive actions (e.g. Brunila, 2009, 2010; Holli, 2003; Lahelma, 2004, 2011; Raevaara, 2005). Gender equality is a political term that is actualised in demands for various kinds of social changes. This is evident when examining equality work, which for the past thirty years has been in the process of becoming organised. A significant amount of equality work has been conducted in co-operation with schools, universities, vocational training, teachers, students, researchers, adult educators, governments and employers (e.g. Haataja et al., 1989; Hynninen and Lahelma, 2010; Lahelma, 2004).

An interesting feature of equality work in Finland is that since the 1970s most of it has been conducted through publicly funded equality projects. In comparison with the 2000s, it appears that the 1980s were a particularly active period for equality projects related to education and training, including particularly the Nordic BRYT AVAA project. The 2000s seem to be an era of programmes, and funding appears to favour large-scale projects with several subprojects and wide cooperation networks (Brunila et al., 2005).

The favouring of projects is a part of a larger societal and market-oriented shift. Particularly after Finland entered the European Union (EU) in 1995, research has suggested a stronger reliance on project-based activities in the public sector (e.g. Rantala and Sulkunen, 2006; Sjöblom, 2009). The history of project work originated from technology-based organisations, and it has been used as a tool to find ways to handle specific operations. Today projects are considered to be a universal solution to all types of problems. I have previously argued that project-based work has permeated the public sector and become a common form of work and of the implementation of welfare politics, including equality work. I have also argued that projects have formed an independent and separate educational genre with a market-oriented and individual-based orientation (Brunila, 2011).

The shift to projects has occurred alongside the shift from government to (new) governance (Ball, 2007; Dale and Robertson, 2009). New governance is a market-oriented attempt to introduce territorially unbounded public and private actors, operating outside of their formal jurisdictions, into political institutions' decision-making processes (cf. Bailey, 2006). The notion of the project society as a form of new governance and as a concept developed by Pekka Sulkunen (Rantala and Sulkunen, 2006), applies to contemporary societies, which rely largely on voluntary contracts between individuals, groups, organisations, enterprises and states. Indeed, Sulkunen (2006) has argued that Finland has shifted into a project society and that projects as an organisational form have become the core of a new kind of power system (Rantala and Sulkunen, 2006).

The shift to publicly funded projects in equality work has also been acknowledged in the other Nordic countries (see Guðbjörnsdóttir, 2010; Pinqus and van der Ross, 2001). Projects as the core of a new type of power system can explain some of the obstacles equality work in Finland has faced, so it is important to analyse the consequences of projectisation. At the moment, when projectisation seems to be applied to its full extent, I find it even more important to show that although equality activities are numerous and operate in very different contexts in education and working life, following the shift to a project society they have been targeted and formed by similar forms of power.

Analytical tools and research data

When equality work is involved, I argue that it is important to address the performative effect of language and discourse with material effects. In exploring the discourses of project-based equality work, there is a need to explore the ways in which certain elements of the discourses have become more powerful than others. This involves examining the use of power. In order to grasp and acknowledge the forms of power that shape equality work, I developed the concept of projectisation (Brunila, 2009). Crucial to the development of this concept was feminist deconstructive and discourse-oriented research, with its emphasis on language, power and meaning as well as meaningful silences that must be heard (Davies 1998; Lather 2003; Naskali, 2003; St. Pierre, 2000).

Projectisation is both a theoretical concept as well as an analytical tool. It represents a disciplinary and productive form of power derived from feminist-oriented research, but also from Michel Foucault (1975/1995), and the Neo-Foucauldian researchers Nikolas Rose and Peter Miller (e.g. Rose and Miller, 2008). It suggests what can be said and thought, but also who can speak, as well as when, where and with what authority. The study of power relations affecting people associated with gender equality work is important, because power relations have material effects on people's lives. As a form of discursive power, projectisation is important to analyse because it is tolerable only on condition that it masks a substantial part of itself. It does not dominate; instead it incorporates those who are subject to it, and is productive in the sense that it shapes and retools its targets (cf. Foucault, 1975/1995).

Before I could look at how one is able to act in order to promote equality, an understanding was needed of how discursive power relations function as a forcible framework within which the subject and action are formed (cf. Butler, 2008). In order to understand why projectisation 'works', and why we end up acting as we do, I utilise the concept of subjectification. According to Bronwyn Davies and her colleagues (2001; see also Davies, 1998), subjectification represents the processes to which we are subjected and through which we actively take up as our own the terms of our subjection. In my analysis, subjectification means the ongoing process in which one is placed, and takes place in the discourses of projectisation (e.g. Brunila, 2009). Subjectification as a part of projectisation involves individuals taking up those discourses through which they and others speak/write as if they were their own. Through these discourses, individuals involved in equality work are made speaking subjects at the same time as they are subjected to the constitutive force of discourses.

I use the concept of discourse as an analytical tool not only to refer to speech and writing but also productive and regulative practices (e.g. Davies, 1998; Foucault, 1975/1995). According to Foucault (2000), power and knowledge are always found embedded together in the discursive regimes of truth. Discourse is a way of representing knowledge about a particular domain at a particular historical moment. It defines the domain and produces the objects of knowledge within that domain (Edwards, 2008, p. 23). I examine the projectisation of gender equality work through an analysis of discursive power, acknowledging the relation between discourse and power in project work as productive and regulative. Such an approach allows one to see how the forms of power work and what effects they have on forming speech, that is, how one must speak in order to be heard.

I utilise the research data collected in 2003-2004 for my doctoral dissertation. This data was produced in an equality project undertaken with fellow researchers Mervi Heikkinen and Pirkko Hynninen (Brunila et al., 2005[49]). The data consists of thirty oral interviews mostly with women who have promoted

---

49 The interviews were conducted by Kristiina Brunila and Mervi Heikkinen as part of the Desegregation of the Labour market-research project (Brunila et al., 2005).

equality for decades and who have also worked in a number of public sector equality projects. The data also includes documents from ninety-nine publicly funded equality projects. By project, I mean short-term, publicly funded by the EU, Finnish government, foundations, associations etc., efforts usually implemented outside the formal educational system and having certain predetermined goals. Instead of focusing on individual projects I would like to broaden the analysis through moving from a focus on who speaks to an emphasis on what is said and how. I utilise the documents of three publicly funded equality projects, as well as interviews with participants, who have devoted themselves to the promotion of equality in education and working life. All have worked in publicly funded equality projects.

Understanding the mechanisms of the projectisation

One era that has left its mark on the definition of equality and its objectives has been the EU policy-making period, a time marked by the emergence of new forms of governance (Outshoorn and Kantola, 2007). When Finland joined the EU, the number of publicly funded projects representing the new forms of governance increased by several hundred. Heli, who has promoted equality with government, in schools and in the context of teacher training, describes the situation when Finland joined the EU: 'When the Ministry of Labour, in accordance with the EU, started to use the concept of good practices in the middle of the project, this directed all of the projects' activities towards a more practically-oriented and more goal-oriented approach'.

As Heli described, the turning to such projects shifted the language of equality towards a new orientation imported from the social, employment and educational policies of the EU, and this orientation began to surface on a national level in the aims of equality projects. In practice, the equality obligation laid down in EU structural policy as a mainstreaming principle was interpreted as directing actions specifically towards women, instead of calling for equality to be integrated into all project activities. In consequence, many projects implemented in Finland after the mid-1990s were specified as so-called women's projects. However, the work towards effecting a change in women's education, training and career choices in terms of equality work goes back to the 1980s when projects began to attract women particularly in technology. It was interesting to discover that technology, in particular, has received more financial resources more than any other sphere of equality work (see Vehviläinen and Brunila 2007).

Projectisation would not have succeeded without heteronormativity (Brunila, 2009). Heteronormativity carries the idea of a hierarchical gender order. It represents a code of behaviour that expects women to behave in a less valued 'feminine' manner, and men in a more valued 'masculine' manner (for more detail see Lehtonen, 2010). In the Finnish project society, projectisation, marketisation and heteronormativity have created a circle of benefit and regulation; they each benefit each other and regulate how equality ought to be talked about in order to be heard.

The people we interviewed were quite critical towards activities targeting individual girls and women. We talked about the assumption of differing characteristics that lead to different treatment, which then produces differences that strengthen the assumption of gender-bound characteristics. Johanna, for example, commented that women in these projects are positioned most often as targets. She wondered: 'To what extent are they there as actors?' Anja, who had worked in several ICT projects, commented: 'Shaping [attitudes] won't make any difference if reality doesn't change alongside.' Anja continued by explaining how the system in projects works:

> They [the evaluators] had written that the objective of the project is to bring more women into the field of technology. I then said that bringing women into technology has never existed in the project plan. In my mind, it has not been the aim of the project. The evaluator, however, continued arguing that it was the goal. This is very contradictory.   (Anja)

Anja's extract shows how the circle in practice works. In the project she describes, as in many similar projects, activities were ultimately aimed at changing girls and women's career choices with respect to the field of technology, regardless of objections (see also Hynninen and Lahelma, 2008; Vehviläinen et al., 2007). Project activities are aimed at directing girls and women towards the more valuable male-centred environment, and as a consequence, the heteronormative gender hierarchy as well as the difference in value between the environments of the two genders persists (Brunila et al., 2005). Furthermore, this tendency can be called market-oriented inclusive politics (e.g. Brunila, 2011). Market-oriented inclusive politics work by inventing and re-inventing the hierarchical order of societal differences based on how capable differences are of benefiting the economy and working life. The projectisation of equality has led to neglect that societal differences such as gender, sexual orientation, ethnicity, class and disability should be recognised as a system of oppression, or intersectional, as feminist research and equality politics have highlighted.

> When equality and diversity are seen as measures of competitiveness, they get more emphasis. From the company point of view, this means that all resources are utilised well and that circumstances are developed to make this happen.   (Equality project's final report, 2000)

As the above extract describes, since joining the EU, equality discourse in Finland has begun to display more market-oriented traits, such as competitiveness, but has also moved to an emphasis on effectiveness measures, evaluations, and the conceptualisation of equality as an export product. Instead of valuing equality itself equality is seen as valuable when harnessed to bigger goals. And the projects' targeting of women has not taken place without tensions:

> Defining the women's point of view caused problems which culminated in conflicts about who owns the project and who gets to define its content. Women's needs were at the centre of the projects but the problem was who gets to define them in different situations.
> (Equality project's final report, 1999)

Projectisation has worked by regulating activities into constant reporting, accounting and self-evaluations. In the equality projects this has conflicted with the more feminist aims, such as the rights of the project target groups to define their own goals and interests themselves.

The above extracts describe the shift Finland has been experiencing. Activity that used to be positioned as central to the objectives of the Nordic welfare state and which was based on grass-roots activism and criticism of the market orientation is more likely now to receive its legitimation from marketisation and to be managed through individual short-term projects. From the perspective of subjectification, this implies that one must submit oneself to marketisation and master the language of the market in order to be heard. Furthermore, mastering the language of the market includes learning the heteronormative gender order. And because of the pre-determined schedule of projects, objectives that used to be the responsibility of the Nordic welfare state and the differing interests of the project partners, projectisised equality work necessarily consists of tensions and conflicts. As a consequence, the discursive field of equality work has become fragmented, as Fanny explains:

> We have these actors, yes, but these field actors, are they sort of acting along their own lines? We have women's research, we have organisations and then we have a few equality consultants, but one can almost say that these equality consultants, and for example these ESF projects, are there in the world of the practical way of working, but are they different worlds nonetheless? (Fanny)

Fanny's extract is crucial because it demonstrates how we are witnessing a shift into a period where the previously influential policy agencies are losing their significance as links between women's movements and the state (cf. Kantola, 2010). This transformation can be linked to changes in the political context, including Europeanisation, welfare state retrenchment and decentralisation, which have had a significant impact in the form of diminishing resources (Brunila, 2009). At the beginning of this article I stated that the Nordic welfare state has been a major supporter of equality work. Having said so, I argue that projectisation has now become a major challenge to the Nordic welfare state. This is not, however, the whole story.

Actively seeking change

At a time when equality issues are harnessed to the aims of economic efficiency and productivity, it is even more important to understand how people who actively seek change have succeeded in negotiating equality matters. Mervi and I began discussing equality work with people who had devoted their lives to the promotion of equality, and we were told rather amasing stories. Based on the discussions one can easily argue that the position of promoting equality has not been an easy one in the 'model country of equality':

> I felt that it wasn't wise to fight a lonely battle against an organisation or their views on these issues—they'd always be stronger. They showed us who's in power. I'm sure everyone in our group has experienced and will share my feeling of a sort of invalidation and belittling. (Lena)

> If some major machinery starts to knock you down and you're alone, it's not an easy spot to be in. (Doris)

As Lena and Doris's extracts describe, their positions have been constantly challenged and marginalised. From the perspective of subjectification, there was a noticeable ambivalence. It was no surprise to discover that people involved in equality work were often tired and generally rather cynical. Lena, for example, who had done equality work in education since the 1980s, wished she had been an ornithologist instead, and Marjorie, who had conducted several equality projects, thought a career in gardening might have been better. Maria expressed tiredness, describing how project-based work forms an endless cycle where 'new' results must be continuously produced.

> You know that, in theory, development projects are like that, but in practice it always comes as a surprise that all of that really happens. That all those sort of clichés really come true.　　　　　　　(Maria)

I, too, observed such processes taking place when I studied equality project activities from the 1970s to the 2000s. Projectisation has worked by producing similar kinds of results as always being 'new'. I interpret the clichés Maria refers to as being the products of projectisation and marketisation, but also as the results of heteronormativity. During thirty years of project-based equality work in Finland, the heteronormative idea of gender has been repeatedly re-invented (Brunila, 2009). Alli has worked with equality issues in various organisations. She gave the following example of the ways heteronormativity functions in practice:

> *Alli:* You have to know how to read the organisation, you have to know how to act, and you have to know the border that you are not allowed to cross if you want to influence the organisation positively.
> *Kristiina:* What do you mean by 'border'?
> *Alli:* If you go to a very patriarchal, masculine organisation that is goal-oriented, the borders are stricter. If you cry in a meeting, you are out. ....
> Or if you are sentimental or say that this is not right, or that childcare is not organised, or if you talk about handiwork or something feminine, out you go.

Alli's example provides an example of heteronormativity as a form of subjectification. The border Alli mentions refers to the need to acknowledge heteronormative discourse and to master it in order to be heard. In this sense, equality work consists of sequences of repeated acts that solidify into the appearance of something that has been present all along. In other words, those involved in equality work do not stand apart from the prevailing norms and conflicting power relations. But as Alli's example also shows, neither heteronormativity nor any form of power relation has to be deterministic. In order to promote equality, one needs to learn the 'right' way to talk so that in becoming objects of the disciplinary forms of power, people also become active subjects.

In spite of the alliance between projectisation, marketisation and heteronormativity, equality work continues to be carried out in different ways. However, as many of the interviewed women mentioned, they are always caught up in various normalising schemes of categorisation and regulation. We discussed how crucial it is to recognise these power relations and to try opening up channels that allow for creating distance to existing identities and identifications with preset meanings and categories. I was grateful for these discussions because they allowed me confront my overly comfortable distance to 'complicated' equality issues (cf. Lather and Smithies, 1997, p. 151) and helped me to avoid seeing myself as 'rescuing' or 'giving voice' to others.

These interviews taught me to begin asking questions about the relations between the subject, agency and politics. More nomadic and fluid perspectives concerning both subject and agency were needed. Facing the discourse of equality work in this way forced me to take more responsibility for the ways I conduct analyses and position myself as a researcher. I began to question, in the same way as Eva Bendix Petersen, how discursive constructions take hold of the body, take hold of desire, and how certain discursive constructions are appropriated while others are discarded and relegated as irrelevant or even threatening (Petersen, 2008, p. 55).

Judith Butler and Bronwyn Davies's accounts of the subject and agency provided a way to understand agency not only as a process of subjectification, but also as an effect and redeployment of power (Butler, 1997; Davies, 1998). If equality work was a regulated process of repetition taking place in discourses, this meant that the possibility exists to repeat things differently. Indeed, according to Butler, it is the very constitutivity of the subject that enables her to act in these power relations, which are not just regulating but also productive. Because the capacity to act is not a possession, there is no need for a pre-existing subject in political agency (Butler, 1997; Pulkkinen, 2003). This released me from having to choose 'sides', such as whether I was for equality or against it. Instead, I realised that as a researcher I am both conditioned by and dependent on the prevailing norms, and at the same time, I need to find my way in research ethically and responsibly (cf. Butler, 2008). As a consequence, I began to see much more when I revisited the interviews. More than anything, promoting equality meant constantly learning to act in various kinds of power relations, as well as utilising them in order to continue the work. Instead of being repressive, equality work entailed ongoing negotiations. Marjorie and Iris described this as follows:

> Conciliating, listening, looking for gaps that let you break through to take the next step in a positive, constructive manner.   (Marjorie)

> It's like having a kind of inquiring touch, like asking if you could think of it this way, if you've ever thought of this or if you've tried that. It's having this inquiring touch, about being interested.   (Iris)

The negotiations that Marjorie, Iris and all the other interviewees so vividly described consist of skills and (tacit) knowledge that I refer to as 'discourse virtuosity' (Brunila, 2009), which is a consequence of parallel but contradictory aims and discourses in equality work; a complex form of competence one performs in order to be heard.

This kind of virtuosity is especially needed when seeking funds for one's own employment, for the next project and for the continuity of equality work. Due to projectisation and in order to receive funding for equality work, one needs to demonstrate the impacts of equality work in market-oriented terms, such as productivity and competitiveness. Sometimes one needs to highlight public discussions, such as concern over boys' underachievement at school, or strict segregation and gender-divisions in education and working life.

Through utilising different discourses, the women were able to introduce equality work in places and situations that might otherwise have been inaccessible (Brunila et al., 2005, p. 59). More importantly, this also enabled negotiating leeway for more feminist aims that avoided marketisation and heternormativity. Johanna described equality work as taking little steps and doing little things, although for me as a researcher these seemed to indicate rather significant changes in one's thinking:

The sudden understanding that is sometimes created in a group. If you give an example like that when are you going to ask a young thirty-year-old if he's got young kids and how much time he spends looking after them. People find it so obvious that his wife's looking after them. These are little things that make people start to think that I see you can look at it that way, too. (Johanna)

When undressed of marketisation, projectisation and heteronormativity, this is what gender equality work in Finland is all about: enabling people to see how gender and other societal differences operate in our society. However, the aim of allowing people to learn to see societal differences as power relations seems dangerous.

Equality work revisited

I began this article by explaining the troubling situation I faced at the outset of my research on equality work. In 2011, in an even more market-oriented project society where equality discourse seems to be being exploited to its full extent, gender equality has continued to remain the responsibility of projects. Even more so than when I began my research, I wish to be able to come up with words in acknowledging discursive power relations that work as long as they stay hidden and unrecognised. I have shown how equality work has become projectised with market-oriented and heteronormative objectives and results, and have argued that projectisation, marketisation and the repeated reinvention of the heteronormative idea of gender have formed an alliance that conflicts with more feminist aims. In order to break out of this circle, it is crucial to acknowledge the forms of power that maintain the circle. The alliance between marketisation, projectisation and heteronormativity calls for a more critical appraisal, not only from the perspective of its effects but also from the perspective of resistance and rebellion.

What I also consider even more important now is to resist writing about equality work as something that can be synthesised into a singular picture that tells the whole truth about equality. Rather, being able to write about equality work as diverse will hopefully encourage readers to begin asking more critical questions. Talking with individuals who have devoted their lives to the promotion of equality within a deconstructive-discursive approach has encouraged finding ways to analyse equality work as a site of constant negotiations, discourse virtuosity and political agency without an essentialist subject. This has enabled me to see that problems concerning equality are not objects but rather the products of different practices, policies and power relations, and therefore always negotiable and changeable. A significant amount of equality work has been done by switching and shifting from one discourse to another, reflecting changes in the political situation and in societal interests. Although this could be considered an obstacle, when different discourses are utilised equality work becomes more possible in contexts that might otherwise be inaccessible to it.

References

Ball, S., (2007) *Education plc: Private sector participation in public sector education*, London: Routledge.

Bailey, D., (2006) Governance or the crisis of governmentality? Applying critical state theory at the European level, *Journal of European Public Policy*, 13(1): 16-33.

Brunila, K., Heikkinen, M., and Hynninen, P. (2005) *Difficult but doable. Good practices for equality work,* Oulu University, Kajaani University Consortium, Adult Education Unit/The National Thematic Network, Kainuun Sanomat Oy, Kajaani.

Brunila, K., (2009) *Parasta ennen. Tasa-arvotyön projektitapaistuminen. [Best Before. The Projectisation of Equality Work.],* Helsingin yliopisto kasvatustieteen laitoksen julkaisuja 222 [Department of Education, University of Helsinki, publications 222], Thesis (Phd), Helsinki: Yliopistopaino.

Brunila, K., (2010) *Sukupuolten tasa-arvo korkeakoulutuksessa ja tutkimuksessa. [Gender Equality in Higher Education and Research],* Sosiaali- ja terveysministeriön selvityksiä 2009:51, Helsinki: Yliopistopaino [University Press].

Brunila, K., (2011) Projectisation, marketisation and therapisation of education, *European Educational Research Journal*, 10(3): 425-437.

Butler, J., (1997) *The psychic life of power: Theories in subjection*, Stanford, CA: Stanford University Press.

Butler, J., (2008) An account of oneself, in Davies, B., (ed.) *Judith Butler in conversation. Analyzing the texts and talk of everyday life*, London: Routledge.

Dale, R. and Robertson, S., (2009) *Globalisation and Europeanisation in education*, Oxford, UK: Symposium books.

Davies, B., (1998) *A body of writing 1990-1999*, Walnut Creek, CA: AltaMira Press.

Davies, B., Dormer, S., Gannon, S., Laws, C., Rocco, S., Lenz Taguchi, H., and McCann, H., (2001) Becoming schoolgirls: The ambivalent project of subjectification, *Gender & Education*, 13(2): 167-182.

Edwards, R., (2008) Actively seeking subjects?, in Fejes, A., and Nicoll, K., (eds.) *Foucault and lifelong learning. Governing the subject,* London: Routledge.

Foucault, M. (1975/1995) *Discipline and punish. The birth of the prison*. London: Penguin Books Ltd.

Guðbjörnsdóttir, G., (2010) Gender in teacher training in Iceland, *ECER Conference*, University of Helsinki, 27 August, Helsinki.

Haataja, A., Lahelma, E. and Saarnivaara, M., (1989) *Se pieni ero: kirja tasa-arvokasvatuksesta.* [That small difference: A book about equality education], Helsinki: Valtion painatuskeskus.

Kristiina Brunila253

Kristiina Brunila253

Holli, A-M., (2003) *Discourse and politics for gender equality in late twentieth century Finland*, Acta Politica 23, University of Helsinki.

Hynninen, P., and Lahelma, E., (2008) Tasa-arvo- ja sukupuolitietoisuutta opettajankoul utukseen.[Equality and gender awareness into teacher education], *Kasvatus*, 39(3): 283-288.

Kantola, J., (2010) Shifting institutional and ideational terrains: The impact of Europeanisation and neoliberalism on women's policy agencies, *Policy & Politics*, 38(3): 353-368.

Lahelma, E., (2004) 20 vuotta koulun tasa-arvotyön alkamisesta—entä nyt? [20 years from the beginning of equality work—what now?], in Taajamo, M., (ed.) *Suunnistuksia. Tiede. Kasvatus. Taide*, Jyväskylä: Jyväskylän yliopisto [University of Jyväskylä].

Lahelma, E., (2011) Sukupuolitietoisuutta kouluun ja opettajankoulutukseen: TASUKO-hankkeesta eteenpäin, [Gender awareness in schools and teacher education], *Kasvatus*, 42(1): 90–95.

Lather, P., (2003) Applied Derrida: (Mis)reading the work of mourning in educational research, *Educational Philosophy and Theory*, 35(3), 257-270.

Lather, P., and Smithies, C., (1997) *Troubling the angels. Women living with HIV/AIDS*, Columbus: Grayden Press.

Lehtonen, J., (2010) Gendered post-compulsory educational choices of non-heterosexual youth, *European Educational Research Journal*, 9(2): 177-191.

Naskali, P., (2003) Dekonstruktio uusien kysymysten avaajana kasvatustieteessä ja yliopistopedagogiikassa. [Deconstruction as a way to open up new questions in educational sciences and university pedagogy], *Kasvatus*, 34(1): 18-29.

Outshoorn, J. and Kantola, J., (2007) *Changing state feminism*. Basingstoke: Palgrave Macmillan.

Petersen, E., (2008) Passionately attached: Academic subjects of desire, in Davies, B. (ed.) *Judith Butler in conversation. Analyzing the texts and talk of everyday life*, London: Routledge.

Pincus, I. and van der Ross, J., (2001) Valtiot, kunnat, tasa-arvo ja poliittinen tahto, in Bergqvist, C., Borchorst, A., Christensen, A-D., Ramstedt-Silén, V., Raaum, N. and Styrkarkársdóttir, A. (eds.) *Tasa-arvoiset demokratiat? Sukupuoli ja politiikka Pohjoismaissa.* [Equal democracies? Gender and politics in the Nordic countries], Helsinki: Edita.

Pulkkinen, T., (2003) *Postmoderni politiikan filosofia.* [Postmodern philosophy of politics], Tampere: Gaudeamus.

Raevaara, E., (2005) *Tasa-arvo ja muutoksen rajat. Sukupuolten tasa-arvo poliittisena ongelmana Ranskan parité- ja Suomen kiintiökeskusteluissa. [Gender Equality and the Limits of Change—Gender Equality as a Political Problem in the Debates on Parity in France and Quotas in Finland]*, Tasa-arvoasiain neuvottelukunta, Sosiaali- ja terveysministeriö, Tane-julkaisuja 7, Helsinki.

Rantala, K. and Sulkunen, P., (eds.) (2006). *Projektiyhteiskunnan kääntöpuolia.* [The Flipsides of the Project Society], Helsinki: Gaudeamus.

Rose, N. and Miller, P., (2008) *Governing the present: Administering economic, social and personal life*, Cambridge, UK: Polity Press.

Sjöblom, S., (2009) Administrative short-terminism: A non-issue in environmental and regional governance, *Journal of Environmental Policy and Planning*, 11(3): 165-168.

St. Pierre, E. A., (2000) Poststructural feminism in education: An overview, *Qualitative studies in education*, 13(5): 477-515.

Vehviläinen, M. and Brunila, K., (2007) Cartography of Gender Equality Projects in ICT. Liberal equality from the perspective of situated equality, *Information, Communication & Society*, 10(3): 384-403.

www.ingramcontent.com/pod-product-compliance
Lightning Source LLC
Chambersburg PA
CBHW061722270326
41928CB00011B/2079